Paolo Bertuletti, Johannes K. Schmees, Fabienne-Agnes Baumann,
Dietmar Frommberger & Francesco Magni (Eds.)



# Vocational Education in European Regions

## Lower Saxony and Lombardy in Comparison

DAAD Deutscher Akademischer Austauschdienst
German Academic Exchange Service

wbv

This book was financed by the German Academic Exchange Service (DAAD) using funds from the Federal Foreign Office (AA), the Norwegian University of Science and Technology (NTNU) University Library, and the Department of Vocational Education Studies at Osnabrück University.

2025 wbv Publikation
a business division
wbv Media GmbH & Co. KG, Bielefeld

Overall production:
wbv Media, Bielefeld,
Auf dem Esch 4, 33619 Bielefeld,
service@wbv.de
**wbv.de**

Cover design: Paolo Bertuletti

ISBN (Print): 978-3-7639-7666-9
ISBN (E-Book): 978-3-7639-7667-6
DOI: 10.3278/9783763976676

Printed in Germany



---

**Bibliographic information of the German National Library**
The German National Library lists this publication in the German National Bibliography; detailed bibliographic data are available on the Internet at http://dnb.d-nb.de.

---

# Contents

# Preface

Comparative studies on vocational education and training (VET) models take different theoretical approaches, and numerous classifications have been developed over time. The problem with these typifications is that they tend to overlook the real-world complexity and for this reason scholars have begun to emphasise case-specific differences within types. Despite the close link that VET systems have with the world of work and local institutions (even when the governance of the system is centralised), the distinctive characteristics of regional VET systems are rarely investigated.

In this book, we summarise the research findings of a collaborative project conducted by VET research teams of the University of Bergamo and Osnabrück University, which was funded by the German Academic Exchange Service (DAAD). The focus of this cooperative effort was on comparative studies of VET in European regions, especially Lombardy (Italy) and Lower Saxony (Germany).

The term 'region' refers to geographical divisions at the subnational level and happens to coincide with the political-administrative boundaries of the region of Lombardy in Italy[1] and the Federal State of Lower Saxony in Germany[2]. It should also be noted that a particular focus of the project was on the apprenticeship systems in both Lower Saxony and in Lombardy. Zooming in on the specificities of these two regional cases has revealed a wealth of insights into the establishment of VET programmes that would otherwise have remained hidden under the conventional blanket of national types.

In her introductory chapter, Fabienne-A. Baumann describes the skill ecosystem approach as a potential lens through which researchers can attend to the regional aspects, rather than those that emerge only at the national level, when investigating VET systems. Although thus far applied only to a limited number of case studies, the concept of the skill ecosystem, when equipped with comprehensive data, can be particularly useful for examining regional VET systems.

Dietmar Frommberger then problematises the focus on dual apprenticeship systems frequently found in research on German VET, arguing that the diversity within German VET should be discussed, especially in terms of comparative approaches. This is justified by the fact that while roughly two-thirds of a cohort in Germany were found to opt for some type of VET at the upper secondary level, only half of them chose the dual apprenticeship system. In Frommberger's view, it is therefore crucial to shed light on other VET programmes.

Regarding the regional level, Tim Migura focuses on the structures and challenges of the dual apprenticeship system that have emerged in Lower Saxony. In particular, he

1 With a population of 9.9 million, Lombardy is the most populated of the 20 administrative regions in Italy.
2 By land area, Lower Saxony is the second largest among the 16 federated states in Germany and twice the size of Lombardy, but with a smaller population of eight million.

discusses the issues of gender-specific interests in occupations, the so-called 'fitting problem', and the high rate of early contract termination, as well as increasing academic drift. Considering the long-term consequences of these challenges on the local as well as the national level, Migura questions why the structural changes required to improve the dual apprenticeship system seem not to be part of any political agenda.

Building on the idea of the diversity of the German VET system and following the regional focus of this book, Silke Lange introduces the landscape of VET schools in Lower Saxony. Specifically, she argues that while they are an integral part of the dual apprenticeship system, VET schools provide a much wider array of educational options for different target groups. In particular, these schools not only vary with respect to the vocational fields they cover and their general organisation, but also in the levels of their offered credentials, which range from vocational preparation for a dual apprenticeship to the so-called bachelor's professional track. Despite these differences, however, Lange argues that these schools share a common purpose of integrating general education with vocational training and fostering personal development alongside the acquisition of occupational qualifications.

In the last contribution which focuses on Lower Saxony, Silke Lange, Kristina Trampe, Christoph Porcher, and Dietmar Frommberger introduce the VET teacher training process used in the region. Departing from the fact that there is a persistent shortage of VET teachers, the authors attribute this outcome to the structural heterogeneity of the VET teacher training programmes. As universities try to increase the attractiveness of their study programmes through alternative study models that fit individual needs, educational pathways to becoming VET teachers are becoming increasingly more confusing. Accordingly, this chapter systematically examines this trend of heterogenisation, analyses its implications, and discusses whether it is still the right solution to attract new students.

Turning to the case of Lombardy, Francesco Magni and Virginia Capriotti explore the VET system in this region within the framework of Italian VET, aiming to highlight both its strengths ('light') and challenges ('shadow'). They argue that the VET system has long been trying to strengthen its links with the world of work, increase the number of students who participate, cope with early school leaving and educational poverty, and improve the quality of learning. They delve into specific regional policies, institutional frameworks, and pedagogical approaches at play, thereby presenting Lombardy as one of the most industrially advanced regions in Italy and thus a microcosm of broader national trends. The paper ends with some recommendations for enhancing the efficiency and inclusivity of the VET system, which would ensure that it continues to meet the evolving needs of the workforce and the economy.

Evelina Scaglia then uses a historical lens to investigate the development of the Italian VET system in general, and the Lombardian VET system in particular. This contribution provides two exemplary cases, taken from the local history of Bergamo, Lombardy, that illustrate the conflict between local and national jurisdiction in Italian VET, where, since unification, the increasing attempt by the state to centralise the governance of the school system has clashed with the Lombardian idea of a more adjusted approach that fits the needs of a successful regional economy and labour market.

In the following chapter, Giada Ragone argues that Lombardy is a laboratory of innovation in VET from a constitutional perspective. While after the 2001 Constitutional Reform, she argues, Italian VET fell under the exclusive legislative authority of the regions, the Italian Constitutional Court played a pivotal role in reshaping the landscape of Italian regionalism by reinterpreting the allocation of legislative competences in favour of the state. This contribution examines the regulatory initiatives implemented by the Lombardy region to establish its own VET system, thereby highlighting how regional innovation and experimentation can contribute to the broader realisation of constitutional rights, including the right to vocational education. Through her analysis, Ragone suggests that innovations tested at the local level can serve as catalysts for transformative changes that can benefit the entire nation.

Paolo Bertuletti and Andrea Potestio make another regional case in their effort to show how and to what extent Lombardy's short-cycle tertiary education system supports innovation. This explorative research, based on semi-structured interviews with representatives of nine higher technical education institutions, reveals that this branch of the regional VET system is not necessarily fully market-driven, despite its strong ties with the world of work, and may instead play a proactive role in contributing to the skill ecosystem and promoting, within certain limits, the development of new professional profiles. As a result, the higher technical education institutions in Lombardy can be seen as 'intentional' agents committed to improving the school-to-work transition through the development of professional profiles that can guide companies in their innovation and growth processes.

In the final chapter, Paolo Bertuletti and Johannes Karl Schmees synthesise the findings presented in the prior chapters in light of the theoretical perspective of skill ecosystems, arguing that Lombardy, much more than Lower Saxony, differs from the overarching model. The authors conclude that by using skills formation systems closer to the territories, regional specifications can be met, and a better alignment of the economy and the VET system can be achieved, with more sustainable outcomes in the long run.

Bergamo, Derby/Trondheim, Munich, and Osnabrück

Paolo Bertuletti, Johannes Karl Schmees, Fabienne-Agnes Baumann,
Dietmar Frommberger, and Francesco Magni

# Theoretical perspective

# Researching vocational education and training from a regional perspective: The skill ecosystem approach

Fabienne-Agnes Baumann

**Abstract:** research on vocational education and training (VET) has long been driven by a desire to make sense of 'national' training systems and to group them into different types representing country cases. However, the study of vocational skill formation at the sub-national level could be highly instructive with regard to the variety within cases and yield explanatory variables for political, economic and social outcomes. The skill ecosystem approach, initially developed by David Finegold, potentially opens a new route to infuse a regional or local scope into analyses of VET. To date, its application has been piecemeal and dominated by metaphorical use rather than further conceptual development and theory building. Departing from a justification for zooming in on sub-national education and training arrangements, this chapter delivers a brief overview of available literature on skill ecosystems and suggests potential pathways for strengthening research in this area.

**Keywords:** Regional Vocational Education and Training; Skill Ecosystem; Social Ecosystem Model; Sub-National Research on Vocational Education and Training.

## 1 Introduction

The desire to describe and understand differences and commonalities in vocational education and training (VET) has produced a considerable body of literature, especially since the 1990s. A multitude of typologies have been developed by scholars from different disciplinary angles mapping, for instance, different learning venues (Blossfeld, 1992), qualification styles (Deißinger, 1995), patterns of regulation (Greinert, 1998, 2008) or degrees of state and firm involvement (Crouch et al., 1999; Busemeyer & Trampusch, 2012). The diversity of approaches to make sense of the cross-national variety of vocational skill formation reflects the inherent interdisciplinary nature of comparative research on VET, while the lack of standardisation and systematisation with a view to its theoretical and methodological underpinnings has also been perceived as problematic (Lauterbach & Mitter, 1998; Lauterbach, 2003)[1]. Still, channelling country cases into typologies has proven to be useful both for assessing and comparing different ap-

1 Lauterbach (2003) suggests tying comparative research in VET to a reference discipline, namely comparative education. However, a key question is whether such a standardisation is at all necessary.

proaches to VET and for reducing real-world complexity. At the same time, typologies tend to gloss over heterogeneity. Scholars of comparative institutional political economy therefore now draw attention to “variety within types” (Busemeyer & Trampusch, 2012), emphasising historicity and tracing the unique politico-economic trajectories that shape the institutions that condition the nature of VET systems in each case. What has thus far received comparatively little scholarly attention is *variety within cases*. This is surprising, as the actual ‘production’ of vocational skills tends to occur in a decentralised manner and to be closely tied to place-based variation in terms of economic structures, politics, actor constellations and education and training entities.

With regard to economic structures, specific conditions of the sector in which training takes place, the size of firms and the strategies on which firms compete have long been recognised as variables impacting VET (see for instance Hall & Soskice, 2001; Brown et al., 2001; Busemeyer & Thelen, 2012; Emmenegger & Seitzl, 2019). However, interlinkages between VET and economic geography have been much weaker. Economic geographers analyse local production networks, economic regions, city economics or clusters (see for instance Cooke et al., 2007; Cooke & Piccaliaga, 2008; Maier et al., 2008; Vicente, 2018). What these different concepts have in common is that they underline that there is no such thing as *the* economy[2]. Instead, diversity in economic structures leads to rural-urban and regional cleavages concerning the allocation and quantity of learning and training venues and respective skill formation opportunities, job prospects, income, as well as other adjacent factors affecting access to or retention in education and training, such as mobility infrastructure and the availability of affordable housing.

What is more, the governance of VET is notoriously complex (Oliver, 2010). The political arena of VET in which key players – notably the state, employers and learners and workers – vie for influence, engage in cooperation and settle conflicts is inherently multilayered. It reflects state structures (e. g., central or federal), different levels of policy-making (supranational, national and sub-national), industrial relations institutions (national or sectoral scope) and the nature of interest organisation (especially associations, unions, and chambers at national and/or regional or sectoral levels) (Busemeyer & Trampusch, 2012; Martin, 2012). Consequently, a wide array of options as to how the governance of VET can be organised exists. In some cases, including Germany and Italy, VET-related tasks are deliberately devolved to sub-national governments, stakeholders or specific governance bodies, among others, to facilitate the consideration of regional specificities. Even where VET governance is highly centralised or where skill formation is based on sectoral or national standards, social practices – thus, the ways in which stakeholders engage with, interpret, and implement the rules of the game – infuse contingency into the reality of VET, which might lead to diverging outcomes ‘on the ground’ (Trampusch, 2014; Emmenegger et al., 2019).

Yet, regional politico-economic specificities are rarely treated as explanatory variables for observed outcomes in VET, and seldom are regional characteristics of VET the

2 Italy (Becattini, 1979, 1991) and Germany (Hardach, 2022) are cases in point here.

object of empirical analysis[3]. A reason for this might be that analytical frameworks that consider VET at a sub-national level are hard to come by. One approach that has stirred scholarly interest in that regard is that of skill ecosystems, first introduced by Finegold (1999) and taken up in various but disparate contributions on skill formation, particularly in Anglophone OECD member states. Buchanan, Anderson and Power (2017, p. 446) observe that "[t]he academic literature on skill ecosystems is growing but limited". The following paragraphs are dedicated to an introduction to Finegold's approach and to an overview of examples from the scattered literature on skill ecosystems. To conclude this chapter, potentials and limitations of this approach are identified and possible pathways for its further development addressed.

## 2 Origins and central tenets

In his seminal contribution on high-skill ecosystems (HSEs), David Finegold builds on the work of industrial geographers, political economists and organisational ecologists. His examination of HSEs was an advancement of the rather broad-brush idea of low-skill/high-skill equilibria introduced in earlier publications (Finegold & Soskice, 1988; Snower, 1994). "Both concepts [equilibria and ecosystems] highlight the interdependence of actors in a system, but in the study of ecosystems the focus is on continual evolution" (Finegold, 1999, p. 63).

Finegold was particularly interested in what he considered 'high skills'. His case studies consequently focus on clusters of healthcare technology, biotechnology and information technology in what is commonly known as Silicon Valley in California. According to Finegold (1999, p. 61) "[a]n HSE is a geographic cluster of organizations (both firms and research institutions) employing staff with advanced, specialised skills in a particular industry and/or technology."

The ecosystem metaphor expresses the notion of distinctiveness in how processes of skill investment and skill creation are organised and sustained in a specific locality. To facilitate the analysis of these processes and of the genesis of HSEs, Finegold offers a framework that consists of four elements considered necessary for the emergence and maintenance of a (high-)skill ecosystem.

Firstly, in order to initiate the development of the ecosystem, a *catalyst* is needed. A catalyst can be an event or another sort of trigger that leads to the founding and accumulation of successful businesses in a certain region. In Finegold's case studies, increased government spending on and demand for research and development, investment by individuals, cheap land, availability of university graduates in combination with proximity of leading research institutions have served as catalysts for the establishment of firms driven by high skills. While contingency is an important aspect in the formation of skill regions, the initiation of skill ecosystems is not random. They depend on the right combination of finance, demand and a well-functioning skills incubator

3 Notable exceptions include the works of Culpepper (2003) and Emmenegger, Graf and Trampusch (2019).

for talent that can take on a leading role in jumpstarting the skill ecosystem. Secondly, the nascent ecosystem needs *fuel or nourishment* to sustain its continuing growth. Commonly, this fodder is new talent attracted to the region as such or to the working conditions and career prospects it offers. Frequently, synergies exist between several such pull factors.

A *supportive host environment* allows the ecosystem to mature. What is needed is appropriate infrastructure (technology, opportunities for further learning and training, and partnerships between businesses and research or training institutions) as well as regulations, policies and programmes beneficial to the clusters or economic regions in which skill ecosystems emerged.

Finegold finds that skill ecosystems are characterised by a *high degree of interdependence*. What differentiates a skill ecosystem from "a group of separate organisms [merely] sharing the same physical space" (Finegold, 1999, p. 66) is that its component parts are mutually interdependent. Cooperation, particularly between firms, and a shared focus on a sector, an industry or technology are deemed essential to build capacities for "collective knowledge creation and diffusion" (Finegold, 1999, p. 70). Finegold's HSE case studies suggest that interdependence or network structures in skill ecosystems can take different forms. Horizontal interdependence exists between firms that specialise in a distinct competency or technology and therefore have to collaborate with other organisations for complementary expertise. Vertical interdependence is prevalent between different links along value chains. Individual networks, as a third form of interdependence, form between individual workers that draw on intermediary enabling structures to meet others "and exchange learning" (Finegold, 1999, p. 71). Such structures can be provided for instance by alumni networks, business or professional associations or through further education and training courses.

The key underlying logic of Finegold's analytical approach is that of a virtuous cycle. Ecosystems "[...] once started, generate a positive, mutually reinforcing dynamic that fuels ongoing knowledge creation and growth and adaptation to changing competitive conditions" (Finegold, 1999, p. 61). Hence, skill ecosystems are thought of as 'self-sustaining'. This does not mean, however, that skill ecosystems are passive entities. To the contrary, they rely on sufficient "adaptive capacity" (Finegold, 1999, p. 73) and need to evolve in order to survive. This capacity can be built or increased by ensuring continuous access to new knowledge through interaction with research or training institutions. Skill ecosystems also benefit if based on different links of a value chain rather than being carried by firms active in a single segment (Finegold, 1999, p. 74).

In this context, Finegold (1999, p. 61) raises important further questions regarding (high-)skill ecosystems: How are they linked to the rest of the economy? What are their outcomes in terms of "wealth and employment generation"?

In the case of HSEs, Finegold (1999, p. 61) argues that "[t]he basic concepts of the firm, individuals' careers, and skill development will be shown to operate differently in these HSEs than in the traditional economy." That is because HSEs, or more precisely the industry clusters, individual entrepreneurs and research institutions that carry them, are sources of innovation and growth for the national economy, underlining their overall economic relevance.

HSEs also generate more jobs directly and exhibit higher salaries than the regional and national average enterprise (Finegold, 1999, p. 64). In areas in which HSEs are located, a multiplier effect also leads to indirect job creation, for instance in services or manufacturing. As a consequence, HSEs exist side by side with jobs requiring lower skills and offering lower wages further down the value chain, with a potential of widening inequalities between the two (Finegold, 1999, p. 65).

# 3 State of research

While Finegold focused on skills for and obtained through high technology and research and development activities, other researchers have demonstrated the applicability of the skill ecosystem approach to contexts different from the Silicon Valley clusters. References to skill ecosystems are mostly found in contributions from Australia, the United Kingdom and the United States (Buchanan et al., 2017). Hitherto available papers frequently conceptualise skill ecosystems as a desired process result. Common objectives of these studies are therefore to identify good practice examples of skill formation or to develop policy recommendations and ideas for reforms geared at skill ecosystem development.

In their analysis of "skills and work in the future" for the New South Wales Board of Vocational Education and Training, Buchanan et al. (2001, pp. 21–22) point to a key argument, since shared by other authors, for linking skill ecosystems also to vocational, intermediate and foundational skills. For them, focusing skills policy on HSEs alone would not be sustainable, as they involve only a minority of a nation's workforce. What is more, a challenge lies in avoiding the inequalities Finegold identified between HSEs and other labour market segments (Buchanan et al., 2001). Consequently, Buchanan et al. (2001, p. 23) conceive of skill ecosystems more generally "[...] as a means of thinking through issues associated with the linkages between work and skill [...]". Instead of drawing on Finegold's approach, they suggest analysing the interaction of several 'interlocking forces' prevalent in regional or sectoral skill ecosystems: business settings including competition strategy, markets and products; institutional and policy frameworks for skill formation; modes of engaging labour, for example, types of contracts and conditions of hiring and firing; the structure of jobs, for instance professional profiles and the organisation of work; and level and type of skill formation, that is access to and locations of training, assessment and certification.

In connection to this alternative way of thinking about skill ecosystems, the authors make two important points to be heeded when analysing skill ecosystems: Firstly, there is an internal diversity to skill ecosystems with regard to the work roles and professional profiles within and across the organisations skill ecosystems are made up of. This notably diverges from Finegold's HSEs in which universities act as transmission belts for a seemingly uniform group of highly skilled talent. Secondly, and in a nod to Finegold's emphasis of the importance of evolution for the survival of skill ecosystems, Buchanan et al. (2001, pp. 22–23) argue that a skill ecosystem approach can also be useful for understanding change in mature economic sectors.

In another Australian contribution, Windsor and Alcorso (2008, p. 11) see skill ecosystems at the centre of a strategy for "[...] developing holistic responses to workforce development". Even though they acknowledge Finegold's work on HSEs, the authors build on three Australian case studies to lay out several strategies for the development of skill ecosystems and provide guidelines for implementation programmes. Windsor and Alcorso (2008, p. 7) studied projects in the sectors of dairy foods manufacturing, disability services and gaming and digital content creation which aimed at the development of sectoral skill ecosystems. They find that when applied in such a prospective fashion, with a skill ecosystem becoming a joint mission, the skill ecosystem perspective can be useful for reaching a desired outcome. In Windsor and Alcorso's cases, the aim was to improve engagement between VET bodies and industry.

Dalziel's 2015 paper problematises skill mismatch in New Zealand. He argues that the main barrier to reducing skill mismatch is a coordination problem between employers and (future) employees. Employers tend to separate investment decisions that ultimately affect competition and production strategies from the available skills base. Learners and workers, in turn, risk investing in skills for which there is no labour market demand (Dalziel, 2015, pp. 1–2, 7). Dalziel therefore advocates for regional skill development systems to become ecosystems that facilitate employee–employer coordination. To this end, he develops an ecosystem framework adapted to fit the coordination problem he studied. What is interesting about Dalziel's work is that he adopts an actor-centred perspective that focuses on the role specific actors play or should play in a skill ecosystem. Dalziel (2015, pp. 10–12) proposes a "New Zealand System of Regional Skill Ecosystems" in which career offices and secondary and tertiary education organisations become "purposefully" acting agents, improving school-to-work transition through career decision and career development guidance and by building regional learning networks.

As can be drawn from the examples sketched above, available literature on skill ecosystems takes them as inspiration, or a lens to adjust their perspective, rather than engaging with Finegold's original analytical model as such.

A more recently emerging body of research, however, has stayed close to Finegold's work but at the same time offers the broadest, most direct conceptual expansion of it yet. The social ecosystem model (Hodgson & Spours, 2016; Grainger & Spours, 2018; Spours & Grainger, 2018; Spours, 2019; Wedekind et al., 2021) departs from the "social exclusionary effects" (Spours, 2019, p. 2) attributed to HSEs and is supposed to offer an inclusive, sustainable alternative that meets the needs of a wide range of learners and stakeholders.

The social ecosystem model aims to connect the spheres of working, living and learning; thus, it takes into account housing, transport, health and social services infrastructure, addresses access to decent jobs and digital developments and seeks to enable active citizenship.

In terms of geography, social ecosystems are area- or place-based rather than tied to clusters or industry regions. Emphasis is placed on "place shaping" through facilitating economic, civic and educational participation instead of the kind of "place utilisation" found in "elite entrepreneurial" HSEs (Spours 2019, pp. 6, 23). Thus far, social ecosystems have been primarily linked to the realities of cities or peri-urban areas. Drawing on the example of London, England, Spours (2019) as well as Spours and Grainger (2018) argue that the social ecosystem model can be particularly useful in supporting urban reform towards decentralisation or polycentric city planning and the strengthening of local economies. The social ecosystem model contains the four elements necessary for skill ecosystems as identified by Finegold and adds to them the dimensions of horizontal and vertical integration and the task of mediation between these dimensions. Verticalities are extensions of the elements 'catalysts' and 'supportive host environment' and comprise national and/or local governments, policy and regulation structures and regional political strategies that (are supposed to) facilitate the development of social ecosystems (Spours, 2019).

The horizontal dimension extends 'interdependent relations' and 'nourishment' to encompass networking and cooperation between local anchor institutions[4], employers and employees or their representative organisations and education and training providers, as well as community participation, and access to digital technologies (Spours, 2019).

While Finegold looked at HSEs in retrospect, examining how they came to be, the social ecosystem model approach is guided by prospective thinking. Social ecosystem models rest on an underlying idea of "mission-led innovation" and are conceptualised as actively "managed" ecosystems (Spours & Grainger, 2018, p. 1). Accordingly, mediation between the vertical and horizontal dimensions is achieved through a mission that is shared by the parties involved and by dedicated social ecosystem leadership, referred to as 45° mediation. It is suggested that collaborative building of social ecosystems be realised along several phases (Grainger & Spours, 2018, pp. 5–8).

In the first phase, the "spatial identity" needs to be determined, including the identification of problems and opportunities, as well as the definition of a joint mission for solving the former and exploiting the latter. The second phase encompasses a mapping exercise that sheds light on existing interrelationships, networks and projects, identifies potential catalysts, and sets in motion knowledge exchange. The first two phases pave the way for the development of a space-based strategy that integrates the area of skills with other relevant areas, such as the local economy, the environment or housing. This is followed by the third stage of network building. In the social ecosystem model, networks between public, private and community organisations concerned with working, living and learning are crucial for shaping the conditions in which social ecosystems can function and flourish. Networks facilitate the identification of shared values and local specificities as bases for the common mission. In phase three, social

4 Buchanan et al. (2020, p. 30) adapt the concept of "local anchor institution" to fit the skill ecosystems perspective. In his case study of Further Education Colleges in Wales, the researcher argues that an anchor institution, alongside its main function, plays a significant and recognised role in a locality by making a strategic contribution to the local economy and supporting a sense of local identity.

ecosystem projects are co-created and implemented. Co-creation is supposed to bring together various stakeholders, including firms, schools, learners, parents, unions, associations and other relevant entities such as chambers, local governments, employment agencies etc. In a final phase, ecosystem outputs such as new forms of learning or innovative work practices are collected and scrutinised.

The logic inherent to the incremental assembly of social ecosystem building blocks represents a time-related or "chrono" dimension that reflects the long-term perspective attached to this approach (Grainger & Spours, 2018, p. 6).

Through its governance- and time-related extensions, the social ecosystem model adds depth to Finegold's approach developed for HSEs. It also shows possibilities for conceptual expansion by linking ecosystem development to stakeholder engagement and co-creation, as well as social innovation and issues of transport and housing. Representing a multi-governance-level multi-actor framework, the social ecosystem model also mirrors the complexity of establishing social ecosystems. It is based on a forward-looking perspective and is therefore rather prescriptive than analytical. Even though Wedekind et al. (2021) have engaged in empirical application of the social ecosystem model, additional research is needed to develop it further.

## 4 Potentials and limitations

To date, research on VET does not present a very thorough understanding of skill formation at sub-national levels, because analyses are also commonly directed at the compilation and aggregation of findings for nation-level types of VET. Considering this, the ecosystem metaphor is helpful for zooming in on sub-national education and training arrangements. Skill ecosystems as a heuristic open a place-based route to researching VET and, provided that extensive data requirements are met, can first and foremost serve as a holistic *mapping tool* that invites researchers to identify and describe the relationships and wider social, political and economic contexts, as well as missing links, that characterise and shape VET in a specific geographic setting.

With a view to its potential for providing an analytical framework for the study of VET at the sub-national level, some caveats exist. Thus far, most research on skill ecosystems is applied and case-study based and, as a consequence, piecemeal rather than cumulative. In addition, skill ecosystems have not travelled far, as the geographical scope of publications has been limited mainly to Australia, the United States and the United Kingdom. Piecemeal application results in incoherence with regard to the object of research, and analytical depth of available literature varies from mapping to retrospective analysis to prospective planning for a skill ecosystem as a desired end-state. The latter function seems to dominate, as ecosystems contributions are frequently geared towards policy-makers. This might explain why the metaphor of the skill ecosystem has above all served as an inspiration; there has been little empirical engagement with the approach to advance it on a conceptual and theoretical level. To talk of *the* analytical approach in the face of the dominance of a metaphorical use over theoretical engagement is actually rather misleading.

An initial conceptual difficulty certainly lies in the delimitation of the geographic scope of the research to be undertaken. There is no blueprint at hand, and hitherto available studies on skill ecosystems reflect above all the scalability of the scope, as they variably focus on cities or metropolitan areas, federated states, sectors or industry clusters. The geographical location of a skill ecosystem is essentially a matter of empirical definition but guided by either political-administrative boundaries or economic geography or by the conjunction of both. In accordance with Finegold (1999), any analysis of a skill ecosystem should address its interconnectedness, be it regional, local or sectoral, with national economic and educational structures.

A further issue is that 'skill' remains a vague concept. Without engaging in a general debate about skills, it is suggested here that rather than qualifying skills as general or specific (see Streeck, 2012 for discussion), high or low (Brown et al., 2001), skills will only be clear from the context of the respective study. Assuming a retrospective analytical perspective, the study of existing skill ecosystems would, with as much precision as possible, take account of which skills exactly are produced within the ecosystem. Drawing loosely on Mournier (2001) a (at this stage non-exhaustive) set of guiding questions might be helpful for pinpointing skills in an ecosystem: How are skills defined, and how is their acquisition assessed? How is skill formation regulated? Where and how are skills acquired (e. g., on the job or in education and training, by public or private organisations)? Does the ecosystem entail initial and/or continuous skill formation?

Apart from resolving conceptual issues, skill ecosystem research will have to progress from description to actual analysis. While Finegold's four building blocks are a good starting point regarding *what* should be the subject of analysis, the *how* of building explanations for observed outcomes is still underdeveloped. Hence, skill ecosystem research would benefit if it were supplied with more sound theoretical underpinnings. It is suggested here that a neo-institutionalist perspective[5] could offer valuable anchors for a theorisation of skill ecosystem analysis. Throughout the past two decades, neo-institutionalist analysis of VET, particularly in the historical institutionalist tradition, has become a sizeable body of VET research. Historical institutionalist research on VET, by way of historical tracing (Beach, 2016; Trampusch & Palier, 2016), reconstructs the genesis and evolution of VET regimes and identifies formative periods that have set countries on their respective paths of vocational skill formation. Historicist analysis with attention paid to "historical junctures" (Thelen, 2004, p. 284) potentially presents research into the emergence of skill ecosystems with a sound analytical scaffolding.

Historical institutionalist research argues that the nature of VET is "strongly conditioned" (Trampusch, 2014, p. 14) by the institutions underpinning VET systems and that these institutions reflect and shape the outcomes of continuing political struggles between key players trying to maintain or change the status quo in the political arena of VET (Thelen, 2004). In skill ecosystem analysis, institutions as "[...] formal or informal procedures, routines, norms and conventions embedded in the organizational struc-

5 Refer to Hall and Taylor (1996) for an overview of neo-institutionalism.

ture of the polity or political economy" (Hall & Taylor, 1996, p. 9) could facilitate the characterisation of the host environment in which the ecosystem is embedded and also serve as explanatory variables for the specific set-up of the ecosystem. In institutionalist research, institutions are expected to shape power relations between, and the preferences and capacities of, key players. They therefore represent variables affecting co-operation and relationships between the actors and organisations involved in the eco-system and, thus, serve to explain different patterns of coordination and how they translate into the very processes of skill formation (Thelen, 2004; Busemeyer & Trampusch, 2012).

In addition, historical institutionalist advances in researching incremental, endogenous institutional change (Streeck & Thelen, 2005; Mahoney & Thelen, 2009) could be helpful in capturing the evolution of skill ecosystems. Institutionalist analysis would identify the mechanisms of reproduction and explain which institutional arrangements are "[...] getting stably reproduced over time and which are subject to renegotiation and why" (Thelen, 2004, p. 296). Focusing on institutional change provides an alternative to Finegold's (1999) argument of self-sustaining ecosystems, arguing that the maintenance and adaptation of skill ecosystems require actual "institutional work"[6] (Lawrence et al., 2009) by the players involved.

## 5 Concluding remarks

Researchers have long been intrigued by the variety that characterises VET across the globe. They have set out to identify the roots of, and to map and explain, commonalities and differences between VET systems, linking VET to the different economic and political propensities countries have at their disposal to build comparative economic advantage, and capacities for innovation and social coherence. In this context, researching variety within cases by way of applying a sub-national analytical lens could generate important insights regarding economic, social and political implications transpiring from regional differences in vocational skill formation. To date, those who are interested in researching VET at a sub-national level find that the analytical bases for such a scope are weakly developed. Finegold's skill ecosystem approach could represent a place to start. While research on skill ecosystems has paved the way to move from HSEs to a broader understanding of skills including VET, more work is needed as regards the theoretical pillars of ecosystem analysis. This chapter has suggested that linking skill ecosystem analysis with neo-institutionalist research, particularly with the growing body of historical institutionalist studies on VET, is a promising endeavour. Future research will have to show whether it comes to fruition.

6 Institutional work is defined as the "[...] 'purposive action of individuals and organizations aimed at creating, maintaining and disrupting institutions'" (Lawrence and Suddaby, 2006, p. 215, as cited in Lawrence, Suddaby and Leca, 2009, p. 1, authors' captions).

## References

Beach, D. (2016). It's all about mechanisms – what process-tracing case studies should be tracing. *New Political Economy, 21*(5), 463–472. https://doi.org/10.1080/13563467.2015.1134466

Becattini, G. (1979). Dal "Settore" industriale al "distretto" industriale. Alcune considerazioni sull'unità d'indagine dell'economia industrial. *Rivista di economia e politica industrial, 1*, 7–21.

Becattini, G. (1991). The industrial district as a creative milieu. In G. Benko & M. Dunford (Eds.), *Industrial change and regional development: The transformation of new industrial spaces*. Belhaven Press.

Blossfeld, H.-P. (1992). Is the German dual system a model for a modern vocational training system? *International Journal of Comparative Sociology, 33*(3–4), 168–181.

Brown, P., Green, A., & Lauder, H. (2001). *High skills: Globalization, competitiveness, and skill formation*. Oxford University Press.

Buchanan, J., Froud, J., Lang, M., Lloyd, C., Smith, B., & Williams, K. (2020). *Enabling renewal: Further education and building better citizenship, occupations and business communities in Wales*. Colleges Wales Research Report. https://www.colleges.wales/image/publications/reports/Enabling%20Renewal%20-%20FE/Enabling%20Renewal%20-%20FE.pdf

Buchanan, J., Anderson, P., & Power, G. (2017). Skill ecosystems. In J. Buchanan, D., Finegold, K. Mayhew, & C. Warhurst (Eds.), *The Oxford handbook of skills and training* (pp. 444–464). Oxford University Press.

Buchanan, J., Schofield, K., Briggs, C., Considine, G., Hager, P., Hawke, G., Kitay, J., Meagher, G., Macintyre, J., Mounier, A., & Ryan, S. (2001). *Beyond flexibility: Skills and work in the future*. NSW Board of Vocational Education and Training. http://hdl.voced.edu.au/10707/62961

Busemeyer, M. R., & Trampusch, C. (2012). *The political economy of collective skill formation*. Oxford University Press.

Busemeyer, M. R., & Thelen, K. (2012). Institutional change in German vocational training: From collectivism towards segmentalism. In M. R. Busemeyer & C. Trampusch (Eds.), *The political economy of collective skill formation* (pp. 68–100). Oxford University Press.

Cooke, P., & Piccaliaga, A. (Eds.), (2008). *Regional development in the knowledge economy*. Routledge.

Cooke, P., De Laurentis, C., Todtling, F., & Trippl, M. (Eds.), (2007). *Regional knowledge economies. Markets, clusters and innovation. New horizons in regional science*. Edward Elgar.

Crouch, C., Finegold, D., & Sako, M. (1999). *Are skills the answer? The political economy of skill creation in advanced industrial countries*. Oxford University Press.

Culpepper, P. D. (2003). *Creating cooperation. How states develop human capital in Europe*. Cornell University Press.

Dalziel, P. (2015). Regional skill ecosystems to assist young people making education employment linkages in transition from school to work. *Local Economy* (Special Issue February 2015), *30*(1), 53–66.

Deißinger, T. (1995). Das Konzept der "Qualifizierungsstile" als kategoriale Basis idealtypischer Ordnungsschemata zur Charakterisierung und Unterscheidung von "Berufsbildungssystemen". *Zeitschrift für Berufs- und Wirtschaftspädagogik, 91*(4), 367–387.

Emmenegger, P., Graf, L., & Trampusch, C. (2019). The governance of decentralised cooperation in collective training systems: A review and conceptualisation. *Journal of Vocational Education & Training, 71*(1), 21–45. https://doi.org/10.1080/13636820.2018.1498906

Emmenegger, P., & Seitzl, L. (2019). Collective action, business cleavages and the politics of control: Segmentalism in the Swiss skill formation system. *British Journal of Industrial Relations, 57*(3), 576–598. https://doi.org/10.1111/bjir.12426

Finegold, D. (1999). Creating self-sustaining high-skill ecosystems. *Oxford Review of Economic Policy, 15*(1), 60–81.

Finegold, D., & Soskice, D. (1988). The failure of training in Britain: Analysis and prescription. *Oxford Review of Economic Policy, 4*(3), 21–51.

Grainger, P., & Spours, K. (2018). *Future of work and education for the digital age: A social ecosystem model: A new paradigm for skills development?* [T20 Argentina 2018] Consejo Argentino para las relaciones internacionales (CARI). https://dera.ioe.ac.uk/id/eprint/34351/

Greinert, W.-D. (2008). *Steuerungsformen von Erwerbsqualifizierung und die aktuelle Perspektive europäischer Berufsbildungspolitik.* Reihe „Jugend und Arbeit – Positionen" der Bertelsmann-Stiftung. http://www.anti-bertelsmann.de/berufsbildung/Bertelsmann Greinert2008.pdf

Greinert, W.-D. (1998). *Das "deutsche System" der Berufsausbildung. Tradition, Organisation, Funktion. Studien zur Vergleichenden Berufspädagogik.* Nomos Verlagsgesellschaft.

Hall P. A., & Soskice, D. (2001). *Varieties of capitalism: The institutional foundations of comparative advantage.* Oxford University Press.

Hall, P. A., & Taylor, R. C. A. (1996). *Political science and the three new institutionalisms.* MPIFG Discussion Paper 96/6. https://pure.mpg.de/rest/items/item_1235717_3/component/file_1235716/content

Hodgson, A., & Spours, K. (2016). *The evolution of social ecosystem thinking: Its relevance for education, economic development and localities: A stimulus paper.* Centre for Post-14 Education and Work, UCL Institute of Education. https://discovery.ucl.ac.uk/id/eprint/1537510/3/Spours_Ecosystem%20thinking%20Stimulus%20Paper.pdf

Lauterbach, U. (2003). Vergleichende Berufsbildungsforschung und vergleichende Erziehungswissenschaft als Referenzdisziplinen? *Zeitschrift für Berufs- und Wirtschaftspädagogik, 99*(4), 514–535.

Lauterbach, U., & Mitter, W. (1998). *Theory and methodology of international comparisons. Vocational education and training – the European research field. Background report – Volume II.* Office for Official Publications of the European Communities.

Lawrence, T., Suddaby, R., & Leca, B. (2009). Introduction: Theorizing and studying institutional work. In T. Lawrence, R. Suddaby, & B. Leca (Eds.), *Institutional work: Actors and agency in institutional studies of organizations* (pp. 1–28). Cambridge University Press. https://doi.org/10.1017/CBO9780511596605

Lawrence, T., & Suddaby, R. (2006). Institutions and Institutional work. In S. R. Clegg, C. Hardy, T. B. Lawrence, & W. R. Nord (Eds.), *Sage handbook of organization studies* (2nd ed., pp. 215–254). Sage.

Mahoney, J., & Thelen, K. (2009). A theory of gradual institutional change. In J. Mahoney & K. Thelen (Eds.), *Explaining institutional change: Ambiguity, agency, and power* (pp. 1–37). Cambridge University Press. https://doi.org/10.1017/CBO9780511806414.003

Maier, G., Tödtling, F., & Trippl, M. (2008). *Regional- und Stadtökonomik 2. Regionalentwicklung und Regionalpolitik. Vierte, aktualisierte Auflage.* Springer-Verlag. https://doi.org/10.1007/978-3-211-75619-5

Martin, C. J. (2012). Vocational training and the origins of coordination: Specific skills and the politics of collective action. In M. R. Busemeyer & C. Trampusch (Eds.), *The political economy of collective skill formation* (pp. 41–67). Oxford University Press.

Mournier, A. (2001): *Three logics of skills in French literature.* Australian Centre for Industrial Relations Research and Teaching Working Paper No. 66. https://ses.library.usyd.edu.au/bitstream/handle/2123/13397/WP66.pdf?sequence=1

Oliver, D. (2010). Complexity in vocational education and training governance. *Research in Comparative and International Education, 5*(3), 261–273. https://doi.org/10.2304/rcie.2010.5.3.261

Snower, D. (1994). *The low-skill, bad-job trap.* International Monetary Fund Working Paper 94/83. https://ssrn.com/abstract=883810

Spours, K. (2019). *A social ecosystem model: Conceptual developments and implications for VET. Working discussion paper.* UCL. https://discovery.ucl.ac.uk/id/eprint/10082170/

Spours, K., & Grainger, P. (2018). *A social ecosystem model: A new paradigm for skills development? G20 insights.* Global Solutions Initiative. https://www.global-solutions-initiative.org/policy_brief/a-social-ecosystem-model-a-new-paradigm-for-skills-development/

Streeck, W. (2012). Skills and politics: General and specific. In M. R. Busemeyer & C. Trampusch (Eds.), *The political economy of collective skill formation* (pp. 317–352). Oxford University Press.

Streeck, W., & Thelen, K. (2005). Introduction: Institutional change in advanced political economies. In W. Streeck & K. Thelen (Eds.), *Beyond continuity: Institutional change in advanced political economies* (pp. 1–39). Oxford University Press.

Thelen, K. (2004). *How institutions evolve: The political economy of skills in Germany, Britain, the United States, and Japan.* Cambridge University Press.

Trampusch, C., & Palier, B. (2016). Between X and Y: How process tracing contributes to opening the black box of causality. *New Political Economy, 21*(5), 437–454. https://doi.org/10.1080/13563467.2015.1134465

Trampusch, C. (2014). Collective skill formation: A historical analysis of the least-likely case New Zealand. *Journal of Vocational Education & Training, 66*(2), 135–155. https://doi.org/10.1080/13636820.2014.894934

Vicente, J. (2018). *Economics of clusters: A brief history of cluster theories and policy*. Palgrave Pivot.

Wedekind, V., Russon, J., Ramsarup, P., Monk, D., Metelerkamp, L., & McGrath, S. (2021). Conceptualising regional skills ecosystems: Reflections on four African cases. *International Journal of Training and Development, 25*(4), 347–362. https://doi.org/10.1111/ijtd.12251

Windsor, K., & Alcorso, C. (2008). *Skills in context. A guide to the skill ecosystem approach to workforce development*. New South Wales Department of Education and Training (Ed.). https://www.voced.edu.au/content/ngv%3A12460

## Short portrait of the author

**Fabienne-Agnes Baumann** is a Researcher for the Institut für Innovation und Technik (iit) and consultant at the VDI/VDE-IT in Munich. Her research focuses on the politics of vocational education and training and on international comparison of vocational training systems and training reforms.
Contact: baumann@iit-berlin.de

# The case of Lower Saxony

# Diversity at a glance: Vocational education and training in Germany, between standardisation and fragmentation

DIETMAR FROMMBERGER

**Abstract:** In Germany, although the well-known 'dual apprenticeship system' is predominant, initial and continuing/higher education and training are offered in a multitude of variants, with their own regulations, governance, learning venues, and targets. Therefore, the nation's great success in terms of employment and the training of a skilled workforce, normally attributed to the company-based dual apprenticeship system, must be interpreted as the result of a much more complex vocational education and training (VET) provision, wherein heterogeneous offerings are able to satisfy different company qualification needs, societal and educational demands, and individual interests. Moreover, consideration should be given to whether a more pronounced overall perspective on the design of VET may improve the system as a whole.

**Keywords:** Dual Apprenticeship; Germany; Higher Vocational Education and Training; School-Based Vocational Education and Training; Vocational Education and Training.

## 1 Vocational education and training as part of the education system in Germany

In attempts to provide a comprehensive presentation of education systems, a distinction is usually made between the areas of general education, higher education, and vocational education and training (VET). Often, the area of (general, academic, and vocational) continuing education is also added, as is special or inclusive education. In detail, these areas are made up of very different general, higher education, and VET programmes, which often differ significantly internationally, particularly when considering the transitions between these different educational areas. This article focuses on the area of VET, including higher VET. However, the fact that there are intersections between general, vocational, and higher education is also kept in view here. These intersections are expressed, for example, by the fact that a VET programme awards a further general education qualification in addition to a vocational qualification. Furthermore, there is a growing tendency to combine VET and higher education qualifications, for example, through so-called dual study programmes.

Another analytical approach to the overall representation of education systems lies in the distinction between formal, non-formal, and informal opportunities. Formal education is usually organised, recognised, or regulated by the state. Non-formal offerings are often organised by the private sector. These systems are predominantly aimed at the provision of certificates and degrees that are not otherwise integrated into the overall education system. Informal learning processes are those that are not standardised and that take place 'along the way' in the context of work or everyday life. In many countries, there have been strong efforts to identify and assess these informal learning processes (and learning outcomes) through various instruments (e. g. competence assessment) to link them to the non-formal and formal education system. The non-formal and informal VET programmes are therefore, unlike the formal programmes, not integrated into the institutional framework of the VET system and do not follow any inter-company standards (e. g. curricular principles, additional or compatible qualifications, or qualification requirements for the staff providing the training).

This article mainly focuses on formal VET offerings. Accordingly, the many non-formal offerings, as well as the very significant and comprehensive informal qualification practices and learning experiences that are currently provided, are not taken into account here.

## 2 Transitions from school to vocational education and training: The five sectors following general education

At the end of lower secondary school, a large proportion of pupils transfer to a special VET programme to obtain a full professional qualification. In addition, many pupils transfer to a VET programme after the lower secondary level to catch up on or acquire an additional general education qualification (e. g. a higher education entrance qualification) and then transfer to another VET programme for professional qualification. A relatively high number of pupils who, after lower secondary education, attend general upper secondary education and acquire a higher education entrance qualification there (e. g. at grammar schools or comprehensive schools) also transfer to special VET programmes for professional qualifications. Thus, in certain initial VET programmes (e. g. in the commercial training or nursing occupations), there are many young adults who have previously acquired a higher education entrance qualification.

This phenomenon is typical of individual educational choice behaviour in Germany. Internationally, however, this progression through the various upper secondary-level programmes and the long stay at this level of education is relatively unusual. Overall, about two-thirds of a student cohort in Germany were found to have completed some form of VET at the upper secondary level (Autor:innengruppe Bildungsberichterstattung, 2022, p. 131). However, only half of the group that had left lower secondary education and transferred to a programme in the area of VET elected to pursue a track within the so-called dual apprenticeship system (Autor:innengruppe Bildungsberichterstattung, 2022, p. 167). This is why it is so important to attend to those VET programmes that exist aside from dual apprenticeship programmes for a full understanding of VET in Germany.

In the following sections, we briefly describe the different initial VET programmes that students attend after the lower or upper secondary level of general education. Generally, we distinguish between five different VET sectors at the upper secondary level in Germany:

- Company-based dual apprenticeship programmes;
- School-based dual VET programmes;
- Vocationally-oriented and partially qualifying VET programmes;
- VET programmes for people with learning difficulties and disabilities (i. e. vocational rehabilitation); and
- VET programmes at upper VET schools.

The VET programmes in these five sectors are very diverse. In detail, there are many different variants and characteristics that have emerged in various states and at the regional and local levels. We will shed some insight into this diversity below.

## 2.1 Company-based dual apprenticeship programmes

Company-based dual apprenticeship programmes are the main focus of initial VET opportunities in Germany. The central feature is the close proximity of the learning processes to the area of work in a particular company based on a training contract between the apprentice and the company. In this case, school leavers apply for a training place offered by a company. Thus, the transition from general education to VET takes place in the apprenticeship market. Training companies alone decide to whom they will offer an apprenticeship contract on the basis of their own preferences. The only formal prerequisite for an apprenticeship is the completion of compulsory full-time schooling.

For many decades, this apprenticeship market was characterised above all by the fact that there were significantly more young people applying than there were apprenticeships available. This allowed the companies to make their selections, to a large extent, on the basis of their own individual criteria. Many young people did not receive an offer at all, or at least none that corresponded with their interests. For some years now, however, this situation in the apprenticeship market has been subject to significant change. Specifically, the supply market has been increasingly transitioning into a demand market, and many apprenticeship spots remain unfilled. The reasons for this lie in demographic changes and, thus, in the smaller number of school leavers. In addition, however, educational choices have also been changing. The appeal of dual apprenticeships has diminished, and young people are increasingly opting for more attractive VET options in order to acquire university entrance qualifications that cannot directly be obtained in the dual apprenticeship system.

The contractual training relationship between the training company and the apprentice is linked to instruction at the VET school. There, trainees from the same training occupations but different training companies in a certain region are usually taught in class groups specific to the occupation. Accordingly, the instruction that takes place here is related to the specific training occupation and the associated occupational field, as well as to subjects of general education.

VET in these company-based dual apprenticeships has a long tradition. In fact, this approach has its origins in the guilds' apprenticeships of craftsmen and commercial assistants. Over time, especially in the first decades of the 20th century, this approach to qualification was transferred to industry. The supplementation of learning in the company with the attendance of VET schools also solidified into an established practice during this period. The first comprehensive legal regulation for in-company training came in the form of the Vocational Training Act of 1969. Prior to this, in-company qualifications had been regulated by various trade laws. The 1969 Act attempted to standardise in-company learning to ensure minimum quality standards. The Act also made a decisive contribution to the protection of young trainees from being abused as cheap labour. In addition, the link between learning in the company and at the VET school was further institutionalised. Trainees were henceforth released from work to attend VET schools. Amendments to this nationwide Vocational Training Act were made in 2005 and 2020. Parallel to this legal regulation of in-company qualification, learning in VET schools has been subject to regulation by the school laws of the federated states due to the federal structure.

There are about 320 different training occupations (*Ausbildungsberufe*) in the company-based dual programme. In recent decades, the number of training occupations has decreased significantly, and the curricula have become broader and broader. Today, many specialisations concerning the working processes in companies are accounted for through special ranges of the curricula (Bretschneider & Schwarz, 2015). In general, a distinction is made between two-year training occupations on the one hand and three- or three-and-a-half-year training occupations on the other, which are classified in the German Qualifications Framework at Level 3 and Level 4, respectively.

As a rule, VET in the company-based dual apprenticeship system primarily takes place in a training company and is combined with attendance in a VET school. In-company qualifications are often supplemented by courses at inter-company VET centres (*überbetriebliche Berufsbildungsstätten*, ÜBS). Because many training companies cannot cover the breadth of the training requirements of the curriculum, these inter-company learning centres supplement in-company VET. In principle, VET in this system takes place in at least three typical learning venues: in the company, in the inter-company training centre, and in the VET school. However, there are other variants, such as joint training (i. e. the combination of different companies for the training of a trainee) or specialised school forms, in which a training contract is concluded with a VET school, and the in-company practice then takes place through various internships.

Through VET in the company-based dual system, it is possible to acquire further general school-leaving qualifications on the basis of a certain minimum performance in VET schools. These general school-leaving qualifications are limited to lower secondary education. The acquisition of a higher education entrance qualification on the basis of this company-based route is not yet common in Germany.

The proof of a successful apprenticeship in the company is provided by passing a final examination for which the chambers are responsible. These chambers, which include the Chamber of Crafts, the Chamber of Agriculture, and the Chamber of Industry and Commerce, among others, are public organisations that represent businesses. In a sense, they are successor institutions to traditional guilds. According to the Vocational Training Act, they are responsible for monitoring the quality of VET for the companies involved. Therefore, they are also responsible for the final examinations. Accordingly, they award certificates for vocational qualifications, such as a journeyman's certificate or a skilled worker's certificate.

Traditionally, VET in a company-based dual apprenticeship system has been very popular. For decades, many young people in Germany have chosen this form of VET, including graduates of upper secondary education. The social recognition of this VET path is relatively high, and the subsequent employment opportunities and professional development possibilities are good. For many companies and sectors, dual apprenticeships are a central form of recruiting and developing skilled workers. When taking a closer look, however, the company and technical requirements and training quality across the various occupations vary greatly. Specifically, there are training occupations with higher requirements, for which companies predominantly recruit graduates from upper secondary education. Furthermore, there are training occupations for young adults who have acquired low or no school-leaving qualifications. Overall, the heterogeneity of trainees is very pronounced between the different training occupations, but also within the same ones. In the dual apprenticeship system, there are school leavers without school-leaving certificates, those with lower secondary school-leaving certificates, and those with upper secondary school-leaving certificates, as well as drop-outs, adult apprentices, and others.

As already indicated above, clear changes have been observed in the apprenticeship market for this system for almost 10 years. Over time, the number of training contracts has tended to decline (Christ et al., 2023). Companies looking for trainees are now faced with the challenge of finding suitable prospects. Whereas in earlier times, companies were still able to select the young people they considered suitable from a large number of applications, this situation has changed significantly in recent years. In the meantime, school leavers can choose their training spots in many regions and training occupations. In the existing research, this market mechanism (formerly a supply market, but today a demand market) is described as a 'fitting problem' (Matthes et al., 2014). In other words, there is a mismatch between the expectations of the training companies and the interests and prerequisites of the applicants, so that as a result, fewer apprenticeship contracts are able to come about. In this regard, the article by Tim Migura in this volume takes a closer look at the developments in the training market in the federated state of Lower Saxony.

### 2.2 School-based dual vocational education and training programmes

Typical examples of school-based dual VET programmes are those for health and care professionals (e. g. nursing professionals) or educational professionals (e. g. nursery or curative education nurses). Therapist occupations (e.g. physiotherapist, occupational therapist, and speech therapist) are also included in this group. These vocational training programmes are very popular and in high demand, with a trend that continues to grow. At the same time, the demand for skilled workers in these personal service occupations is very high.

These programmes are often referred to as school-based training programmes, as the overall responsibility for the training lies with VET schools (*Berufsfachschulen*). School leavers apply to these specialised VET schools for a training spot. In fact, this system could also be considered exemplary of a 'dual' VET programme, as it combines vocational and school-based learning with extensive learning phases in companies. Learning in the company (e.g. in hospitals, geriatric care facilities, day-care centres, or therapeutic facilities) is combined with learning in a VET school, as in the case of the company-based dual apprenticeship system (see above). In these cases, school-based learning takes place in VET schools. These VET schools are private or public and are often closely linked to companies, so the coordination of learning processes between the company and the VET school works relatively well.

Some of the VET schools for most of these health professions are publicly funded and are then a type of school within a public VET school. However, most of them are VET schools run by independent or private organisations (e.g. churches or hospitals), which are generally recognised by the state. These VET schools of independent or private sponsorship are then not subject to the supervision of the Ministries of Education and Cultural Affairs, but rather to the Ministries of Health or Social Affairs in the states. These school-based dual VET programmes are regulated by specific occupational licensing laws (federal laws) or the school laws of the federated states, and in some cases by further federal legislation. The federal occupational licensing laws (e.g. the Nursing Professions Act), which apply in particular to the health and healing professions, stipulate that the exercise of an occupation in this area requires, among other things, training, which is concluded with a state examination; on the basis of these occupational licensing laws, training and examination ordinances (e.g. the Nursing Professions Training Ordinance) are usually issued, which include more detailed provisions on training, such as the duration, structure, and subject matter of the training and examination; requirements for training centres and examination boards; and prerequisites for admission to training.

In addition to the school-based dual VET programmes above, the federated state school laws regulate different VET programmes at specialised VET schools, which are located at public VET schools (*berufsbildende Schulen*, BBS). Examples include auxiliary and assistant training in health and care (e.g. geriatric care assistant and care assistant) and training in the education and social professions (e.g. educator and curative education nurse). Other examples consist of training in the so-called assistant occupations, which fall into the areas of laboratory technology, communication, and design technology, as well as secretarial work and foreign languages.

Entry into all tracks of school-based dual VET is dependent on certain minimum general education qualifications. The VET schools are the lead learning venue that guides the learners through the training together with the companies. However, all these programmes fall under other legal regulations, specifically the school laws of the federated states and the various federal occupational licensing laws, and not under the Vocational Training Act. Therefore, they are not referred to in Germany as VET in the 'dual apprenticeship system'. Furthermore, in the official statistics, these school-based dual VET programmes are subsumed under full-time school-based VET. However, due to the very high importance of in-company training in these programmes, this widespread understanding is misleading. One of the strengths of these school-based dual VET programmes compared to those offered in the company-based dual apprenticeship system is that in the former case, VET can be combined with further general education qualifications, and in some cases also with a higher education entrance qualification. This immensely increases the attractiveness of these programmes.

### 2.3 Vocationally-oriented and partially qualifying vocational education and training programmes

Many young people who would like to start VET after attending a general lower secondary school do not find a training place in one of the abovementioned company-based or school-based dual programmes in Germany. Often, they do not meet the school requirements for entering such a programme or do not meet the expectations of the companies to secure an apprenticeship contract. They also often do not meet the school requirements for further general education. Fortunately, VET programmes are available for these young people, which serve to further develop their learning skills at school and impart a vocational orientation and further general education qualifications.

In essence, all programmes aim to support young people in making a transition from school to work or gainful employment. In this respect, these VET programmes are subsumed under the so-called transition system. They serve the purpose of vocational orientation and the acquisition of a first or further general school-leaving certificate, such as a lower secondary school-leaving certificate. In addition, the offerings in the transition system ensure that many pupils are able to fulfil the requirements of their compulsory schooling.

This particular VET offering is diverse and group oriented in focus. It is offered by state VET schools or private training providers. The programmes offered by private training providers are often financed by the Federal Employment Agency. The target groups are very different. For some years, the proportion of refugee groups in these programmes has been increasing. However, overall, the proportion of learners in this transition system has been decreasing for several years. This is due to demographic developments and, in connection with this, to the fact that a change to the company-based dual apprenticeship programmes has become more likely.

Typical vocational training offerings provided by the transition system are as follows:

- There are one- and two-year courses at public VET schools, which are referred to as the so-called vocational preparation year (*Berufsvorbereitungsjahr*). These programmes have different names in different federated states. In Lower Saxony, for instance, these VET programmes are called *Berufseinstiegsschule* (BES). These programmes are also offered as language and integration classes, which are tailored to refugees in particular. Public VET schools are very engaged in taking care of all the different refugees in Germany. These one- and two-year programmes of the *Berufseinstiegsschule* are mainly offered as full-time school programmes. In some cases, internships are provided. The main aim of these programmes is to place school leavers into a company-based dual apprenticeship. After that, it will be possible for them to obtain a lower general secondary school-leaving certificate.

- Another typical offering is the *Berufsvorbereitende Bildungsgänge* (BvB); these courses are offered by private training providers and financed by the Federal Employment Agency. The main focus is on general skills development and vocational orientation (Beer, 2022).
- Another option is based on an internship called *Einstiegsqualifizierungen* (EQ). These are in-company internships lasting between six and twelve months. These measures are also financed by the Federal Employment Agencies. These internships are supposed to be credited toward a company-based dual apprenticeship afterwards.
- Next to the abovementioned different tracks, there are various other offerings, such as school-based vocational oriented tracks to obtain a first school-leaving certificate or an orientation for a company-based or school-based dual programme. These many different options within the transition system are often financed on the basis of being programmes for young people with special needs by the federal state, federated states, or locally.
- In addition, there are other offerings that vary greatly nationwide, statewide, or even regionally and locally. With a multitude of programmes, attempts have been made to enable young people to connect to further development. Nevertheless, this 'jungle' of measures is hard to keep track of. A systematic integration of the transition system into an overall vocational system and further efforts to create greater transparency are not yet apparent.

## 2.4 Vocational rehabilitation for people with learning difficulties and disabilities

The spectrum of VET provision for people with an impairment or disability and a special need for support is diverse. First, there are those offerings that are part of the VET programmes described above and are therefore to be understood as fully or partially inclusive (e.g. those provided in the company-based dual system or in the transition system; see the following explanations). There are also vocational rehabilitation services that are exclusively aimed at this target group (e.g. *Berufsförderwerken*). The people for whom these offerings exist are also very diverse. Since their impairments are very different, the diagnosis of the specific learning impairment, disability, and need for support is decided on a case-by-case basis. Determining the need for support is, therefore, a very important task and is often taken over by the Federal Employment Agency.

However, transitions often take place without explicit identification of support needs and based on previous assessments of limitations. Therefore, the concrete transitions for this target group from general education to the various forms of VET and vocational rehabilitation strongly depend on individual support conditions and are thus very divergent. Also, because the general education special school in Germany ends after the tenth grade, and a reorientation takes place afterwards, close personal support is needed but often lacking.

Typical offerings for people with learning impairments and disabilities are part of the system of company-based dual apprenticeship programmes (Beer, 2023, p. 38). These offerings are based on § 66 of the Vocational Training Act (BBiG) and § 42r of the Crafts Code (HwO). They are so-called specialist trainee or worker training programmes (e. g. for a specialist trainee kitchen worker or specialist trainee warehouse worker). The training regulations are based on those that exist for other programmes (e. g. kitchen specialist, cook, or warehouse specialist) but are adapted to the requirements of the target group. Model regulations are available from the Federal Institute for Vocational Education and Training (BIBB). The competent bodies, in particular the chamber organisations, can define specific requirements and examination modalities. In fact, there are very different regulations in the various chamber districts, and there is actually no systematic coordination between them concerning these programmes.

VET according to § 66 BBiG/§ 42r HwO is subordinate to regular VET according to the Vocational Training Act and is therefore subject to admission restrictions. Before taking up training as a worker or skilled tradesperson, the lack of aptitude for regular VET must therefore be determined. This is done by the Vocational Psychology Service of the Federal Employment Agency. High demands are placed on the suitability of the training companies and the training staff. As a rule, the suitability of the training staff must be proven by an additional qualification specific to rehabilitation. The training companies often cooperate with a training provider (e. g. a *Berufsförderwerk* or *Berufsbildungswerk*). While the company-based learning that takes place on the basis of these regulations can be understood as inclusive, the actual learning often does not take place in VET school classes specific to the training occupation. Therefore, training is generally not as inclusive as it may appear.

## 2.5 Vocational education and training programmes at the upper vocational school level

These programmes in upper VET schools comprise the *Berufliche Gymnasium* (VET high school), the *Fachoberschule* (FOS), and the *Berufsoberschule* (BOS). The central function of these three types of school-based learning systems is to provide a higher education entrance qualification, including a general qualification for university entrance. These school forms are related to a specific occupational field, such as health and social work, electrical engineering, or business. The curriculum is therefore also related to one of these occupational fields. In addition, typical general education subjects are taught.

The vocational tracks are offered at state VET schools. Many pupils who did not attend the *Gymnasium* or another type of school with an upper cycle in general secondary education and who wish to acquire a higher education entrance qualification change to a type of school in the vocational upper cycle. Traditionally, these vocational upper secondary school programmes have been developed to offer persons who first completed vocational training after lower secondary school with the opportunity to acquire a higher education entrance qualification, which was granted in connection with the introduction of universities of applied sciences in the 1970s. In the meantime, however, many young people switch to vocational upper secondary school directly after lower secondary school.

Vocational high school lasts three years and leads to a general higher entrance qualification. The FOS is offered as a two-year or one-year programme. The two-year option includes a work placement that lasts a total of one year. The one-year variant is purely academic and is for those who have previously completed vocational training. In both variants, the university entrance qualification for universities of applied sciences is acquired. The BOS is a further school year that follows on from the FOS and generally leads to a higher education entrance qualification.

# 3 Higher vocational education and training

Higher VET provision (*Berufliche Weiterbildung, Berufliche Fortbildung,* or *Aufstiegsfortbildung*) aims to provide higher-level VET qualifications and builds on the VET qualifications and professional experience that have already been obtained. These continuing VET qualifications are intended to contribute to advanced professional careers, accompanied by an increase in responsibility in the area of company expenditure. In addition, these higher VET degrees are linked to entrance qualifications for higher education based on the regulations for university admission found in the higher education laws of the federated states. In this respect, graduates of higher VET can acquire a higher education entrance qualification, which allows them to take up a course of study without having previously acquired a school-based higher education entrance qualification (e.g. Abitur).

The offerings of higher VET must be distinguished from the numerous offerings of in-company higher VET. The latter are to be understood as informal or non-formal and are usually related to very company-specific qualification needs. Higher VET programmes are linked to formal qualifications that are subject to state or state-recognised regulations. Therefore, higher VET qualifications are also associated with additional entitlements in the higher education system. The higher VET sector in Germany has become increasingly standardised and transparent in recent years. This shift has been born out of the intention to strengthen the VET pathway as a whole.

The spectrum of higher VET is very diverse and broad (similar to the area of initial VET; see above). In addition to the nationwide regulations based on the Vocational Training Act and the Crafts Code, there are others based on special occupational classification laws, as well as a large number of state-specific regulations based on the school laws of the federated states. Furthermore, a large number of regional regulations are issued by chambers and relate to the specific chamber districts. The central areas of higher VET provision are summarised below (Frommberger & Schmees, 2024).

### 3.1 Higher VET on the basis of federated state school laws

Higher VET programmes on the basis of the school laws of the federated states in Germany are offered at public VET schools (*Berufsbildende Schulen, Fachschulen,* and *Fachakademien*). These programmes usually last two to three years, with a scope of about 2,400 hours of instruction. The courses that impart bindingly defined content are offered in different formats (full-time and part-time; KMK, 2021).

A state-recognised examination is held for this school-based higher VET. The titles of the school-based programmes include, for example, 'state-certified technician' or 'state-certified business economist'. The federated states may also provide the title of 'Bachelor Professional', combined with the designation of the relevant subject area. Entry requirements include completion of initial VET and several years of professional experience. The completed VET can be school-based dual VET according to federated state law or company-based dual apprenticeships according to BBiG or other regulations (e. g. regulated VET in the health and care sector).

The higher VET qualifications obtained at school enjoy a high reputation and are known to open up professional advancement and career paths. These qualifications are classified at Level 6 in the German Qualifications Framework (DQR).

### 3.2 Higher vocational education and training on the basis of the Vocational Training Act (BBiG) and the Crafts Code (HwO)

The BBiG and the HwO are federal laws that regulate company-based VET. In addition to company-based dual apprenticeships, these federal laws also regulate a diverse range of higher VET programmes, namely the range that is the responsibility of chamber organisations.

Higher VET, according to BBiG/HwO, should "make it possible to maintain and adapt or expand one's ability to act and to advance professionally" (§ 1 para. 4 BBiG, transl. by the author). As a result, a distinction is made between adaptation and upgrading one's education and training. Adaptation training serves to ensure that one can adapt or maintain their vocational knowledge and skills, among other things, as a reaction to social or technical changes. In contrast, the purpose of upgrading one's education and training is to expand the ability to act professionally or to advance professionally, and thus to gain higher professional qualifications.

Prerequisites for admission to an examination are the relevant initial VET and several years of professional experience. The completed initial VET may be a school-based or company-based VET programme or another option, such as regulated initial VET in the health and care sector. However, admission is usually also possible if several years of relevant professional experience can be proven. Formally, attendance in preparatory courses is not required for this higher VET examination.

The higher VET courses are based on the nationwide regulations in the BBiG (§ 53 BBiG) or on the regional regulations of the chambers (§ 54 BBiG). In the commercial sector, the qualifications usually include the designation *Fachwirtin/Fachwirt*, whereas the designation *Industriemeisterin/Industriemeister* is used in the industrial sector, and *Handwerksmeisterin/Handwerksmeister* is applied in the crafts sector. The regulations contain examination requirements, including admission requirements and examination procedures (Hagen, 2019, p. 403). In contrast to the regulations in the company-based dual apprenticeship system, which contain a binding education and training framework plan, a framework plan for the design of the examination preparation courses and their scope of hours is all that is recommended for higher VET. The examination is taken at the chambers, and analogous to the final examination of the apprenticeships, the chamber sets up corresponding examination boards for this purpose (§ 56 BBiG).

As mentioned above, a course is not formally necessary for admission to the examination. To prepare for the final examination, however, preparatory courses are offered on the free market by various private training providers. These courses are fee based and do not follow any explicit quality standards. The course fees are either paid by the companies (if there is a corresponding company interest) or financed by the participants themselves. Financial support is possible through an education voucher (for people who cannot bear the costs due to their income) or within the framework of the so-called *Aufstiegs-BAföG'* (Federal Ministry of Justice, 2020). Preparatory courses are offered on a full-time or part-time basis as classroom or distance-learning courses.

In 2020, there were 202 regulations at the federal level for higher VET in accordance with the Vocational Training Act or the Crafts Code. In addition to these regulations at the federated level, there were 746 chamber regulations (Schneider & Waechter, 2021). A positive aspect of this structure is that there are regional specialisation options.

With the last amendment to the BBiG, which came into force on January 1, 2020, a new legal designation was established for upgrading higher VET in the form of higher VET. The aim was to establish this option more strongly as a brand and to promote social recognition in the national context on the one hand and international comparability on the other. In line with DQR Levels 5 to 7, higher VET comprises three levels. The first level is referred to as a 'Certified Occupational Specialist' qualification (Level 5). The scope of learning to acquire the skills, knowledge, and abilities for this level should amount to at least 400 hours (§ 53b BBiG). The second level operates under a 'Bachelor Professional' designation (Level 6). The scope of learning for acquiring the skills, knowledge, and abilities in this case should amount to at least 1,200 hours (§ 53c BBiG). The third level of higher VET is called the 'Master Professional' (Level 7). The scope of learning for acquiring the skills, knowledge, and abilities for this designation should amount to at least 1,600 hours (§ 53d BBiG).

For higher VET on the basis of BBiG, these specifications regarding the scope of teaching hours are optional and not mandatory requirements. For higher VET on the basis of the federated states, all the regulations are mandatory, and the scope of teaching hours is also much higher. Admission to the examination for higher VET on the basis of BBiG is possible without these explicit learning achievements and instead on the basis of the admission requirements based on the higher VET regulations, which are related to professional experience. In contrast, admission to the examination for higher VET on the basis of the federated states requires that these hours of instruction be obtained.

### 3.3 Higher vocational education and training in the nursing and health care professions

For this set of programmes, the focus is on the area of higher VET that follows on from the initial VET offerings for the nursing and healthcare professions, which are regulated on the basis of occupational licensing laws. In addition to the many different informal and on-formal offerings, of which there are a large number in this sector, there are offerings that allow for one's qualifications to be upgraded. These fall under higher VET ordinances or higher VET laws, which exist in different forms in federated states. In Lower Saxony, for example, there is the Lower Saxony Health Professions Act (NGesFBG), which is the responsibility of the Federal State Ministry of Health and Social Affairs. There are no concrete designations for higher VET that follow on from the relevant initial VET programmes. The spectrum of degrees is diverse, and a clear order does not exist (Bensch & Greening, 2021, pp. 8–9). For example, a typical higher VET offering in the nursing sector would be higher education and training to become a palliative care specialist, which is regulated by law in some federal states, but not in others (Bensch & Greening, 2021, p. 9). The German Nursing Education Council has published a model for further education and training regulations for the nursing professions (MWBO PflB) to provide some orientation amidst this confusion (Deutsches Institut für angewandte Pflegeforschung, 2017, cited in Bensch & Greening, 2021).

### 3.4 Vocational reeducation and retraining

In Germany, vocational retraining is usually assigned to the area of higher VET. The so-called *Umschulung* is usually taken up by people who have been unemployed for a long time or who can no longer work in their previous occupations due to health impairments. Vocational retraining can be financially supported according to the regulations of the Social Code III (§§ 81–87 SGB III).

Strictly speaking, retraining is considered an initial VET under these regulations. However, since these are persons who by and large possess a VET qualification and work in this occupation, this offering of vocational retraining is subsumed under higher VET. The people involved in these programmes are often much older. Accordingly, they usually complete this vocational retraining together with other younger students in a typical school-based or company-based initial VET offering.

Vocational retraining is intended to enable people to take up another occupation (§ 1 para. 5 BBiG) or, in other words, to qualify them for an occupation other than the one they have been engaged in up to now. Retraining may be directed towards a qualification recognised under the BBiG (§ 60 BBiG) or towards other (regional) vocational retraining qualifications regulated by the chambers (§§ 58, 59 BBiG). In addition, vocational retraining also takes place for other qualifications not regulated by the BBiG, as in the case of the health sector described above (Frommberger & Schmees, 2024).

## 4 Final remarks

Ultimately, this article shows how diverse VET is in Germany. Initial and higher VET is offered in a multitude of variants. The regulation of these offerings is determined on the part of different legal bodies, combined with different standards for quality assurance. In addition, even within the various offerings, such as the company-based dual apprenticeship system, the concrete characteristics can vary greatly from region to region or from sector to sector. Company-based training provisions and the link with VET school learning can be organised very differently from other programmes. It is not uncommon, for instance, in the company-based dual apprenticeship system for training to be offered outside of a training company, as in the case of school-based variants or joint forms. So-called school-based initial or higher VET is also offered in very different forms in the various federated states in Germany. Likewise, the concrete offerings of higher VET (e.g. preparatory courses and examinations) differ significantly across the country. In addition, there are many differences in the implementation of initial VET and higher VET in various federated states and municipalities. Furthermore, studies on the quality of VET have shown clear differences in relation to different company sizes or occupational areas (Ebbinghaus et al., 2010). However, it was not possible to examine these differences in detail in this article.

In the overall system of VET presented here, the company-based dual apprenticeship system of initial VET is a central determining factor in the course of one's future trajectory in VET. In quantitative terms, this system is of high importance; approximately half of those young people who switch to initial VET after leaving school start in this system (Autor:innengruppe Bildungsberichterstattung, 2022, p. 167). The company-based dual system traditionally enjoys a high level of social recognition and represents an opportunity for many companies to recruit skilled workers. Overall, about 20 % of German companies participate in the company-based dual apprenticeship system (BMBF, 2022, p. 28). The larger the companies, the more likely it is that they will participate in this system. However, in recent years, it has also become increasingly clear that this system is losing its appeal. Specifically, fewer young people are choosing this variant of VET, and fewer companies are providing such training (BIBB, 2022, pp. 183–190). Another striking fact is that just under 38 % of the participants are female (BIBB, 2022, pp. 84–85). The content of the company-based dual apprenticeship system is thus still related to traditional industrial and craft occupations.

To fully understand the VET system in Germany, it is essential to consider the interplay of the different offerings. For instance, the company-based dual apprenticeship system can only develop its strengths because it is part of an overall system, and therefore its weaknesses need be compensated for by other offerings. For example, the company-based dual system is often said to have the advantage of making a significant contribution to relatively low youth unemployment. In fact, however, this system can only be associated with this advantage because the other subsystems, such as the many offerings in the transition system, provide for those young people who have not found a place in the company-based dual apprenticeship system.

These different VET programmes, therefore, stand side by side and are to be understood as comprising an overall system. They represent alternative VET pathways with which different company qualification needs, societal educational demands, and individual interests can be satisfied. The different offerings fulfil different functions, as they serve the interests of the school leavers pursuing an educational pathway and a professional career on the one hand, and provide opportunities for the companies looking for skilled workers on the other. The different offerings compete with each other, complement each other, and compensate for each other's deficits. They follow different legal foundations and quality standards, and their financing modalities and many other structural elements also differ significantly. Unfortunately, only selected aspects of this complex configuration could be addressed in this article; for further details, see Frommberger and Schmees (2024).

The subsystems of the overall VET system are constantly being developed. They are in a permanent state of reorganisation and change, both in terms of content and structure. New initial and higher VET profiles are being developed, and existing initial and higher VET profiles are being reorganised against the background of changing requirements and demands. The various legal foundations, such as the Vocational Training Act, occupational licensing laws, or school laws, are being amended to ensure new quality standards. In addition, new formats of provision are being introduced to link different vocational and educational functions. One example of this is the dual study programme, which combines bachelor's degrees with VET qualifications.

These changes in the structure and design of the various VET programmes serve to accommodate new demands and meet shifting needs. They are the result of permanent VET policy debates and negotiations, as well as academic discourse and research findings. VET policy debates and decisions on the further development of VET generally take place separately – here with a view to the different subsystems of VET outlined above. This situation is closely related to the different legal frameworks and responsibilities to which the subsystems are subject. This means, for example, that VET that falls under the Vocational Training Act is usually discussed and changed independently of other VET offerings in Germany.

From an analytical perspective, and against the background of this VET policy and structural fragmentation, the question arises as to what advantages and disadvantages are associated with this patchwork of VET in Germany. On the one hand, these diverse offerings have grown historically, and they function side by side in a form that has been tried and tested over time. They therefore cover very different needs and requirements. On the other hand, whether a more pronounced overall perspective on the design of VET could go hand-in-hand with possibilities for improving the system as a whole should be considered.

Stronger cooperation between the different offerings is also conceivable, for example, in the form of joint VET offers. The dual study programme is an example of this, as it links VET with a completely different educational sector, namely higher education. Other examples would be the stronger connection of the VET variants with the vocational upper secondary school (for the purpose of further developing the vocational baccalaureate) or the cooperation of different VET institutions, such as an inter-company VET centre with VET schools. Conceptually, it would also make sense to relate the different initial and higher education and training offerings much more closely to each other and to map them into an overall system. This could significantly increase the transparency of VET provision in Germany.

At this point in time, it must be assumed that people in Germany lack a systematic overview of the overall system of VET. Most people are not aware of the variety of offerings, for example, of a local VET school alongside the many other municipal offers. In this respect, increasing transparency could improve the number of transitions into VET. One example of such an attempt to map the overall structure of VET emerged in the Netherlands (Busse & Frommberger, 2016). In the Netherlands, in the 1990s the company-based and school-based initial and higher VET pathways were combined into a nationwide qualification structure. The central reference points of this qualification structure are the qualifications, content standards, and level allocations. In addition, every initial or higher VET programme takes place through a combination of school-based and company-based learning (i. e. it has a dual structure). However, the concrete form this takes, for example, with regard to the temporal scope of school-based and company-based learning, or with regard to the lead learning location of the school or company, can vary. Regardless of the remaining complexity, this integrated presentation of the overall cluster of VET offerings in Germany should lead to a higher degree of transparency.

## References

Autor:innengruppe Bildungsberichterstattung. (2022). Bildung in Deutschland 2022. Bielefeld.

Beer, M. (2022). Benachteiligtenförderung in der Berufsvorbereitenden Bildungsmaßnahme – die "BvB" als "Schaltstelle zwischen Schule und Arbeitswelt" oder "dysfunktionales Dauerprovisorium" im Übergangssystem? *bwp@ Berufs- und Wirtschaftspädagogik, 42,* 1–29. https://www.bwpat.de/ausgabe42/beer-2_bwpat42.pdf

Beer, M. (2023). Begleitete Übergänge in die Berufsausbildung. Theoriereduzierte Ausbildungsgänge für junge Menschen mit Lernbeeinträchtigungen in Deutschland und der Schweiz. *Schweizerische Zeitschrift für Heilpädagogik, 29*(1), 36–42. https://doi.org/10.57161/z2023-01-06

Bensch, S. & Greening, M. (2021). Fort- und Weiterbildung in der Pflege und im Hebammenwesen. In I. Darmann-Finck & K. Sahmel, K. (Eds.), *Pädagogik im Gesundheitswesen.* Springer Verlag Deutschland. https://doi.org/10.1007/978-3-662-61428-0_37-1

BIBB. (2022). Datenreport zum Berufsbildungsbericht 2022. *Informationen und Analysen zur Entwicklung der beruflichen Bildung, Bonn.* https://www.bibb.de/dokumente/pdf/Datenreport%202022_02052022_mit%20Schutz.pdf

BMBF (Bundesministerium für Bildung und Forschung). (2022). *Berufsbildungsbericht 2022.* Bonn.

Bretschneider, M., & Schwarz, H. (2022). Die Ordnung der Berufsbildung als vergeblicher Versuch – Ausbildungsordnungen zwischen Standards und Aushandlung. *bwp@ Berufs- und Wirtschaftspädagogik, 29,* 1–18. http://www.bwpat.de/ausgabe29/bretschneider_schwarz_bwpat29.pdf

Federal Ministry of Justice. (2020). Gesetz zur Förderung der beruflichen Aufstiegsfortbildung – Aufstiegsfortbildungsförderungsgesetz. Berlin.

Busse, G., Frommberger, D., & Meijer, K. (2016). Niederlande. Internationales Handbuch der Berufsbildung. Bonn.

Christ, A., Schuß, E., Milde, B., & Granath, R.-O. (2023). *Die Entwicklung des Ausbildungsmarktes im Jahr 2022.* Bonn: Bundesinstitut für Berufsbildung.

Deutsches Institut für angewandte Pflegeforschung (Eds.). (2017). Systematik von Fort- und Weiterbildungen der professionellen Pflege in Deutschland. http://bildungsrat-pflege.de/wp-content/uploads/2014/10/2017-11.24.-DBR_DIP_P%C3%A4sentation_Heterogenit%C3%A4t-pflegerischer-Fort-und-Weiterbildungen.pdf

Ebbinghaus, M., Krewerth, A., Beicht, U., Eberhard, V., Flemming, S., & Granato, M. (2010). *BIBB-Forschungsverbund zur Ausbildungsqualität in Deutschland.* Gemeinsamer Abschlussbericht.

Frommberger, D., Schmees, J. K. (2024). Deutschland. Internationales Handbuch der Berufsbildung. Bonn.

Kultusministerkonferenz. (Ed.). (2021). Rahmenvereinbarung über Fachschulen. Beschluss der Kultusministerkonferenz vom 07.11.2002 i. d. F. vom 17.06.2021. https://www.kmk.org/fileadmin/veroeffentlichungen_beschluesse/2002/2002_11_07-RV-Fachschulen.pdf

Matthes, S., Ulrich, J. G., Krekel, E. M., & Walden, G. (2014). *Wenn Angebot und Nachfrage immer seltener zusammenfinden. Wachsende Passungsprobleme auf dem Ausbildungsmarkt: Analysen und Lösungsansätze.* Bundesinstitut für Berufsbildung.

Schneider, V., & Waechter, M. (2020). Regelungen des Bundes und der zuständigen Stellen für die berufliche Fortbildung. In Bundesinstitut für Berufsbildung (Ed.), *Datenreport zum Berufsbildungsbericht 2020. Informationen und Analysen zur Entwicklung der beruflichen Bildung.* Bonn. https://www.bibb.de/datenreport/de/datenreport_2020.php

Von Hagen, J. (2019). Regelungen der zuständigen Stellen für die berufliche Fortbildung und Umschulung. In Bundesinstitut für Berufsbildung (Ed.), *Datenreport zum Berufsbildungsbericht 2019. Informationen und Analysen zur Entwicklung der beruflichen Bildung.* Bonn. https://www.bibb.de/datenreport/de/datenreport_2019.php

## Short portrait of the author

**Dietmar Frommberger** has been Professor (full) of Vocational Education at Osnabrück University since 2017. He previously held a professorship at the University of Magdeburg. His research interests include comparative aspects of vocational education and training (VET) research, especially with an international focus, as well as structures and functions of VET in Germany.
Contact: dietmar.frommberger@uni-osnabrueck.de

# Structures and challenges of the dual apprenticeship system in Lower Saxony

Tim Migura

**Abstract**: Dual apprenticeship training enjoys a high status in Germany and is widely recognised and respected around the world as a robust model for vocational education. Nevertheless, challenges with this system have arisen over time. This chapter explores some of these challenges and presents how training in the dual apprenticeship system is developing in Germany. These challenges include gender-specific selection behaviour in training, the difference between the supply and demand of training places, and the problem of early contract termination. Furthermore, it focuses on the increasing demand for academic education and the decreasing demand for vocational education. The state of Lower Saxony is examined in more detail from a regional perspective. Finally, the dual study programme is presented as a hybrid model between academic and vocational education.

**Keywords:** Academisation; Challenges; Dual Apprenticeship; Dual Study Programmes.

## 1 Introduction

From an international perspective, and in considering the systematisation of the vocational education and training (VET) landscape, Germany is characterised first and foremost by its dual apprenticeship system. Greinert (1995, p. 15), for instance, has categorised Germany's training system as a state-controlled market model. This classification is characterised above all by the strong presence of the dual training system, in which both the VET schools and the training companies provide training but remain subject to the extensive regulations of the state. However, there are forms of training in Germany that do not belong to the dual apprenticeship system, but which are assigned to the school-based VET system. According to Greinert's system, these should be categorised under a separate model, and they do not belong to the state-controlled market model. Greinert (1995) also points out that Germany's categorisation as a state-controlled market model does not reflect all facets of the VET system; nevertheless, it does illustrate that the VET system is primarily associated with the dual apprenticeship system in the broader dialogue in Germany.

Germany's dual apprenticeship system has been held up worldwide as a model of a successful training system (Lassnigg, 2015). In the international discourse, the low youth unemployment rate is attributed to the success of the dual system. However, in reality, this unemployment rate is primarily due to the diversity of the German VET system and the variety of support measures on offer (Lassnigg, 2015, pp. 92–93). Nevertheless, this positive image of dual education serves as an argument in favour of its exportation, which is why there were frequent efforts in the past to implement the system in other countries. However, is the dual apprenticeship training system in Germany as outstanding and future-proof as it appears in the international discourse? This article aims to provide some insights into the current developments in dual apprenticeship training in an attempt to answer this question.

The focus of this article is on dual apprenticeship training at the subnational level. For this purpose, the selected indicators and developments are related to the federated state of Lower Saxony. Although a large part of dual apprenticeship training is regulated at the national level, a considerable measure of control is also assigned at the level of single federated states. This, in turn, implies that differences can arise among the federated states and regions.

This chapter opens with an overview of the dual apprenticeship system in Germany and highlights its quantitative importance (Section 2). This section is followed by a description of the organisation of dual apprenticeship training at the federal, federated, and regional levels, with the aim of making the possibility of regional structuring more apparent (Section 3). The following section presents some of the challenges associated with dual education in Lower Saxony (Section 4). These challenges include gender-specific selection behaviour, the difference between the supply of training places and the demand for them, the problem of early contract terminations, and the increasing demand for academic education alongside a decreasing demand for VET. In response to these challenges, the dual study programme is presented as a hybrid model between VET and academic education as an exemplary approach to the promotion of VET (Section 5).

## 2 Overview of the dual apprenticeship system in Lower Saxony

In 2021, 152,528 people entered the education and training market in Lower Saxony. This puts Lower Saxony in fourth place in a national comparison. Only the federated states of North Rhine-Westphalia (335,460), Baden-Württemberg (245,956) and Bavaria (210,873) were able to integrate more newcomers in the training system (Destatis, 2022, Tab. ZÜ1.1). Those sections associated with VET, transition, and other sectors like university studies and upper secondary education for the acquisition of higher education entrance qualifications at VET schools are included in this number.

Figure 1 shows a selected representation of Lower Saxony's VET system in quantitative terms, which clearly underlines the outstanding presence of dual apprenticeship training.

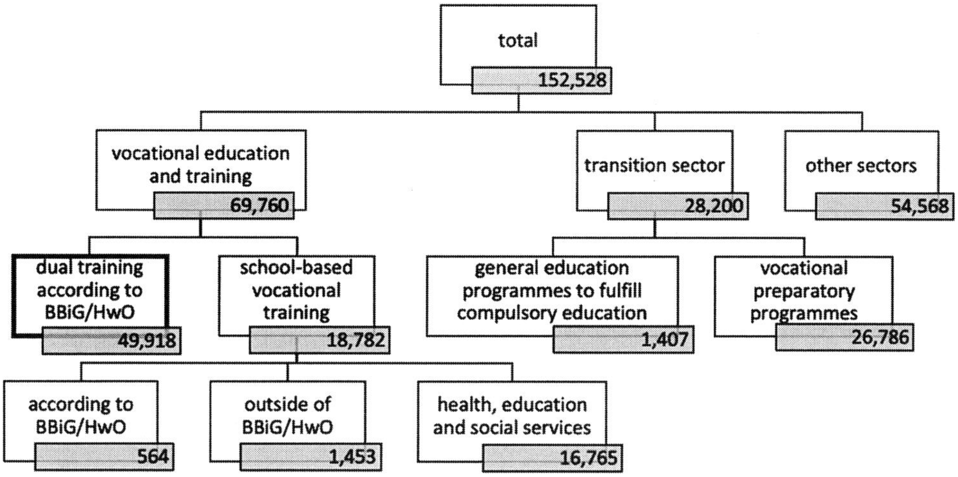


**Figure 1:** Reduced representation of the proportions of new entrants in selected VET systems in Lower Saxony in 2021

*Note:* Data obtained from Destatis, 2022, Table 4_NI.

The largest part of the VET sector is taken up by dual apprenticeship training. This dual apprenticeship model primarily covers apprenticeships in industry, the craft sector, commerce, and agriculture. However, dual apprenticeship training is also present in all other business sectors. The training usually lasts between two and three and a half years and does not have any specific entry requirements (Standing Conference of the Ministers of Education and Cultural Affairs of the Länder in the Federal Republic of Germany [KMK], 2019, p. 147). Hence, it is essentially open to people who do not have a formal school-leaving qualification. The central feature of this system is the combination between the learning location of the VET school as a theoretical component and the practical learning location of the training company. The separation of the learning locations automatically results in a division of governance, since the school system is controlled by the federated states, but the company-based components of dual apprenticeship training are regulated at the federal level (see Figure 2). Although the learning locations are controlled at different levels, they are obliged to work together within the framework of learning cooperation (BBiG, 2020, § 2). For detailed information on the organisation and structure of dual apprenticeship training in Germany, please refer to the contribution by Dietmar Frommberger in this volume.

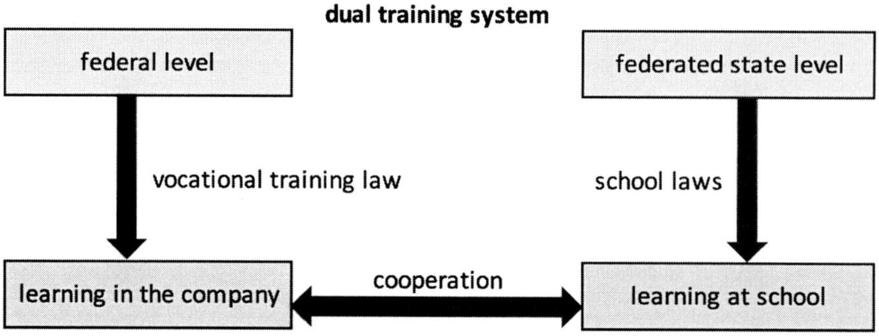


**Figure 2:** Simplified figure of the structure of dual apprenticeship training

## 2.1 Characteristics of the vocational education and training system

Looking at the distribution of trainees in the entire VET system, it is noticeable that they are unequally distributed across the areas of responsibility in Germany and Lower Saxony. A comparison between Lower Saxony and Germany as a whole (including Lower Saxony) reveals that, apart from minor deviations, Lower Saxony has a similar distribution of trainees in comparison to Germany. Specifically, there is only a lower number in the area of industry and commerce; otherwise, the numbers are distributed uniformly among the other areas of responsibility, which are all slightly above the overall German cross-section (see Table 1). In general, it is noticeable that the areas of industry and commerce, as well as the skilled trades, account for the largest percentage of the training market in Germany and Lower Saxony. This is followed by trainees in the free professions, which include pharmacists, tax consultants, and lawyers, as a few examples (Federal Institute for Vocational Education and Training [BIBB], 2023, p. 34). Maritime shipping and home economics occupations account for a very small share of training. As Lower Saxony is considered an agricultural state and ranks second in Germany in terms of the area used for agriculture and third in terms of the number of farms (Destatis, 2021), this likely influenced the slightly higher percentage in the area of agriculture. Nevertheless, this figure cannot be used to infer the exact quantity of workers in agriculture, since a large proportion of agricultural labour (2012: 62 %; 2020: 57 %) is performed by family members, and almost one in four agricultural business managers or farm managers in Lower Saxony (2012: 23 %; 2020: 24 %) have no formal training in the field, and only practical experience (Dahl, 2012, pp. 72–73; Krampf, 2021, pp. 641–643).[1] Although in Lower Saxony, other economic sectors also have employees without VET, the percentage of employees in agriculture is lower (Landesamt für Statistik Niedersachsen, 2022a).

1 Training in non-agricultural areas, such as business administration, is not included these percentages.

**Table 1:** Distribution of newly concluded training contracts in Lower Saxony in 2022 by area of responsibility

| Sector/ region | Industry and commerce sector | Craft sector | Public service | Agriculture sector | Free professions sector | Home economics sector | Maritime shipping sector |
|---|---|---|---|---|---|---|---|
| Lower Saxony | 50.93 % | 30.63 % | 3.21 % | 4.27 % | 10.51 % | 0.38 % | 0.06 % |
| Germany | 56.04 % | 28.02 % | 2.95 % | 2.80 % | 9.87 % | 0.30 % | 0.02 % |

*Note*: Data obtained from BIBB, 2023, p. 37.

An evaluation of the trainee's highest general school-leaving qualification in the dual apprenticeship system shows that the values of Germany and Lower Saxony are only slightly different. Overall, in Lower Saxony, most trainees had a lower and higher secondary school-leaving certificate or comparable school-leaving certificate (69.15 %). It is noteworthy that, in percentage terms, a very small proportion had no school-leaving qualifications (2.64 %). Despite the possibility of gaining access to higher academic education, a considerable proportion still opted for VET (25.16 %). This results in a very heterogeneous picture with regard to the previous school education of the trainees (Destatis, 2022, Tab. 4_NI).

The following section takes a closer look at the relation between the demand for and supply of training. The extended supply-demand ratio (eANR) is used for this purpose. As of September 30 of each year, the number of training places on offer is compared with the number of registered applicants. Those in demand include all young people who have signed a new training contract and those who are registered as still looking for a training place as of the reporting date (BIBB, 2023, pp. 14–15). In the eANR, the number of training places offered is divided by the number of training places demanded, and the result is multiplied by a factor of 100. If the calculated value is above 100 as a reference number, the amount of training places on offer in the region is greater than the number of training places in demand, and if the value is below the targeted number, the sum of training places in demand is greater than the number of training places on offer (BIBB, 2023, pp. 14–15).

In Lower Saxony, the value of the eANR for 2022 was 94.8 (BIBB, 2023, p. 18). Accordingly, applicants outnumbered the training places on offer. In this respect, Lower Saxony differs from the average for Germany as a whole, where the value is 101.6 as a calculated number, which means that there are marginally more training places offered than registered applicants (BIBB, 2023, p. 18). Nevertheless, even within Lower Saxony, there are major differences. Parts of eastern Lower Saxony in particular show values that indicate a clear oversupply of training place seekers (e. g. Hannover: 88.7; Celle: 86.6). The northern regions show a slight oversupply of applicants (e. g. Stade: 96.0; Emden-Leer: 94.8). In contrast, the supply of training places in southwestern Lower Saxony exceeds demand (e. g. Nordhorn: 107.4; Vechta: 103.6). The Osnabrück region, which is also located in the southwest of Lower Saxony, has the most balanced relationship between training supply and training demand in Lower Saxony, with a value of 101.4 (BIBB, 2022a, n. p.).

# 3 General conditions of dual apprenticeship training

The previous section highlighted the quantitative importance of dual apprenticeship training in Lower Saxony. The following section presents some of the relevant legal instruments and actors involved in shaping dual apprenticeship training in Germany. The explanations are divided into the levels of the federal state (Germany), the federated state (Lower Saxony), and the units below the federated state (regions in Lower Saxony).

## 3.1 Regulation of dual apprenticeship training at the national state level

The legal basis for practical training is specified in the Vocational Training Act (BBiG, 2020) and therefore on the federal level. For professions in the crafts and trades, the Crafts and Trades Code (HwO) applies at the national level. Formally, apprentices conclude a training contract with the training company. Among other things, the duration of the training probationary period, weekly working hours, vacation, entitlement, and remuneration are specified in this contract (BBiG, 2020, § 11). The Vocational Training Act stipulates the rights and obligations of trainers and trainees and defines the suitability of training facilities and personnel. The trainees' obligations include following the instructions of the training personnel, keeping written or electronic training records, attending VET school, and safeguarding company secrets (BBiG, 2020, § 13). Training companies, in contrast, are obliged to provide all the necessary work equipment free of charge to protect the trainees from damage, to employ suitable training personnel, and to pay remuneration (BBiG, 2020, § 14). For the latter, a minimum level of remuneration must be observed, which increases at a minimum with each year of training (BBiG, 2020, § 17, I–II). In companies, trainees must be supervised by suitable instructors. A trainer is considered suitable if he or she is professionally and personally suitable (BBiG, 2020, § 28, I), has not seriously or repeatedly violated the law (BBiG, 2020, § 29), has successfully completed the equivalent training, and can demonstrate appropriate practical experience in the occupation (BBiG, 2020, § 30). The examination of professional competence is regulated and specified by an ordinance of the Federal Ministry of Education and Research. The Ordinance on Trainer Qualification (AusbEignV or AEVO) describes the specific fields of action for the planning, implementation, and monitoring of VET (AusbEignV, 2009, § 2). The ordinance links this qualification to the successful completion of a written and a practical examination (AusbEignV, 2009, § 4).

Recognition of training occupations also takes place at the national level. The Federal Ministry for Economic Affairs and Climate Action or the relevant ministries assigned to the occupational field in cooperation with the Federal Ministry of Education and Research can recognise VET by means of ordinances and then formulate them into training regulations. These regulations lay down the basic principles of the training occupation, which are then binding for the implementation of the training (BBiG, 2020, § 5).

### 3.2 Regulation of dual apprenticeship training at the federated state level

To ensure that the cooperative structure between the VET school and the company is maintained, Article 15 of the Vocational Training Act requires companies to release their trainees to attend VET school classes. This is regulated at the federated state level by school laws. Each of Germany's 16 federated states has its own school laws.

The Lower Saxony School Act (NSchG) applies, which defines the rights and duties of students and teachers, divides up the state's school system, and describes other formal guidelines for the operation of schools and teaching, applies in Lower Saxony. Institutionally, the Lower Saxony Ministry of Culture and the Lower Saxony State Education Authority are the main bodies that regulate the operation of VET schools. The KMK acts as a coordinating body between the states. In this self-coordinating body, coordination takes place with the aim of ensuring the greatest possible uniformity in the state laws governing school education. This is intended to ensure greater mobility and the equivalence of qualifications. However, the KMK agreements do not have the character of direct legislation. Rather, they are agreements that the federated states can voluntarily convert into their own laws (Hölterhoff, 2022, p. 10). Nevertheless, the KMK is involved in relevant educational decisions, such as the development of framework agreements, some of which are also binding on the states.

Framework curricula serve as the basis for the implementation of VET in schools. They are implemented by the KMK in a joint procedure with the federated government (KMK, 2019, p. 152). They contain objectives, content specifications, and time guidelines for the school-based part of specific training occupations. The federated states are responsible for developing regulations for inter-occupational subjects (KMK, 2021, p. 10). They also have the option of adopting the occupation-related framework curricula directly or of incorporating partial changes into state-specific framework guidelines (KMK, 2021, pp. 9–10). At the level of the federated states, these framework guidelines form the direct basis for teaching at VET schools (NSchG, 2023, § 122, II). This gives the federated states a certain degree of freedom to take account of regional particularities. In addition, it is clear that the federated states do not have absolute decision-making power over educational decisions in school-based VET. This is due to the fact that the federated states must comply with the minimum provisions of the framework guidelines, which are determined in cooperation with the other federated states and the federated state government.

### 3.3 Regulation of dual apprenticeship training at the regional level

The Vocational Training Act defines the competent bodies that monitor the implementation of vocational training preparation, vocational training, and vocational retraining (BBiG, 2020, § 76). Their duties also include the examination of the suitability of training companies (BBiG, 2020, § 32) and the co-organisation of the trainees' (final) examinations (BBiG, 2020, §§ 39–47). According to Article 71 of the Vocational Training Act, these bodies are primarily chambers (e. g. Chamber of Industry and Commerce or Chamber of Agriculture). The chambers are usually public law corporations and represent the interests of the business community in some regional company-based VET decisions (Hölterhoff, 2023, p. 16). The chambers are divided into different districts, reflecting their regional focus. For example, the Chamber of Industry and Commerce in Lower Saxony is divided into seven further chamber districts (Industrie- und Handelskammer Niedersachsen, n. d., n. p.) The population of the districts ranges from about 500,000 inhabitants in the district of East Frisia and Papenburg in the northwest of Lower Saxony to about 2.6 million inhabitants in the district of Hanover in the southeast. The other districts have an average of one million inhabitants, including the district of Osnabrück-Emsland-Grafschaft Bentheim (Industrie- und Handelskammer Niedersachsen, n. d.) Co-determination at the regional level is exercised, among other things, through the VET Committee, which is set up by the chambers and consists of six employer representatives, six employee representatives (usually sent from unions), and six teachers from VET schools (BBiG, 2020, §77). The VET Committee must be consulted and informed about all important VET matters, including changes in the content of the training, adjustments to the contract model, the number and results of examinations conducted, and the implementation of new regional forms, contents, and methods pertaining to VET (BBiG, 2020, §79).

# 4 Challenges of the dual apprenticeship system

Despite the quantitative importance of the (dual) apprenticeship system, the VET landscape in Lower Saxony faces some challenges. These include gender-specific interests in training, mismatches, early contract termination rates, and increasing competition from the higher education sector. These challenges are described in more detail in the following sections.

## 4.1 Gender-specific interests in training

A gender breakdown of the training sectors in Lower Saxony shows clear disparities in the distribution of training places. While training in the free professions (89.71 %) and in home economics (83.87 %) is strongly dominated by women, the sectors of maritime shipping (0.00 %), craft trades (18.99 %), and agriculture (28.61 %) have very low proportions of women (see Table 2).

**Table 2:** Newly concluded training contracts by gender and area of responsibility in Lower Saxony in 2022

| | Total | Industry and commerce sector | Craft sector | Public service | Agriculture sector | Free professions sector | Home economics sector | Maritime shipping sector |
|---|---|---|---|---|---|---|---|---|
| Total | 48,576 | 24,741 | 14,877 | 1,560 | 2,076 | 5,103 | 186 | 30 |
| Pct. of women | 36.66 % | 35.61 % | 18.99 % | 54.62 % | 28.61 % | 89.71 % | 83.87 % | 0.00 % |

*Note:* Data obtained from BIBB 2023, pp. 41–44.

Table 3 shows the top ten training occupations chosen by men and women in Lower Saxony. An analysis of the ten most frequent occupations shows that women are most likely to choose medical-related and commercial occupations. Overall, 53.4% of all women who started training in Lower Saxony in 2022 chose the first ten occupations in the ranking below. A total of 26.7% fell into the top three occupations of medical assistant, office management assistant, and dental assistant. Measured against all male trainees in these occupations, the share of men in Lower Saxony is 2.3% in the occupations of medical assistant (0.2%), office management assistant (1.9%), and dental assistant (0.2%; BIBB, 2022b, Tab. 68).

By contrast, men are more likely to be found in technical occupations. Overall, however, men are not so strongly distributed among the ten most frequently selected occupations; rather, they are more broadly distributed, with only 39.5% of male trainees in the 10 most frequently selected occupations. This number is 13.9% below that for women. Overall, only 1.4% of all women chose the occupations of motor vehicle mechatronics technician (0.9%), electronics technician (0.3%), and mechanic for sanitary, heating, and air-conditioning technology (0.2%) (BIBB, 2022c, Tab. 69).

**Table 3:** Rankings of apprenticeship occupations for women and men in Lower Saxony in 2022

| Rank | Women | Percentage of all women | Men | Percentage of all men |
|---|---|---|---|---|
| 1 | Medical assistant | 10.0% | Automotive mechatronics technician | 7.2% |
| 2 | Office management assistant | 8.6% | Electronics technician | 5.3% |
| 3 | Dental assistant | 8.1% | Mechanic for sanitary, heating, and air-conditioning systems | 5.0% |
| 4 | Salesperson | 6.2% | IT specialist | 4.9% |
| 5 | Retail saleswoman | 5.0% | Warehouse logistics specialist | 3.2% |
| 6 | Industrial clerk | 4.4% | Salesperson | 3.1% |
| 7 | Tax clerk | 3.2% | Retail salesman | 3.0% |
| 8 | Administrative assistant | 3.0% | Carpenter | 2.7% |
| 9 | Wholesale and foreign trade management assistant | 2.6% | Industrial mechanic | 2.7% |
| 10 | Hairdresser | 2.3% | Industrial clerk | 2.6% |

*Note:* Data obtained from BIBB, 2022b, 2022c.

In Lower Saxony's dual apprenticeship system as a whole, female participation in training has also been declining since 2013. While the share of women in dual apprenticeship training was still 41.24% in 2013, it was only 36.66% in 2021 (Destatis, 2022, Tab. 3.1_Total, Tab. 3.2_Female). Dionisius et al. (2018, pp. 47–50) posit that the decline in quotas can be attributed to an unfavorable development of the number of training places available in occupations that are more frequently chosen by women and in the change in the educational interests of female school leavers, who tend to remain in the school education system (Destatis, 2022).

In order to attract a greater number of women to skilled trades at the regional level, the chamber of skilled trades in Lower Saxony have initiated a series of initiatives and projects designed to disseminate information about the job profiles in question and enhance their appeal to women, with the objective of increasing the representation of women in these roles. For example, the Osnabrück Chamber of Skilled Crafts (Handwerkskammer Osnabrück – Emsland – Grafschaft Bentheim) is promoting an initiative entitled 'Strong Women for Strong Skilled Crafts' (Handwerkskammer Osnabrück – Emsland – Grafschaft Bentheim, n. d.)

### 4.2 Fit problem

In addition to gender-specific factors, there are others that influence the match between trainees and companies. In addition to characteristic-based mismatches, regional or occupational fit problems can also contribute to the fact that trainees and companies may not often find each other. However, at 57 %, the most common reason for a mismatch between companies and trainees is barriers related to characteristics like a lack of skills on the part of the applicant, inadequate training conditions, or insufficient developmental prospects on the part of the company (Seeber et al., 2019, pp. 257–258).

Over time, there has also been an increase in mismatches in terms of occupational aptitude. This accounts for 27 % of the total and manifests itself in training place applicants applying for occupations that are not offered or for which there are not enough places available (Seeber et al., 2019, p. 258). Geographical mismatches, however, are a minor but still significant factor, with a share of 16 %. Especially in Lower Saxony, one of Germany's largest states, it is a challenge for trainees to find their desired occupation in their local area (Seeber et al., 2019, p. 258).

Over the course of time, it can be seen that the number of personality-based fit problems has decreased (since 2009: -24 %). In contrast, occupational fit problems have risen at a similar rate (since 2009: +23 %; Seeber et al., 2019, p. 258). These developments thus show that the supply of training places in particular is becoming increasingly incompatible with the wishes and expectations of young people. One possible explanation lies in the increased relevance and strengthening of career guidance programmes, which provide young people with a better ability to make good career choices and a firmer idea of their desired occupations (Niedersächsisches Kultusministerium, 2022, n. p.)

### 4.3 Early termination of contracts

Another challenge in Lower Saxony concerns the high contract cancellation rate. This rate is made up of trainees whose training contracts were terminated during their training. However, not all of these contract terminations represent dropouts; contract changes are also included in this calculation. Accordingly, an uncertain proportion of these individuals remain in the dual apprenticeship system (Uhly, 2023, pp. 46–52).

Overall, 26.7 % of training contracts in Germany were terminated prematurely. The rates in Lower Saxony are largely in line with the national average. Within all the various occupational sectors, high rates of termination are evident, with the exception of the public sector, where, on average, one in four contracts is terminated prematurely. The highest rates are found in the skilled trades and the free professions, where an average of one in three contracts is terminated (see Table 4). Lower Saxony is slightly above the national average in terms of premature contract terminations (Seeber et al., 2019, p. 92).

**Table 4:** Contract termination rates in Lower Saxony in 2021

| Region | Total | Industry and commerce sector | Craft sector | Public service | Agriculture sector | Free professions sector | Home economics sector |
|---|---|---|---|---|---|---|---|
| Lower Saxony | 27.8% | 24.4% | 34.3% | 5.5% | 24.9% | 32.4% | 23.9% |
| Germany | 26.7% | 23.5% | 33.6% | 7.1% | 24.8% | 30.9% | 29.3% |

*Note:* The Data is from BIBB 2023, p. 150.

The larger share (16.9 %) of premature contract terminations takes place after the probationary period (BIBB, 2023, p. 149). The probationary period is a limited timeframe at the beginning of the training period, usually lasting between three and six months, during which employees prove their suitability for the job. During this period, the employer is allowed to dismiss the employee without valid reason. In light of such circumstances, it is therefore worth taking a closer look at the reasons for early contract terminations.

The reasons for the early contract termination vary depending on the perspective. In a survey by Lange and Goncharova (2020, pp. 6–9), 167 apprentices and 133 companies in a particular chamber district were asked about the reasons for the early termination of contracts in this region with respect to the industrial and commercial sector. The three most frequently cited reasons for trainees terminating their contracts were the working atmosphere, misunderstandings, and working conditions. Employers, in contrast, mainly criticised apprentices' absenteeism, misconceptions, and reorientation. It is clear that the views of the companies and the trainees differ and are only partially compatible (see Figure 3).

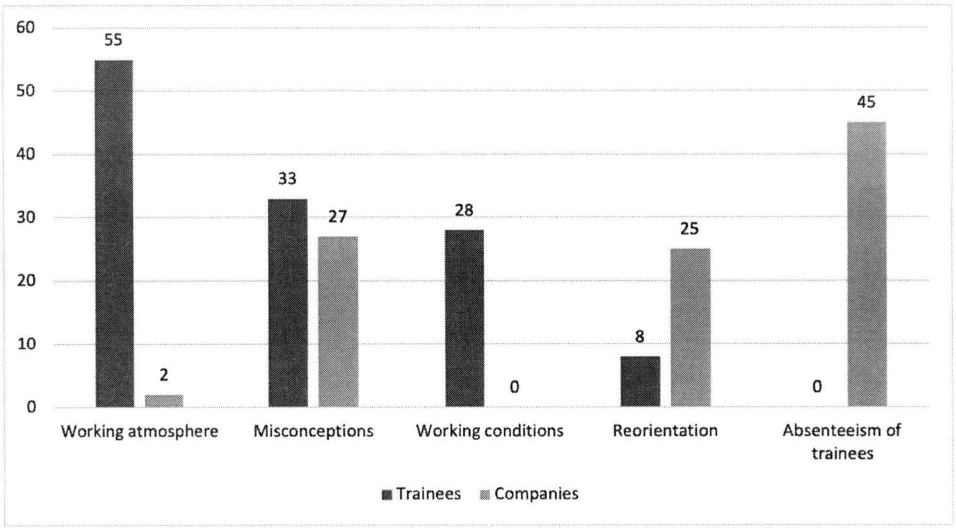


**Figure 3:** Selected reasons for early contract terminations in the district of the Chamber of Industry and Commerce of Osnabrück, Emsland and Grafschaft Bentheim

*Note:* Data obtained from Lange & Goncharova, 2020, p. 8.

Other reasons for early contract termination included the trainees' lack of motivation, unreliability, or a lack of training maturity (Lange & Goncharova, 2020, p. 8). In Lower Saxony, training contracts in the dual apprenticeship system are terminated particularly often in the occupational groups of cleaning (58.7 %), hotel and catering (46.8 %), food trade (43.2 %), and medical assistance (42.9 %; Seeber et al., 2019, p. 95). Patterns have also emerged in relation to previous education with regard to early contract termination. Most contracts are terminated prematurely by young people with no more than a lower secondary school-leaving certificate. The fewest contracts are terminated prematurely by young people with university entrance qualifications (Seeber et al., 2019, pp. 95–96).

## 4.4 Academic drift

In addition to the VET options already described, specially qualified students have the opportunity to take up university studies. For some years now, the number of university entrants in Germany has been rising, with the result that more potential employees with academic qualifications are entering the labour market (BIBB, 2023, pp. 80–81). This shift has been accompanied by changes in the educational and employment structures. Theoretical-systematic knowledge and skills are increasingly coming to the fore as a result of the changes in academic educational backgrounds and are thus increasingly shaping modern occupational fields and requirements (Alesi & Teichler, 2013, p. 19; Severing & Teichler, 2013, p. 10). Similarly, a growing number of vocationally oriented degree programmes are being developed, which are now competing with traditional VET (Severing & Teichler, 2013, p. 8). In this context, there is increasing talk of the academisation of education and employment (Alesi & Teichler, 2013, p. 19).

In addition to the increasing number of people with higher education qualifications over the last two decades, the same period shows a declining trend in the number of VET students, especially apprentices (BIBB, 2023, pp. 80–81). For example, the number of students in Germany has risen by 30.8 % since 2005, while the number of trainees in VET has fallen by 7.7 % over the same period (BIBB, 2023, pp. 82–83). In the dual apprenticeship system, the number of trainees has fallen even more substantially by 14.1 % since 2005 (BIBB, 2023, p. 82). Although more people are currently opting for VET programmes than for academic study programmes, the difference between students and trainees has narrowed between 2005 and 2022 (Alesi & Teichler, 2013, pp. 19–20; BIBB, 2023, pp. 19, 77–78). Different trends emerge for Lower Saxony (see Table 5). In the area of the free professions and in the public sector, the figures have been rising overall since 2012. In all other professional sectors, there has been a significant decrease in the number of employees. A particular dip can be seen between 2019 and 2020, when the number of trainees fell rapidly due to the COVID-19 pandemic. This decline was not reversed in 2022, which is likely due to the reduced participation of companies in training, especially small and medium-sized enterprises, which themselves had to contend with the effects of the pandemic in their own ways (BIBB, 2023, pp. 196–197).

**Table 5:** New VET contracts concluded in Lower Saxony by area of responsibility between 2012 and 2022

| Year | Total | Industry and commerce sector | Craft sector | Public service | Agriculture sector | Free professions sector | Home economics sector | Maritime shipping sector |
|---|---|---|---|---|---|---|---|---|
| 2012 | 58,236 | 32,136 | 17,766 | 1,230 | 2,028 | 4,671 | 336 | 69 |
| 2013 | 56,382 | 30,855 | 17,070 | 1,287 | 2,022 | 4,725 | 372 | 51 |
| 2014 | 55,812 | 30,456 | 16,926 | 1,410 | 2,091 | 4,506 | 348 | 75 |
| 2015 | 54,753 | 29,301 | 16,812 | 1,419 | 2,175 | 4,479 | 324 | 63 |
| 2016 | 54,663 | 29,460 | 16,695 | 1,449 | 2,235 | 4,494 | 291 | 42 |
| 2017 | 54,702 | 28,977 | 16,908 | 1,545 | 2,319 | 4,611 | 294 | 48 |
| 2018 | 55,641 | 29,700 | 17,310 | 1,494 | 2,217 | 4,611 | 270 | 39 |
| 2019 | 54,192 | 28,842 | 16,605 | 1,662 | 2,103 | 4,674 | 258 | 45 |
| 2020 | 46,788 | 24,228 | 14,376 | 1,545 | 2,040 | 4,296 | 267 | 33 |
| 2021 | 48,648 | 24,084 | 15,654 | 1,509 | 2,247 | 4,875 | 240 | 36 |
| 2022 | 48,576 | 24,741 | 14,877 | 1,560 | 2,076 | 5,103 | 186 | 30 |
| 2012–2022 | −16.59 % | −23.01 % | −16.26 % | +26.83 % | +2.37 % | +9.25 % | −46.64 % | −56.52 % |

*Note:* Data obtained from BIBB 2013, p. 32; 2014, p. 33; 2015, p. 32; 2016, p. 34; 2017, p. 35; 2018, p. 32; 2019, p. 36; 2020, p. 45; 2021, p. 39; 2022, p. 36; 2023, p. 37.

The number of school leavers from general and VET schools with direct admission to higher education in Lower Saxony remained almost unchanged between 2013 and 2020 (Landesamt für Statistik Niedersachsen, 2020, p. 69; 2022b, p. 70). In 2020, however, the number of people entitled to study fell sharply as a result of the COVID-19 pandemic (Landesamt für Statistik Niedersachsen, 2022b, p. 70). Until then, the number of students at universities had developed positively, in contrast to the declining number of apprentices (Landesamt für Statistik Niedersachsen, 2020, p. 77; Niedersächsisches Ministerium für Wissenschaft und Kultur, 2021, p. 2). One group of first-year students that has grown strongly in the last 10 years is that of students who obtained their higher education entrance qualification through VET rather than through the general school system. These numbers more than doubled from 2009 (1,135 first-year students) to 2019 (3,090 first-year students; Niedersächsisches Ministerium für Wissenschaft und Kultur, 2021, p. 7). In Lower Saxony, they will mainly attend universities (1,624) and universities of applied sciences (1,158; Niedersächsisches Ministerium für Wissenschaft und Kultur, 2021, p. 8).

Overall, according to the data presented, there is a trend towards embarking on university studies among young people who have either obtained a higher education entrance qualification at school or who have secured a higher education entrance qualification on the basis of their professional vocational qualifications. Some chambers are therefore launching marketing campaigns in newspapers, on social media, and on television to promote VET, for example, by highlighting international facets or cognitive occupational requirements in the skilled trades in ways that would appeal to the interests of young people (Handwerkskammer Osnabrück – Emsland – Grafschaft Bentheim, 2023, n. p.).

At a more structural level, the increasing trend towards higher qualifications has led to attempts to link VET with higher education. One such approach is the dual study programme. Another is the upgrading of higher VET through the newly introduced titles of 'Bachelor Professional' and 'Master Professional', which also imply some equivalence with academic degrees.

## 5 Between vocational and academic education: Dual study programmes

In what follows, the dual study programme as a means of linking VET and higher education is presented as an exemplary approach to the promotion of VET.

In dual study programmes, there is a close link between academic learning content, locations, and vocational-practical learning areas (Frommberger, 2019, p. 46). This should lead to a higher degree of cooperation between the practical learning locations (e. g. companies) and the theoretical learning locations (e. g. universities of applied sciences), thereby establishing a closer connection between theory and practice (Wolter, 2016, p. 40). These learning locations can be linked in terms of curricula and administration. Within this context, dual study programmes can be used for initial training on the one hand and for continuing training on the other hand (Wissenschaftsrat, 2013, p. 9). Initial training implies basic training in order to obtain a vocational qualification. Further training describes training that takes place following a professional qualification in order to gain more competences and authorisations. In the following, only those models in which the learning locations are linked will be discussed. With regard to initial training, a dual study programme can be *training-integrated*, which means that VET is directly linked to the study programme, so that the student can obtain both VET and an academic degree at the bachelor level at the end of his studies (Wissenschaftsrat, 2013, p. 10). Alternatively, the second type of dual study programme in initial training is the *practice-integrated* type, which is characterised by a pure bachelor's degree programme, but with a relatively high proportion of practical experience provided through programmes such as internships (Wissenschaftsrat, 2013, p. 10).

With regard to the further training segment, there are also two types of dual study programmes. On the one hand, there is the *job-integrated* study programme. This is closely linked to the student's professional field of activity and therefore establishes a content-related link between theory and practice. On the other hand, the *practice-integrated* type is also used in the continuing education sector. Continuing education and training programmes can be both bachelor's and master's degree courses (see Table 6).

**Table 6:** Reduced system of dual study programmes in Germany

| | Type | Characteristics | Degree |
|---|---|---|---|
| **Initial training** | Training-integrated | VET programme is integrated in the study structure | VET qualification and academic degree |
| | Practice-integrated | Higher amount of practical internships | Academic degree |
| **Further training** | Job-integrated | High linkage to specific professional fields | Academic degree |
| | Practice-integrated | Higher number of practical internships | Academic degree |

*Note:* Data obtained from Wissenschaftsrat, 2013, p. 9.

In Lower Saxony, practice-integrating and training-integrating programmes predominate, and more than 80 % are bachelor's courses of study (Nickel et al., 2022, pp. 79, 141). The distribution of training-integrating (44.1 %) and practice-integrating courses of study (52.8 %) is quite balanced in Lower Saxony (Nickel et al., 2022, p. 141). In terms of subject matter, the dual courses of study are predominantly technical-economic and scientific-mathematical in nature (Nickel et al., 2022, p. 86).

Since 2011, a total of 32 dual study programmes have been added in Lower Saxony, which corresponds to an increase of 50 % (see Table 7). However, the number of students has only increased by a quarter. Compared to developments in Germany as a whole, where the number of dual study programmes and students has almost doubled, developments in Lower Saxony appear to be lagging behind. However, it should be noted that Lower Saxony already had an above-average number of dual study programmes and dual students in 2011 (BIBB, 2023, p. 192).

**Table 7:** Distribution of dual study programmes in initial training

| Year | Lower Saxony | | Germany | |
|---|---|---|---|---|
| | Study programmes | Students | Study programmes | Students |
| 2011 | 64 | 4,622 | 879 | 59,628 |
| 2022 | 96 | 5,854 | 1749 | 120,517 |
| Development 2011–2022 | +50 % | +26.66 % | +98.98 % | +102.11 % |

*Note:* Data obtained from BIBB, 2023, p. 192.

A survey of students' motivations for choosing the dual study programme showed that the main reason was to have good career prospects after completing their studies. They also emphasised the practical aspects of the programme. A close link between theory and practice is therefore very important to dual students. In this way, dual students gain in-depth insights into the practical fields of an activity and establish theoretical and practical links between the learning content. This is also reflected in the fact that students as a whole attach great importance to being prepared for working life (Nickel et al., 2022, pp. 196–200). The motives for career choice show that a high degree of practical orientation is important to many young people (Nickel et al., 2022, p. 200). Because of the simultaneous trend towards higher qualifications, dual study offers a good intersection between an academic degree and the interlocking dimension of theoretical and practical VET content.

However, the duality of the learning locations is often accompanied by an increased workload for the students, who have to reconcile study content and practical phases or training with their respective personal circumstances. Almost a third of dropouts from dual study programmes can be attributed to this increased workload (Nickel et al., 2022, pp. 212–213). These dropout motives are particularly prevalent in work-study programmes, where students have to complete their studies in addition to their training-related work in the company (Nickel et al., 2022, p. 213).

A closer look at the reasons given by companies in Lower Saxony for participating in a dual study programme reveals that the main motivation is practical relevance (Nickel et al., 2022, p. 251). This means that learning content is not taught on a purely theoretical level, but can instead be applied and reflected upon in practice. In view of the increasing shortage of skilled workers, cooperating companies see the dual study programme above all as an opportunity to bind young people with university entrance qualifications to their own companies at an early stage and to familiarise them with company processes and contexts during their dual study programme in Germany. At the same time, some companies have become more attractive to young people with a desire for higher qualifications through their participation in dual study programmes. These young people are more likely to be employed by the company after completing their studies if they have already been intensively familiarised with in-company processes as part of the dual study programme (Nickel et al., 2022, p. 252).

Overall, it is clear that the concept of dual study meets the needs of both students and companies. Students have the opportunity to gain higher qualifications and practical experience at the same time, and companies can acquire new trainees and future skilled workers through their participation in dual study programmes and thus benefit from the higher qualification. For this reason, dual study programmes are often described as the 'best of both worlds' between the academic and VET paths. However, it remains to be seen how the dual system will develop from here, and whether it will continue to grow.

## 6 Conclusion

The dual apprenticeship training system continues to dominate the German VET system. However, a number of challenges have emerged that affect the attractiveness and further development of dual apprenticeship training. Gender-specific interests in training, a growing problem of unsuitability, a high number of early contract terminations, and increasing academic drift are just a few examples. The demands of the labour market on companies and young people are also changing. Modern work and training models are popular, gender stereotypes in society are being steadily dismantled, and the flexible reconciliation of leisure time and work or training is becoming increasingly important in society. To make dual apprenticeship training fit for the future and to strengthen its attractiveness, it is necessary to address these problem areas, so that there will continue to be a supply of skilled workers in industry, the skilled trades, and other training areas. While there have been campaigns to promote the attractiveness of the training sector, these are primarily designed as image campaigns and do little to change the structural framework that still prevails. It is therefore surprising that so few structural changes are being implemented in the dual system, despite declining numbers of skilled workers and training places, given that these developments could have long-term consequences for the supply situation in Lower Saxony, but also in Germany as a whole (for a discussion, see Klassen & Schmees, 2022).

Finally, it should be noted that the descriptions presented here are exemplary of the region of Lower Saxony. Nevertheless, Lower Saxony is not the only region affected by these challenges. Rather, comparable developments and key figures can be observed in all other German federated states. The dual study approach presented in this article is just one example of a model in the German training system that responds to the needs of companies and young people. More broadly, it is an example of how VET is affected by academisation, and how it can develop further under these circumstances.

## References

Alesi, B. & Teichler, U. (2013). Akademisierung von Bildung und Beruf. Ein kontroverser Diskurs in Deutschland. In E. Severing & U. Teichler (Eds.), *Akademisierung der Berufswelt?* (pp. 19–39). Bundesinstitut für Berufsbildung. https://www.agbfn.de/dokumente/pdf/a12_voevz_agbfn_13_2.pdf

Ausbilder-Eignungsverordnung (AusbEignV) of January 21, 2009 (BGBl. I S. 88).

Berufsbildungsgesetz (BBiG) in the version of May 4, 2020 (BGBl. I S. 920), last amended by Article 10a of the Act of August 16, 2023 (BGBl. 2023 I Nr. 217).

Bundesinstitut für Berufsbildung. (2013). *Datenreport zum Berufsbildungsbericht 2013. Informationen und Analysen zur Entwicklung der beruflichen Bildung.* Bundesinstitut für Berufsbildung. https://datenreport.bibb.de/media2013/BIBB_Datenreport_2013.pdf

Bundesinstitut für Berufsbildung. (2014). *Datenreport zum Berufsbildungsbericht 2014. Informationen und Analysen zur Entwicklung der beruflichen Bildung.* Bundesinstitut für Berufsbildung. https://www.bibb.de/dokumente/pdf/BIBB_Datenreport_2014.pdf

Bundesinstitut für Berufsbildung. (2015). *Datenreport zum Berufsbildungsbericht 2015. Informationen und Analysen zur Entwicklung der beruflichen Bildung.* Bundesinstitut für Berufsbildung. https://www.bibb.de/dokumente/pdf/bibb_datenreport_2015.pdf

Bundesinstitut für Berufsbildung. (2016). *Datenreport zum Berufsbildungsbericht 2016. Informationen und Analysen zur Entwicklung der beruflichen Bildung.* Bundesinstitut für Berufsbildung. https://www.bibb.de/dokumente/pdf/bibb_datenreport_2016.pdf

Bundesinstitut für Berufsbildung. (2017). *Datenreport zum Berufsbildungsbericht 2017. Informationen und Analysen zur Entwicklung der beruflichen Bildung.* Bundesinstitut für Berufsbildung. https://www.bibb.de/dokumente/pdf/bibb_datenreport_2017.pdf

Bundesinstitut für Berufsbildung. (2018). *Datenreport zum Berufsbildungsbericht 2018. Informationen und Analysen zur Entwicklung der beruflichen Bildung.* Bundesinstitut für Berufsbildung. https://www.bibb.de/dokumente/pdf/bibb_datenreport_2018.pdf

Bundesinstitut für Berufsbildung. (2019). *Datenreport zum Berufsbildungsbericht 2019. Informationen und Analysen zur Entwicklung der beruflichen Bildung.* Bundesinstitut für Berufsbildung. https://www.bibb.de/dokumente/pdf/bibb_datenreport_2019.pdf

Bundesinstitut für Berufsbildung. (2020). *Datenreport zum Berufsbildungsbericht 2020. Informationen und Analysen zur Entwicklung der beruflichen Bildung.* Bundesinstitut für Berufsbildung. https://www.bibb.de/dokumente/pdf/bibb_datenreport_2020.pdf

Bundesinstitut für Berufsbildung. (2021). *Datenreport zum Berufsbildungsbericht 2021. Informationen und Analysen zur Entwicklung der beruflichen Bildung.* Bundesinstitut für Berufsbildung. https://www.bibb.de/dokumente/pdf/bibb-datenreport-2021.pdf

Bundesinstitut für Berufsbildung (2022a). *Angebots-Nachfrage-Relation (erweiterte Definition). Stand der Daten: 07.12.2022.* https://www.bibb.de/de/168901.php

Bundesinstitut für Berufsbildung. (2022b). *Rangliste 2022 der Ausbildungsberufe nach Neuabschlüssen in Niedersachsen. Männer. Tabelle 68.* Stand: 07.12.2022. https://www.bibb.de/dokumente/pdf/naa309/naa309_2022_tab068_1land.pdf

Bundesinstitut für Berufsbildung. (2022c). *Rangliste 2022 der Ausbildungsberufe nach Neuabschlüssen in Niedersachsen. Frauen. Tabelle 69.* Stand: 07.12.2022. https://www.bibb.de/dokumente/pdf/naa309/naa309_2022_tab069_1land.pdf

Bundesinstitut für Berufsbildung. (2022d). *Datenreport zum Berufsbildungsbericht 2022. Informationen und Analysen zur Entwicklung der beruflichen Bildung.* Bundesinstitut für Berufsbildung. https://www.bibb.de/dokumente/pdf/Datenreport%202022_20102022_online.pdf

Bundesinstitut für Berufsbildung. (2023). *Datenreport zum Berufsbildungsbericht 2023. Informationen und Analysen zur Entwicklung der beruflichen Bildung.* Bundesinstitut für Berufsbildung. https://www.bibb.de/dokumente/pdf/bibb_datenreport_2023_korr_11102023.pdf

Dahl, S. (2012). Leben und Arbeiten in der Landwirtschaft. *Statistische Monatshefte Niedersachsen, 66* (2), pp. 64–73. https://www.statistik.niedersachsen.de/download/64408

Destatis (2021). *Landwirtschaftliche Betriebe insgesamt und Betriebe mit ökologischem Landbau nach Bundesländern.* https://www.destatis.de/DE/Themen/Branchen-Unternehmen/Landwirtschaft-Forstwirtschaft-Fischerei/Landwirtschaftliche-Betriebe/Tabellen/oekologischer-landbau-bundeslaender.html

Destatis (2022). *Bildung und Kultur. Integrierte Ausbildungsberichterstattung. Anfänger:innen, Teilnehmer:innen und Absolvierende im Ausbildungsgeschehen nach Sektoren/Konten und Ländern. 2021.* https://www.destatis.de/DE/Themen/Gesellschaft-Umwelt/Bildung-Forschung-Kultur/Schulen/Publikationen/Downloads-Schulen/integrierte-ausbildungsberichterstattung-5211201217005.xlsx?__blob=publicationFile

Dionisius, R., Kroll, S. & Ulrich, J. G. (2018). Wo bleiben die jungen Frauen? Ursachen für ihre sinkende Beteiligung an der dualen Berufsausbildung. *Berufsbildung in Wissenschaft und Praxis, 47*(6), pp. 46–50. https://www.bwp-zeitschrift.de/dienst/publikationen/de/9484

Frommberger, D. (2019). Berufliche und hochschulische Bildung im Wandel – Entwicklungen zwischen Annäherung, Differenzierung und Öffnung. In B. Hemkes, K. Wilbers, & M. Heister (Eds.), *Durchlässigkeit zwischen beruflicher und hochschulischer Bildung,* volume 1, pp. 36–59. Bundesinstitut für Berufsbildung. https://www.bibb.de/veroeffentlichungen/de/publication/download/9753

Greinert, W.-D. (1995). *Das duale System der Berufsausbildung in der Bundesrepublik Deutschland: Struktur und Funktion* (2nd ed.). Holland + Josenhans.

Hölterhoff, D. (Ed.), (2022). *Zur Berufsbildungspolitik der KMK. Beiträge zur Bedeutung der Beruflichen Bildung sowie der dazugehörigen politischen Bildung.* Helmut-Schmidt-Universität Hamburg. https://doi.org/10.24405/14320

Hölterhoff, D. (2023). Akteure beruflicher Bildung im Rahmen einer Regionalentwicklung. Versuch einer kritischen Betrachtung. *bwp@ Berufs- und Wirtschaftspädagogik – online, 44.* https://www.bwpat.de/ausgabe44/hoelterhoff_bwpat44.pdf

Handwerkskammer Osnabrück – Emsland – Grafschaft Bentheim. (n. d.). *Starke Frauen für ein starkes Handwerk.* https://www.hwk-osnabrueck.de/wp-content/uploads/Broschüre-Frauen-im-Handwerk-Osnabrück.pdf

Handwerkskammer Osnabrück – Emsland – Grafschaft Bentheim. (2023). Neue Kampagne zeigt Vielfalt und Stärken des Handwerks. https://www.hwk-osnabrueck.de/neue-kampagne-zeigt-vielfalt-und-staerken-des-handwerks/

Industrie- und Handelskammer Niedersachsen (n. d.). *Gebietsatlas Niedersachsen.* https://www.ihk-n.de/ueberuns/mitglieder-894002

Klassen, J. & Schmees, J. K. (2022). Wandel in der Krise? Eine Analyse der Plenardebatten zum dualen System der Berufsausbildung in der COVID-19-Pandemie. In M. Eckelt, T. Ketschau, J. Klassen, J. Schauer, J. K. Schmees, & C. Steib (Eds.), *Berufsbildungspolitik: Strukturen – Krise – Perspektiven* (pp. 157–177). wbv. https://doi.org/10.3278/9783763972623

Standing Conference of the Ministers of Education and Cultural Affairs of the Länder in the Federal Republic of Germany (2019). *Das Bildungswesen in der Bundesrepublik Deutschland 2018/2019. Darstellung der Kompetenzen, Strukturen und bildungspolitischen Entwicklungen für den Informationsaustausch in Europa.* https://www.kmk.org/fileadmin/Dateien/pdf/Eurydice/Bildungswesen-dt-pdfs/dossier_de_ebook.pdf

Standing Conference of the Ministers of Education and Cultural Affairs of the Länder in the Federal Republic of Germany (2021). *Handreichung für die Erarbeitung von Rahmenlehrplänen der Kultusministerkonferenz für den berufsbezogenen Unterricht in der Berufsschule und ihre Abstimmung mit Ausbildungsordnungen des Bundes für anerkannte Ausbildungsberufe.* https://www.kmk.org/fileadmin/veroeffentlichungen_beschluesse/2021/2021_06_17-GEP-Handreichung.pdf

Krampf, K. (2021). Niedersachsens Landwirtschaft verändert sich. *Statistische Monatshefte Niedersachsen,* 75 (11), pp. 632–644. https://www.statistik.niedersachsen.de/download/177400

Landesamt für Statistik Niedersachsen (2020). *Niedersachsen-Monitor. 2020.* Hannover: Landesamt für Statistik Niedersachsen. https://www.statistik.niedersachsen.de/download/161518

Landesamt für Statistik Niedersachsen (2022a). *LSN-Online. Tabelle K70I5930. Sozialversicherungspflichtig Beschäftigte am Arbeitsort in Niedersachsen. 30.06.2022.* https://www1.nls.niedersachsen.de/statistik/html/default.asp Landesamt für Statistik Niedersachsen (2022b). *Niedersachsen-Monitor. 2022.* Hannover: Landesamt für Statistik Niedersachsen. https://www.statistik.niedersachsen.de/download/190492

Lange, S. & Goncharova, A. (2020). *Ausbildungsabbrüche und vorzeitige Vertragslösungen im IHK-Kammerbezirk Osnabrück – Emsland – Grafschaft Bentheim.* https://www.ihk.de/blueprint/servlet/resource/blob/4781096/c87373ba1f2ed3e3c175812c75e0db47/short-paper-ausbildungsabbrueche-final-data.pdf

Lassnigg, L. (2015). The Political Branding of Apprenticeship into the "Dual System": Reflections about Exporting the Myth of Employment Transition. In A. Heikkinen & L. Lassnigg (Eds.), *Myths and Brands in Vocational Education* (pp. 78–98). Cambridge Scholars Publishing.

Nickel, S., Pfeiffer, I., Fischer, A., Hüsch, M., Kiepenheuer-Drechsler, B., Lauterbach, N., Reum, N., Thiele A.-L. & Ulrich, S. (2022). Duales Studium. Umsetzungsmodelle und Entwicklungsbedarfe. wbv. https://doi.org/10.3278/9783763971718

Niedersächsisches Kultusministerium (2022). *Neue Bund-Land-Vereinbarung in Niedersachsen: Berufliche Orientierung an allgemeinbildenden und berufsbildenden Schulen und Übergang in die Ausbildung werden weiter gestärkt.* https://www.mk.niedersachsen.de/startseite/aktuelles/presseinformationen/neue-bund-land-vereinbarung-in-niedersachsen-berufliche-orientierung-an-allgemein-bildenden-und-berufsbildenden-schulen-und-ubergang-in-die-ausbildung-werden-weiter-gestarkt-211618.html

Niedersächsisches Ministerium für Wissenschaft und Kultur (2021). *Leistungsbericht der niedersächsischen Hochschulen.* https://www.mwk.niedersachsen.de/leistungsbericht/landesregierung-legt-leistungsbericht-der-niedersaechsischen-hochschulen-vor-149614.html

Niedersächsisches Schulgesetz (NSchG) in the version of March 3, 1998 (Nds. GVBl. S. 137), last amended by Article 8 of the Act of May 3, 2023 (Nds. GVBl. 80).

Seeber, S., Wieck, M., Baethge-Kinsky, V., Boschke, V., Michaelis, C., Busse, R. & Geiser, (2019). *Ländermonitor berufliche Bildung 2019. Ein Vergleich der Bundesländer mit vertiefender Analyse zu Passungsproblemen im dualen System.* wbv. https://doi.org/10.3278/6004750w

Severing, E. & Teichler, U. (2013). Akademisierung der Berufswelt? Verberuflichung der Hochschulen? In E. Severing & U. Teichler (Eds.), *Akademisierung der Berufswelt?* (pp. 7–18). Bertelsmann. https://doi.org/10.25656/01:7986

Uhly, A. (2023). *Erläuterungen zum Datensystem Auszubildende (DAZUBI) Auszubildenden-Daten, Berufsmerkmale, Berechnungen des BIBB. Berufsbildungsstatistik der statistischen Ämter des Bundes und der Länder (Erhebung zum 31. Dezember). Berichtsjahr 2022. Stand 17. Oktober 2023.* Bundesinstitut für Berufsbildung. https://www.bibb.de/dokumente/pdf/dazubi_daten.pdf

Wissenschaftsrat (2013). *Empfehlungen zur Entwicklung des dualen Studiums. Positionspapier. Drs. 3479–13.* https://www.wissenschaftsrat.de/download/archiv/3479-13.html

Wolter, A. (2016). Der Ort des dualen Studiums zwischen beruflicher und akademischer Bildung: Mythen und Realitäten. In U. Faßhauer & E. Severing (Eds.), *Verzahnung beruflicher und akademischer Bildung. Duale Studiengänge in Theorie und Praxis* (pp. 39–60). Bertelsmann. https://www.bibb.de/dienst/publikationen/de/7940

## Short portrait of the author

**Tim Migura** is a Research Associate at Osnabrück University in the Department of Vocational Education Studies. His research focuses on developments in the academisation and Europeanisation of health professions in Austria, Germany and Switzerland.
Contact: tim.migura@uos.de

# Diversity of vocational schools in Lower Saxony

Silke Lange

Abstract: despite greatly changed educational flows, vocational education and training (VET) still has high social status in Germany. Embedded in the formal education system, VET schools make an important contribution but are often underestimated. The educational opportunities at VET schools catch pupils who have left the general school system without a school-leaving certificate or who have not succeeded in making the transition to vocational training. They offer vocational and further education programmes. Furthermore, they deepen and broaden the general education of their students. They award school and vocational qualifications and enable pupils to 'catch up' on school-leaving qualifications and to acquire further school-leaving qualifications. The article describes the different types of VET schools in Lower Saxony and the pupils at these schools.

**Keywords**: Diversity; Educational Opportunities; School System; VET Schools.

## 1 Introduction

Vocational education and training (VET) still enjoys high social status in Germany – despite greatly changed educational flows between academic and vocational education. While the demand for apprenticeships from those willing to participate in vocational training increased in Germany, particularly in the 1970s to 1980s, the number of training contracts concluded fell from the mid-1980s as a result of a demographically induced decline in school leavers (Althoff, 1999; Hillmert, 2004). After a slight expansion phase, the number of apprentices has been declining again since the early 2000s (Dietrich et al., 2004; Troltsch, 2011; Matthes et al., 2017), which is linked to a long-term trend towards higher qualifications in school-based (upper secondary general school) and academic programmes (Althoff, 1999; Matthes et al., 2017).

Embedded in the formal education system in Germany, VET schools make an important proposition. They offer courses that prepare graduates of general education schools for VET or enable them to complete compulsory schooling, to catch up on general education qualifications and to acquire vocational qualifications. Both within Germany and when viewed from abroad, VET schools are often underestimated, on the one hand because it is difficult to grasp the complexity of the VET system in Germany (Frommberger, in this volume), and on the other hand because they are often reduced to their offers in the dual apprenticeship system. However, VET schools actually provide an institutional framework for a *variety* of VET school types. Thus, the educational landscape is diverse and "[...] has only one thing in common: All types of VET schools claim to combine general with vocational education and personality development with qualification" (Clement, 2010, p. 63; author's transl.)

When trying to describe the VET schools, difficulties arise: Since the education system in Germany is subject to the political power of the federated states (*Bundesländer*), it is at least partly shaped by state-specific offers and characteristics. In this respect, despite framework agreements agreed upon by and valid for all states (KMK 2010a, 2010b, 2020b, 2021a, 2021b, 2022), there are "inconsistently ordered objects with partly state-specific school types" (Wittmann, 2009, p. 96; author's transl.; also KMK, 2023) and "diverging educational pathways, access entitlements and, above all, certificates in these school types" (Wittmann, 2009, p. 96; author's transl.) as well as permanent changes to their legal basis that are "in part difficult to comprehend and [...] require a look at the relevant ordinances of the states" (Wittmann, 2009, p. 96; author's transl.). And as different as the programmes are, as heterogeneous is their clientele. Youths and (young) adults with different educational, professional and social backgrounds learn together at VET schools. In some cases, school attendance is compulsory for learners, while others attend voluntarily in order to acquire educational and/or vocational qualifications.

This chapter addresses this diversity of VET schools from the perspective of both supply and demand. The supply perspective is characterised by the types of schools and courses of education, which are presented as individual offers and placed in the overall context of VET schools as educational institutions. The heterogeneity of those seeking education is traced on the basis of statistical data in relation to the types of schools presented. Because the chapter was written as part of a cooperation project between the universities of Bergamo and Osnabrück, the descriptions refer to the situation in Lower Saxony, thus reducing the exploration of complexity outlined above and relating it to the situation in one state only.

## 2 The school system in Lower Saxony

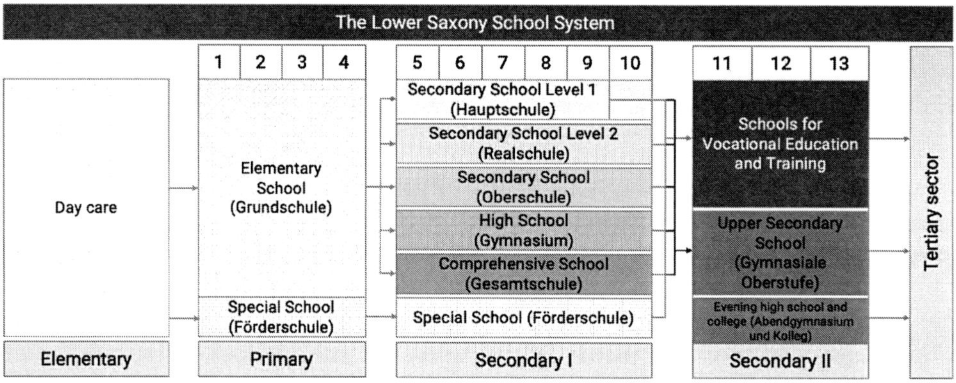


**Figure 1:** The Lower Saxony School System

*Note*: Adapted from MK NI, 2020, p. 2.

The school system in Lower Saxony is – as it is nationwide – a multi-level system characterised by common educational pathways at the elementary and primary levels[1] which are then differentiated at the lower and upper secondary levels as well as at the tertiary level (Fig. 1; also MK NI, 2020). As for the secondary level, pupils are taught in different types of schools (Fig. 1) that provide a lower secondary education in levels one (*Hauptschule, Oberschule, Gesamtschule*) and two (*Realschule, Oberschule, Gesamtschule*) or upper secondary general (*Gymnasium, Oberschule, Gesamtschule*) or vocational education (VET schools).

After completing the lower secondary level, pupils take a final examination to obtain a lower secondary school-leaving certificate level one (*Hauptschulabschluss*) or two (Mittlerer Schulabschluss) or an extended lower secondary school-leaving certificate (*erweiterter Sekundarabschluss I*). Pupils in an upper secondary school do not have to take this examination; by transferring to the eleventh grade, they fulfil the requirements of the extended lower secondary school-leaving certificate. If the pupils do not transfer to the eleventh grade, they can be awarded a lower secondary school-leaving certificate. After successful completion of the upper secondary school, pupils acquire the general higher education entrance qualification (*Allgemeine Hochschulreife*; MK NI, 2015, p. 3).

In the school year of 2020/21, a total of approximately 1.09 million pupils were educated at 3,699 schools by 91,963 teachers in Lower Saxony. Among them, 237,206 (22.9 %) were educated at 250 VET schools (6.8 %) by 14,522 (15.8 %) VET teachers (LSN, 2023a, 2023b, 2023c, 2023d). In all, 132 (52.8 %) of the VET schools in Lower Saxony are publicly funded. In the financial year 2020, the state of and municipalities in Lower Saxony together invested around 7.4 billion euros in schools (DESTATIS, 2022a, p. 128), which corresponds to EUR 8,100 per pupil (DESTATIS, 2022a, p. 129). At the VET schools, investment in education per pupil was EUR 5,300, EUR 700 below the national average of investments in VET schools (ibid.). Lower Saxony thus invests comparatively little in its VET schools.

In the same year, a total of 76,319 pupils left general schools in Lower Saxony, 60.6 % of them with a lower secondary school-leaving certificate (level one: 13.5 %; level two: 44.5 %) and 33.4 % with a higher education entrance qualification (LSN, 2023 f). The proportion of school leavers without a lower secondary school-leaving certificate was 6.0 % (LSN, 2023 f) and thus only slightly below the national average (6.2 %; DESTATIS, 2023a). Overall, Lower Saxony has a fairly high proportion of school leavers with a lower secondary school-leaving certificate level two, which "from the point of view of companies offers a favourable reservoir of potential training candidates" (Seeber et al., 2019, p. 253; author's transl.). However, due to the proximity to the city states of Bremen and Hamburg, which are very well positioned in terms of infrastructure, a broader training offer is potentially available to Lower Saxony's school leavers. "For companies close to these states' borders, this can [...] lead to higher competition

1 Children can be enrolled in special schools at the primary level, and Lower Saxony is one of the states in Germany where a comparatively large number of children are still enrolled directly in special schools (Autor:innengruppe Bildungsberichterstattung, p. 115).

for apprentices, as both city states are highly attractive to young people from Lower Saxony" (Seeber et al., 2019, p. 254; author's transl.)

When transferring to the upper secondary level and following educational programmes at the upper secondary level, adolescents and young adults have access to various educational programmes at VET schools. In 2020/21, 118,494 persons entered VET school programmes (LSN, 2023b), including 4.6 % without a school-leaving certificate, 18.7 % with a lower secondary school-leaving certificate level one and 56.9 % with a lower secondary school-leaving certificate level two or an extended lower secondary school-leaving certificate. In all, 15.1 % of those entering VET schools had a higher education entrance qualification (LSN, 2023b). Accordingly, the VET schools in Lower Saxony offer important learning/education opportunities, especially for school leavers without or with only a lower secondary school-leaving certificate.

## 3 Offers of vocational schools in Lower Saxony

The VET schools in Lower Saxony have various tasks. In general, they should

- "impart a vocational capacity to act which combines professional competence with general skills of a humane and social nature;
- develop professional flexibility to cope with the changing demands in the world of work and society, also with regard to the growing together of Europe;
- develop the readiness for further and continuing education;
- promote the ability and willingness to shape one's own life and to act responsibly in public life" (MK NI, 2020, p. 28; author's transl.)

In order to meet these requirements, instruction at the VET schools should be "implemented according to the didactic-methodical concept of action orientation" (Supplementary provisions for the VET school system, EB-BbS Niedersachsen), whereby school type-specific characteristics are taken into account. The individual types of VET schools can be distinguished on the basis of several characteristics. As a rule, the characteristics 'access requirements', 'framework conditions and curricular requirements' (e. g. on duration and form of instruction[2]) as well as 'qualifications awarded' are used to differentiate the offers. From the certificates awarded, individuals derive 'unconditional rights' to participate in further general education (usually through the attainment of school-leaving qualifications) or VET (usually through the attainment of vocational qualifications) (Kell, 1982, pp. 291–292; Wittmann, 2009, p. 95). Furthermore, certificates confer "conditional rights to occupy certain positions in the hierarchy of tasks and jobs in the economic system and/or to perform certain functions in the political-social system" (Kell, 1982, p. 291; author's transl.) This is because certificates are "a prerequisite for applying for certain positions, for which they indicate suitability, without, however, implying a legal claim to such a position" (Wittmann, 2009, p. 95; author's transl.)

2 The form of instruction refers to the learning time spent at a VET school: It is possible to provide only part of the learning time at school (part-time) or to learn full or quasi-full time at the VET school (DESTATIS, 2023).

In the following, the various types of VET schools in Lower Saxony are briefly characterised on the basis of the above-mentioned features, and their pupils are described on the basis of school statistics data from the Lower Saxonian State Office for Statistics (Landesamt für Statistik Niedersachsen; LSN).

### 3.1 Part-time VET school (Berufsschule)

**Table 1:** Summary characteristics of the part-time VET school

| | |
|---|---|
| **Target group** | Apprentices to compulsory VET school attendance |
| **Access requirements** | Vocational training contract in the dual apprenticeship system |
| **Form of instruction** | Part-time |
| **Duration** | 2 to 3.5 years |
| **Awarded certificates** | VET school-leaving certificate in combination with a secondary school-leaving certificate |

The "showpiece" (Baethge, 2005, p. 526; author's transl.) of the VET system is the dual apprenticeship system, that is, training in a vocationally recognised occupation within the framework of the Vocational Training Act (BBiG), in which in-company training in a private or public training company is combined with school-based training in a public VET school. For Lower Saxony, the dual apprenticeship system is particularly important for securing skilled labour. The employment structure in Lower Saxony, which area-wise is one of the largest federated states in Germany, is dominated by employees with a vocational or further training qualification (Lower Saxony 2020: 64.7%; Germany: 60.5%), while the proportion of employees with a university degree is comparatively low (Lower Saxony 2020: 13.5%; Germany: 17.7%; for Lower Saxony: LSN, 2023e; for Germany: DESTATIS, 2023b). The employment system in Lower Saxony thus relies very heavily on vocationally or non-academically qualified skilled workers (Seeber et al., 2019, p. 252).

School-based training in the dual apprenticeship system takes place at VET schools in the school type of part-time VET schools (*Berufsschule*). Formally, there are no requirements in terms of school-leaving qualifications to take up apprenticeship in the dual apprenticeship system. Training companies decide at their own discretion whether to hire apprentices. Nevertheless, it is evident that the chance of finding an apprenticeship is closely linked to the school-leaving certificate (Seeber et al., 2019, p. 31–32.; Dohmen et al., 2023).

Dual apprenticeship training lasts between two and three and a half years – depending on the training occupation. During the training period, the training company with which a trainee concludes the vocational training contract is obliged to release the trainees for part-time VET school; the trainees are obliged to attend the part-time VET school during the vocational training in the dual apprenticeship system (§ 13 in conjunction with § 15 para. 1 BBiG). Instruction at the part-time VET school comprises 12 hours per week per training year. It can be taught either regularly on one or two days a week (part-time instruction), bundled on several days alternating with non-instruction weeks (bundled part-time instruction) or as full-time instruction in connected sections of at least one week (block instruction) (EB-BbS).

In the classroom, apprentices in training-occupation-related specialist classes[3] are "promoted in their vocational competences by means of in-service instruction, professionally relevant to the occupation" (Heinrichs et al., 2023, p. 8; author's transl.) by imparting "the basic theoretical training required for the occupation" (KMK 2020a, p. 15; author's transl.) and integrating offers for the further development and deepening of general education (KMK, 2021a). In Lower Saxony, the inter-occupational learning area comprises the subjects German, a foreign language, politics, physical education and religion (EB-BbS). The occupation-related learning area, which refers to the training occupations, is subdivided into learning fields that are based on the cross-state framework curricula (KMK, n. d.)

Anyone who has successfully attended the part-time VET school acquires a VET school-leaving certificate (*Berufsschulabschluss*) (§ 33 para. 1 in conjunction with Annex 1 & § 23 para. 2 BbS-VO). Successful completion of vocational training is certified by the respective regional chamber[4] organisation after the training examination is passed (vocational qualification; § 37 in conjunction with § 71 BBiG). In Lower Saxony, trainees who have successfully completed training can acquire a lower secondary school-leaving certificate (level one or two) or the entrance qualification to universities for applied science (*Fachhochschulreife*). A lower secondary-leaving certificate is awarded to anyone with the VET school-leaving certificate and the vocational training certificate (level one for a two-year training and level two for a three-year training). In order to acquire the entrance qualification for universities of applied sciences, a supplementary training course must be attended parallel to the school-based training (§§ 25–29 BbS-VO).

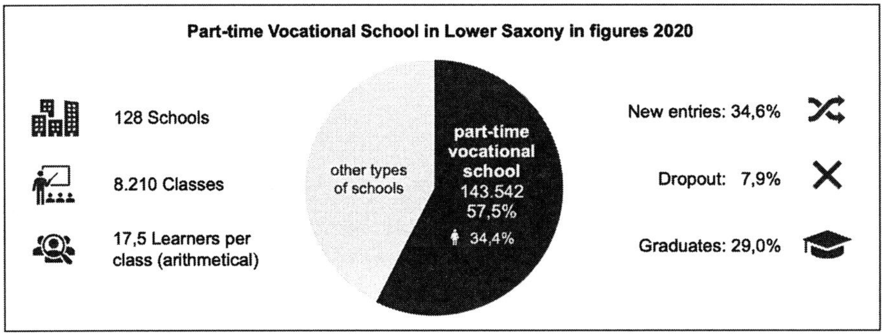


**Figure 2:** Part-time VET school in Lower Saxony in figures (2020)

*Note:* The data is from LSN, 2023a.

3 As a rule, classes at *Berufsschule* should be formed on a year-by-year basis for training occupations. In order to avoid classes that are too small, specialised classes can also be formed from trainees who are being trained in occupations that have an affinity. Affine occupations are those that have significant similarities in content (§ 1b par. 1 & 2 BbS-VO).

4 In the dual vocational training system in Germany, chamber organisations, e. g. the chambers of commerce and industry, are responsible for monitoring and certifying vocational training programmes (sf. § 76 BBiG).

In the school year 2020/21, around half of the VET schools in Lower Saxony (51.2 %) offered vocationally related specialist classes in the part-time VET school. A total of 143,542 apprentices were educated in these classes, which accounts for 57.5 % of the students at VET schools. The part-time VET school is thus the largest type of VET school in Lower Saxony in terms of learner numbers (Figure 2). This is not a state-specific phenomenon but is also true for Germany as a whole (Frommberger & Lange, 2018, p. 12). At only 34.4 %, the proportion of female apprentices at the part-time VET school was significantly lower than that of male apprentices (Figure 2). The fact that women are represented to a lesser extent in the dual apprenticeship system nationwide is regularly noted in the VET Report of the Federal Ministry of Education and Research (Bundesministerium für Bildung und Forschung; BMBF). In 2020, the proportion of female apprentices in Germany as a whole was 36.4 % (BMBF, 2023, p. 56).

Approximately 34.6 % of apprentices in the part-time VET school started their training in 2020 (see Figure 2). More than half of the new entrants had a lower school-leaving certificate level one (22.3 %; Germany 23.6 %) or level two (45.1 %; Germany: 45.0 %). The proportion of new entrants with a university entrance qualification was also comparatively high at 23.3 % (Germany: 22.1 %) (Heinrichs et al., 2023, p. 10). Overall, 3.9 % of new entrants to the part-time VET school did not have a school-leaving certificate; this proportion is lower than the nationwide average (5.2 %) (for Lower Saxony: LSN, 2023a; for Germany: DESTATIS, 2022b).

During the school year, 7.9 % of the trainees left the part-time VET school without a corresponding qualification. At the end of the school year, 41,637 students (29.0 %) finished the part-time VET school, of whom 92.7 % were successful and obtained a VET school-leaving certificate. Another 20.1 % obtained a lower secondary school-leaving certificate (level one: 0.9 %, level two: 19.2 %), and 0.2 % acquired the entrance qualification for universities of applied sciences (*Fachhochschulreife*) (LSN, 2023a).

## 3.2 Vocational preparation school (Berufseinstiegsschule)

**Table 2:** Summary characteristics of the vocational preparation school

| | |
|---|---|
| **Target group** | Young people who do not have a lower secondary school-leaving certificate and/or have not been able to enter a vocational training programme |
| **Access requirements** | None |
| **Form of instruction** | Grade 1: full-time: Grade 2: full-time or part-time |
| **Duration** | 2 years |
| **Awarded certificates** | Lower secondary school-leaving certificate level one |

The vocational preparation school is a state-specific type of VET school that exists only in Lower Saxony. It is part of the transition system, which in Germany has taken on the social function of "closing the integration gap of young people who fail to make the transition to fully qualifying VET and/or to gainful employment that secures their livelihood" (Steib, 2020, pp. 169–170; author's transl.). It "imparts to its pupils, in addition to general education, a vocational education which focuses on preparing them for vocational training or for employment" (§ 17 para. 1 NSchG). It is aimed at persons who do not have a lower secondary school-leaving certificate or "who otherwise indicate that they still need to improve their knowledge and skills in order to attain the maturity required to successfully complete vocational training" (§ 17 para. 2 NSchG). In addition, language and integration classes can be set up within the framework of the vocational preparation school. Once sufficient language skills have been acquired, a transfer to class 1 or 2 of the 'regular' vocational preparation school is possible (§ 17 NSChG).

Instruction at vocational preparation schools is full-time in the first year and can be continued full-time or part-time in the second year. It is divided into vocational and inter-occupational learning areas. The vocational learning area relates to vocational content from one of the specialisations of 'health and social work', 'technology' and 'economics' (Annex 2 BbS-VO; EB-BbS) and is taught in qualification modules. Within the framework of qualification modules, basic VET competences from VET courses are taught. They comprise a minimum of 60 and a maximum of 120 hours (EB-BbS). At the end of each qualification module, the pupils take a written and a practical examination (Anlage 2 BbS-VO).

The inter-occupational learning area is taught in the first year in the learning modules 'Communication in the World of Life and Work' and 'Promotion of Basic Knowledge'. In the second year, lessons are given in German, English, mathematics, politics, physical education. and religion (EB-BbS). The final examination in the inter-occupational learning area consists of two written examinations in the subjects German and mathematics. Those who successfully complete the final examinations of the vocational preparation school are awarded lower secondary school-leaving certificate level one (§ 25 in conjunction with Annex 2 BbS-VO).

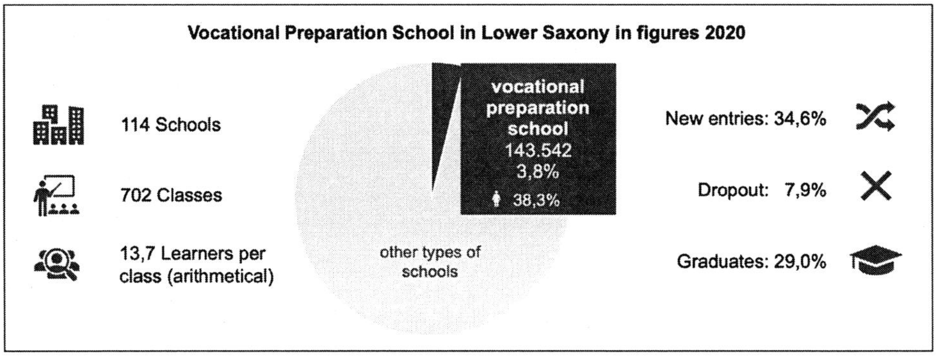


**Figure 3:** Vocational preparation school in Lower Saxony in figures (2020)

*Note:* The data is from LSN, 2023a.

Vocational preparation was offered at 114 VET schools in Lower Saxony (45.6 %) in the school year 2020/21. A total of 9,600 pupils were educated, which represented 3.8 % of the learners at VET schools (see Figure 3). The vocational preparation school is thus the smallest type of VET school in Lower Saxony in terms of the number of pupils. At the vocational preparation school, too, female pupils are clearly underrepresented at 38.3 % (see Figure 3), which is – also nationwide – quite typical for programmes in the transition system (Pimminger, 2012, p. 20). A special feature of the vocational preparation school is the comparatively small classes; in school year 2020/21, the classes had a calculated capacity of only 13.7 learners (see Figure 3), whereas in all other school types of the VET schools there were more (between 17.5 and 23.5).

A total of 4,895 young people entered a vocational preparation school in 2020. Of the new entrants, only 5.6 % had a lower secondary school-leaving certificate; the majority had left the general school system without a certificate (72.5 %) or with a certificate from the special needs education sector (11.9 %) (LSN, 2023a).

The dropout rate of the vocational preparation school is comparatively high at 12.4% in the school year 2020/21. Since the data does not provide any information about the young people's subsequent pathways and the vocational preparation school offer is relatively young, there have been no analyses of the dropout behaviour for this school type yet. However, it can be assumed that at least some of the dropouts can be explained by the transition to vocational qualifying training. At the end of the school year, a total of 7,886 pupils (82.1 %) were able to complete the vocational preparation school, of whom 87.9 % were successful, although only 27.3 % of those were able to obtain lower secondary school-leaving certificate level one (LSN, 2023a).

## 3.3 Full-time VET school (Berufsfachschule)

**Table 3:** Summary characteristics of the full-time VET school

| | |
|---|---|
| **Target group** | Young people who have a lower secondary school-leaving certificate level one and have entered neither further education nor employment or who want to train for an occupation outside of the dual apprenticeship training system |
| **Access requirements** | At least lower secondary school-leaving certificate |
| **Form of instruction** | Full-time or part-time |
| **Duration** | 1 to 3 years |
| **Awarded certificates** | school-leaving certificate<br>Vocational qualification in combination with a lower secondary school-leaving certificate |

The full-time VET school is the most heterogeneous of the VET school types, at least in terms of the structure of provision. It combines various educational offers that

- provide broad-based basic vocational training in preparation for vocational qualifying training that can be credited towards training in the dual apprenticeship system (partially qualifying or *one-year full-time VET school*)
- facilitate the acquisition of a school-leaving certificate (*two-year full-time VET school*) or

- provide a vocational training qualification in an occupation outside the dual apprenticeship system (e. g. biological-technical assistant, socio-educational assistant; *vocationally qualifying full-time VET school*).

The *one-year full-time VET school* (*einjährige Berufsfachschule*) is also part of the transition system and is designed for people with a lower secondary school-leaving certificate level one who were not able to secure an apprenticeship. For some vocational specialisations a lower secondary school-leaving certificate level two is required (Annex 3 BbS-VO). In addition to the subjects German, a foreign language, politics, physical education, and religion, a vocational learning area is taught. The vocational learning area relates to one of seventeen vocational specialisations (agriculture; construction technology; chemistry, physics and biology; printing and media technology; electrical engineering; vehicle technology; colour technology and interior design; floristry; horticulture; gastronomy; home economics and care; wood technology; personal hygiene; food trades; metal technology; textile technology and clothing; economics) (EB-BbS). The content and focus of instruction are oriented by the competences assigned to the respective occupational specialisation. Modes of instruction include both theoretical and practical learning scenarios. The final examination is completed in writing and in practice and relates to the vocational learning area (Annex 3 BbS-VO).

The *two-year full-time VET school* (*zweijährige Berufsfachschule*) is one of the programmes of vocational education leading to a higher school-leaving certificate. In Lower Saxony, it is only offered in the second grade; grade 1 of the two-year full-time VET school is 'replaced' by the one-year full-time VET school (BA, 2022, p. 18). The second year of the two-year full-time VET school can be conducted in one of six vocational specialisations (agriculture; nutrition; home economics and care; social pedagogics; technology; economics) (Annex 3 BbS-VO). As in the one-year full-time VET school, instruction takes place in an inter-occupational learning area, which in the two-year full-time VET school is supplemented by the subject of mathematics. In addition, instruction takes place in a vocational area that focuses on theory, with the exception of the two-year full-time VET school in social pedagogy (*Berufsfachschule Sozialpädagogik*), which includes extensive (420 hours) practical training in a suitable institution (EB-BbS) over the two years. The final examination of the two-year full-time VET school consists of two written tests, one in the subject German or a foreign language and one in the vocational learning area (theory) (Annex 3 BbS-VO).

Alongside the dual apprenticeship system, the *vocationally qualifying full-time VET school* (*berufsqualifizierende Berufsfachschule*) is the second pillar of vocationally qualifying training in the VET system. It is often described as full-time school-based training, although this training also includes extensive practical components (Frommberger, in this volume). The range of training courses offered in the vocationally qualifying full-time VET school includes training occupations regulated under federal law in the health professions (e. g. in nursing, PflBG; in physiotherapy, MPhG) and a wide range of training courses regulated under state law (usually to become a state-certified assistant; KMK, 2023). There are cross-state framework agreements for the programmes regulated by state law (KMK, 2020b, 2022).

In Lower Saxony, vocationally qualifying full-time VET schools are able to offer 19 specialisations: industrial-technical (agriculture, biology, chemistry, electronics, design, information, ship-operational assistance; information technology), commercial (commercial assistance) and socio-pedagogical field (social assistance and socio-pedagogical assistance) fields, as well as health (respiration, voice and speech teacher; ergotherapy; cosmetics; nursing assistance and pharmaceutical-technical assistance) and textiles (fashion and design assistance; tailoring) (Annex 3 BbS-VO). As a rule, people who have at least a lower secondary school-leaving certificate level two can be admitted to the vocationally qualifying full-time VET school. Depending on the specialisation, other (e. g. cosmetics: at least lower secondary school-leaving certificate level one) or additional entry requirements can be defined (e. g. breathing, speaking and voice teacher: additionally, a good vocal quality). Training in the vocationally qualifying full-time VET school lasts between two and three years, depending on the specialisation (Annex 3 BbS-VO). In general, instruction is divided into an inter-occupational and an occupation-related learning area. The occupation-related learning area is subdivided into theory and practice, wherein the practice is usually carried out in the form of work placements in suitable institutions. The inter-occupational learning area generally comprises the subjects German, a foreign language, mathematics, politics, physical education and religion, although there may be subject-specific deviations (EB-BbS). The vocationally qualifying full-time VET school concludes with written and practical final examinations, the number and design of which depend on the chosen vocational specialisation. With the vocational qualification, graduates of the vocationally qualifying full-time VET school can acquire a secondary school-leaving certificate level two or an extended secondary school-leaving certificate, depending on the specialisation and performance (Annex 3 BbS-VO).

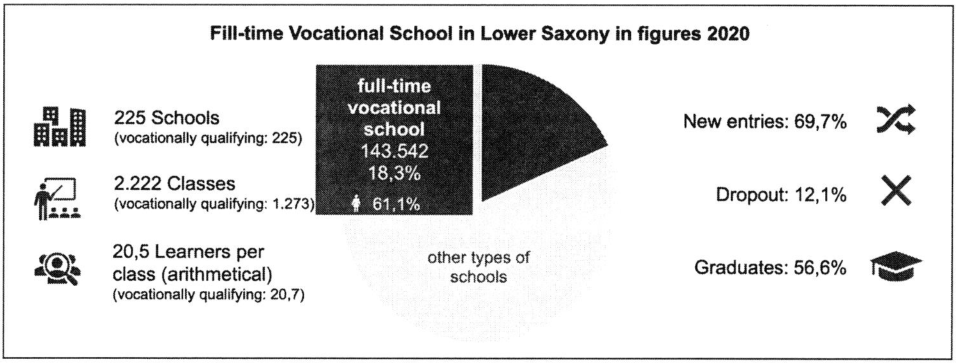


**Figure 4:** Full-time VET school in Lower Saxony in figures (2020)

*Note*: Data from LSN, 2023a.

In the school year 2020/21, 225 VET schools in Lower Saxony (90.0 %) offered educational programmes within the framework of the full-time VET school. At all these schools, pupils were able to obtain a vocational qualification (see Figure 4). Overall, 57.3 % of the schools offered one-year full-time vocational programmes. Attendance at the two-year full-time VET school was possible at 29.3 % of VET schools (LSN, 2023a). A total of 45,549 pupils attended a full-time VET school in 2020, which was 18.3 % of the pupils at VET schools (see Figure 4). The full-time VET school is thus – by some distance – the second most important VET school type in Lower Saxony after the part-time VET school. Within the full-time VET school, pupils in the vocational qualification courses form the largest group (57.9 %). The proportion of women in these programmes is 72.2 % (LSN, 2023a). Training occupations in this vocational subsystem are accordingly more likely to be traditionally female compared to those in the dual apprenticeship system (also Seeber et al., 2019, p. 55).

About two-thirds of the students in a full-time VET school started training in 2020, with the majority of new entrants being in a one-year course (54.1 %). Among both new entrants with a level one (33.9 %) and level two (54.5 %) lower secondary school-leaving certificate, the majority of pupils entered the one-year full-time VET school (LSN, 2023a), possibly in order to acquire occupation-related competences in a corresponding occupational field after an unsuccessful transition to a vocationally qualifying training and to increase their own chances of receiving training in the dual apprenticeship system. In the vocationally qualifying full-time VET school, the majority of pupils had a lower secondary school-leaving certificate level two (60.3 %) or an upper secondary school-leaving certificate (21.3 %; LSN, 2023a).

During school year 2020/21, 12.1 % of the pupils left, which means that the dropout rate at full-time VET school was comparatively high. Unfortunately, the school statistics of the LSN do not provide any differentiated data on this, so it remains unclear in which type of full-time VET school dropout rates were particularly high. Similar to the vocational preparation school, it seems probable that pupils succeeded in transferring to apprenticeships in the dual apprenticeship system during the school year. At the end of the school year, 25,772 pupils left full-time VET school (56.6 %; see Figure 4). In all, 81.3 % of them were successful; 29.5 % of the leavers were able to obtain an additional school-leaving qualification; 3.9 % a lower secondary school-leaving certificate level one; 25.3 % a lower secondary school-leaving certificate level two; and 0.3 % an entrance qualification for universities of applied sciences (LSN, 2023a).

## 3.4 Vocationally oriented upper secondary school and upper VET school (Fachoberschule und Berufsoberschule)

**Table 4:** Summary characteristics of the vocationally oriented upper secondary school and upper VET school

| | |
|---|---|
| **Target group** | Young people who aspire to a higher education entrance qualification |
| **Access requirements** | Vocationally oriented upper secondary school: lower secondary school-leaving certificate level two<br>Upper VET school: entrance qualification for universities of applied sciences |

*(Continuing table 4)*

| | |
|---|---|
| **Form of instruction** | Vocationally oriented upper secondary school: full-time or part-time<br>Upper VET school: full-time |
| **Duration** | Vocationally oriented upper secondary school: 2 years<br>Upper VET school: 1 year |
| **Awarded certificates** | Vocationally oriented upper secondary school: entrance qualification for universities of applied sciences<br>Upper VET school: subject-linked or general higher education entrance qualification |

The vocationally oriented upper secondary school (*Fachoberschule*) and the upper VET school (*Berufsoberschule*) are school types for the focus-related expansion and deepening of general education with the aim of acquiring higher school-leaving qualifications. The vocationally oriented upper secondary school comprises school years 11 and 12 and aims at the acquisition of the entrance qualification for universities of applied science (§ 18 NSchG; KMK 2010b). The upper VET school comprises school years 12 and 13 and leads to the acquisition of the subject-specific higher education entrance qualification, e. g. for universities (§ 18a NSchG; KMK 2010a). In Lower Saxony, grade 12 of the upper VET school is run as grade 12 of the vocationally oriented upper secondary school (Annex 6 BbS-VO), which means that the upper VET school is only offered for school year 13.

The vocationally oriented upper secondary school and upper VET school in Lower Saxony offer various vocational specialisations. The vocationally oriented upper secondary school offers six specialisations: business and administration (with a focus on business, administration and legal services as well as information technology); technology (with a focus on construction technology, information technology and mechatronics); health and social occupations (with a focus on health care as well as social education); design; nutrition and home economics; and agricultural economics, biotechnology and environmental technology (Annex 5 BbS-VO). The upper VET school can be continued in these subjects, with exception of design, for which no upper vocational programme is offered.

The vocationally oriented upper secondary school can be attended by persons with at least a lower secondary school-leaving certificate level two, after a completed vocational training or following employment. The upper VET school can be entered by people with an entrance qualification for universities of applied sciences and work experience (or completed vocational training) or by graduates of the vocationally oriented upper secondary school.

Grade 11 of the vocationally oriented upper secondary school consists of part-time courses (12 lessons per week in the vocationally related and inter-occupational area) and an extensive work placement (960 hours in total). The inter-occupational learning area comprises German, English, mathematics, science (only grade 12), politics, physical education and religion (EB-BbS). This Grade 11 can be replaced by relevant vocational training or sufficient relevant work experience. People with a vocational qualification or sufficient work experience can therefore be admitted directly to grade 12. In grade 12, learners acquire in-depth subject-related competences in the inter-occupational and occupation-related learning areas in full- or part-time courses. Grade 12 ends with a written final examination in German, English and mathematics as well as in the vocational learning area (Annex 5 BbS-VO). Upon successful completion of the vocationally oriented upper secondary school, pupils acquire the entrance qualification for a university of applied sciences (§ 29 BbS-VO) and also the entrance requirements for the upper VET school.

In grade 13 of the upper VET school, learners deepen their competences in the inter-occupational and occupation-related learning area (EB-BbS). After successful written examinations in the subjects German, English and mathematics as well as in the vocational learning area (Annex 6 BbS-VO), pupils receive the subject-linked higher education entrance qualification (§ 30 BbS-VO). In addition, a supplementary examination in a second foreign language can be taken, which enables the acquisition of the general higher education entrance qualification (§ 31 in conjunction with Annex 6 BbS-VO).

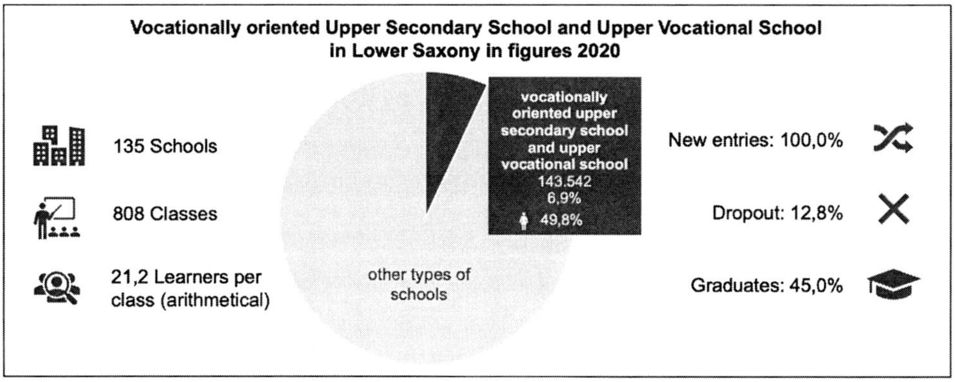


**Figure 5:** Vocationally oriented upper secondary school and upper VET school in Lower Saxony in figures (2020)

*Note:* Data from LSN, 2023a.

In the school year 2020/21, applicants for the vocationally oriented upper secondary school in Lower Saxony had a choice between 130 schools (52.0 % of VET schools), but upper secondary schooling could only be continued at 5 VET schools (2 %) (see Figure 5). These figures already indicate that the demand for the upper secondary programme is not as high as that for vocationally oriented upper secondary programmes.

In 2020, 17,106 learners (6.9 % of learners at VET schools) were taught at a vocationally oriented secondary school and 62 learners (0.02 % of learners at VET schools) at an upper VET school (LSN 2023a). In the school statistics, the learners at both are considered new entrants every school year (LSN, 2023a) – it is unclear why this is the case. According to the statistics, about half of the learners leave the vocationally oriented secondary school and the upper VET school every year, while the dropout rate is about 10.0 %. The destination of the other students remains unclear.

In school year 2020/21, pupils of the vocationally oriented secondary school almost exclusively had a lower secondary school-leaving certificate level two (99.6 %). The remaining learners had a foreign school-leaving certificate or another school-leaving certificate (at least equivalent to the lower secondary school-leaving certificate level two). The pupils at the upper VET school all had the entrance qualification for universities of applied science (LSN, 2023a). The pupils were taught in a total of 808 classes, of which only 6 were at an upper VET school. Arithmetically, 21.3 people on average studied together in the classes of the vocationally oriented secondary school and 10.3 in the classes of the upper VET school (see Figure 5). At the latter class sizes were small due to low enrolment.

During the school year, 2,173 learners dropped out of a vocationally oriented secondary school (12.7 %) and 17 learners dropped out of an upper VET school (27.4 %) (LSN, 2023a). At the end of the school year, 7,680 pupils finished the vocationally oriented secondary school (44.9 %), of whom 88.4 % were successful and were able to acquire the entrance qualification for higher education and thus the entrance requirements for the upper VET school. The upper VET school was completed by 50 people (80.6 %), of whom 47 were successful and even acquired the general higher education entrance qualification (LSN, 2023a).

## 3.5 Vocational high school (Berufliches Gymnasium)

**Table 5:** Summary characteristics of the vocational high school

| | |
|---|---|
| **Target group** | Young people who want to acquire the general higher education entrance qualification and choose a vocational focus in the process |
| **Access requirements** | Extended lower secondary school-leaving certificate or promotion to the upper secondary school level |
| **Form of instruction** | Full-time |
| **Duration** | 3 years |
| **Awarded certificates** | General higher education entrance qualification |

The vocational high school is a vocational-oriented alternative to the upper secondary level at general education schools (*gymnasiale Oberstufe*). Like the upper secondary level at the general schools, the vocational high school enables pupils with an extended lower secondary school-leaving certificate or an equivalent diploma to acquire the general higher education entrance qualification within a three-year programme. It is also divided into the introductory phase (grade 11) and the qualification phase (grades 12 and 13). In contrast to the upper secondary level at general education schools, students at the vocational high school choose a vocational focus in the qualification phase, which prepares them for the world of work. Courses are offered in the fields of economics, technology (with a focus on construction technology, electrical engineering, mechatronics, metal technology, information technology, or design and media technology) and health and social occupations (with a focus on agricultural economics, ecotrophology, health care or social pedagogy). People who have acquired the entrance qualification for universities of applied sciences at VET schools in the same subject area and have learned a second foreign language in at least four consecutive school years may be directly admitted to the qualification phase of the vocational high school (Annex 7 BbS-VO).

Full-time instruction takes place – as in the upper secondary level at general education schools – in the introductory phase in class groups and in the qualification phase in school year-related learning groups. The results of the qualification phase are included in the examination results for the general higher education entrance qualification (*Allgemeine Hochschulreife*). The (written) exam is taken in five subjects, with the first being the chosen vocational focus area. As in the upper secondary level at general education schools, the subjects of the vocational high school are assigned to three fields of activity (linguistic-artistic, social-scientific and mathematical-scientific-technical subjects), from each of which at least one subject must be chosen (Annex 7 BbS-VO).

If the examination results (results of the qualification phase and results of the exam) are satisfactory, graduates of the vocational high school acquire the general higher education entrance qualification (§ 31 in conjunction with Annex 7 BbS-VO). In the focus area of social pedagogy (specialisation health and social occupations), a vocational qualification in social pedagogical assistance (state-certified social pedagogical assistant) can be acquired alongside the general higher education entrance qualification under certain conditions (Annex 7 BbS-VO).

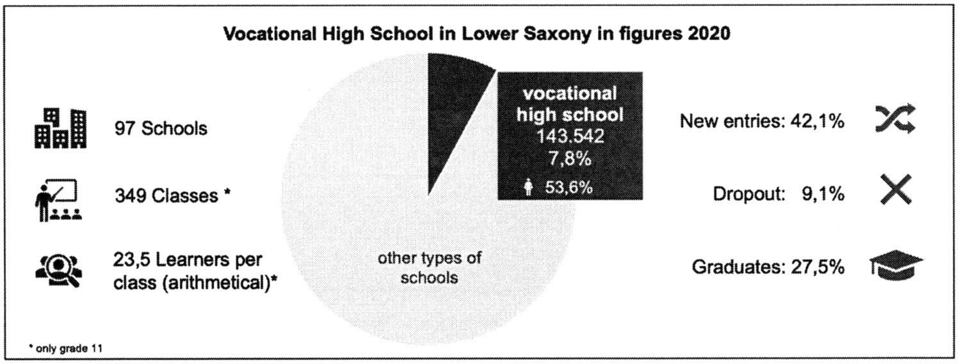


**Figure 6:** Vocational high school in Lower Saxony in figures (2020)

*Note*: Data from LSN, 2023a.

Attendance at vocational high school was possible at 97 VET schools (38.3 %) in Lower Saxony in the school year 2020/21. A total of 19,502 pupils (7.8 % of learners at VET schools) attended the upper secondary course in vocational high school, of whom slightly more than half were female (53.6 %; Figure 6). Most new entrants (99.4 %) had an extended lower secondary school-leaving certificate, and a few had an entrance qualification for universities of applied sciences or subject-linked higher education entrance qualification (*fachgebundene Hochschulreife*) (0.5 %; LSN, 2023a). At the end of the school year, 5,365 pupils (27.5 %) left the vocational high school; the success rate was astonishingly high at 98.4%. Overall, 83.6 % of the graduates were able to obtain the general higher education entrance qualification. However, the vocational high school plays a subordinate role in the acquisition of the general higher education entrance qualification in Lower Saxony. In the school year 2020/21, a total of 29,979 people in Lower Saxony acquired the general higher education entrance qualification (LSN, 2023 f, 2023 g), but only 14.9 % of them attended a vocational high school.

## 3.6 Professional school (Fachschule)

**Table 6:** Summary characteristics of the professional school

| | |
|---|---|
| **Target group** | People who want to qualify for management tasks or self-employment |
| **Access requirements** | Completed vocational training and/or relevant work experience |
| **Form of instruction** | Full-time |
| **Duration** | 3 years |
| **Awarded certificates** | Vocational qualification in combination with a general higher education entrance qualification |

The professional school is a type of school that belongs to the tertiary sector. It includes further vocational and continuing education and aims to qualify skilled workers with vocational experience for management tasks or self-employment (KMK, 2021b, p. 4). In Lower Saxony, there are 27 specialisations to choose from (construction technology; mining technology; drilling, conveying and pipeline technology; electrical engineering; paint and varnish technology; heating, ventilation and air conditioning technology; wood technology; information technology; vehicle technology; food technology; machine technology; mechatronics; medical technology; metal construction technology; mill construction, grain and feed technology; shipbuilding technology; stone technology; environmental protection technology; agricultural technology; agricultural economics; business administration; hotel and catering trade; wood design; home economics; social education; therapeutic care; therapeutic pedagogy; and seafaring) (Annex 8, 9 BbS-VO).

The prerequisite for attending the professional school is a lower secondary school-leaving certificate level two, a relevant, completed vocational training and a VET school-leaving certificate or equivalent qualification. Other (e. g. mining technology: relevant vocational training and at least five years of relevant professional experience) or additional admission requirements may be defined for each specialisation (e. g. curative education: additional proof of personal reliability and health suitability). The courses at the professional school can be offered on a full-time or part-time basis. Depending on the specialisation, they last between one and three years (Annex 8 BbS-VO).

Instruction at the professional school comprises an interdisciplinary and a subject-related area. The subject-related learning area aims to expand vocational action competence and is related to the specialisation. The interdisciplinary area serves to expand cross-occupational competences (KMK 2021); in Lower Saxony, it generally comprises the subjects German, English, science, mathematics and politics and is partly supplemented by the subject human resource management/vocational and work education (EB-BbS).

The professional school concludes with a written examination and a practical examination, the number and design of which depend on the chosen specialisation. With acquisition of the further vocational certificate, graduates can, under certain conditions, acquire the entrance qualification for universities of applied sciences (Annex 8, 9 BbS-VO).

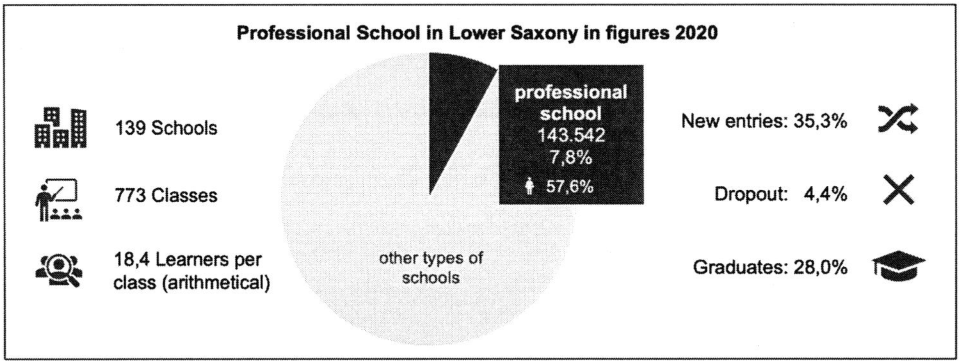


**Figure 7:** Professional school in Lower Saxony in figures (2020)

*Note:* Data from LSN, 2023a.

At 139 VET schools in Lower Saxony (55.6 %), people with vocational experience were able to attend a professional school in school year 2020/21. A total of 19,502 learners (7.8 % of all learners at VET school) were educated at a professional school in Lower Saxony, more than half of whom were female (57.6 %; see Figure 7). Just under 7,000 learners (35.3 %) started their course of education at a professional school in 2020. The majority of new entrants had a lower secondary school-leaving certificate level two (69.4 %), and the proportion of new entrants with a higher education entrance qualification was 29.4 %.

The dropout rate during the professional school year was very low at 4.4 % compared to the other types of VET schools. A large proportion of the pupils who opted for further education and training at the professional school also completed it by the end. In the school year 2020/21, 5,453 people were able to complete their advanced/continuing education at the professional school, of whom 98.6 % were successful. In all, 76.0 % acquired the entrance qualification for universities of applied sciences together with the further vocational certificate.

# 4 Organisational structures at vocational schools

With the types of schools described heretofore, VET schools offer a broad range of education for different target groups, although they differ, sometimes significantly, in the breadth of the offer and their size. Due to their diversity, VET schools are generally regarded as "a special type of school" (Sloane et al., 1998, p. 228; author's transl.) under which different school types are subsumed. The structure of the VET school system is divided vertically according to school types and horizontally in terms of content of different occupational areas (Kell, 2006, p. 90) (see Figure 8).

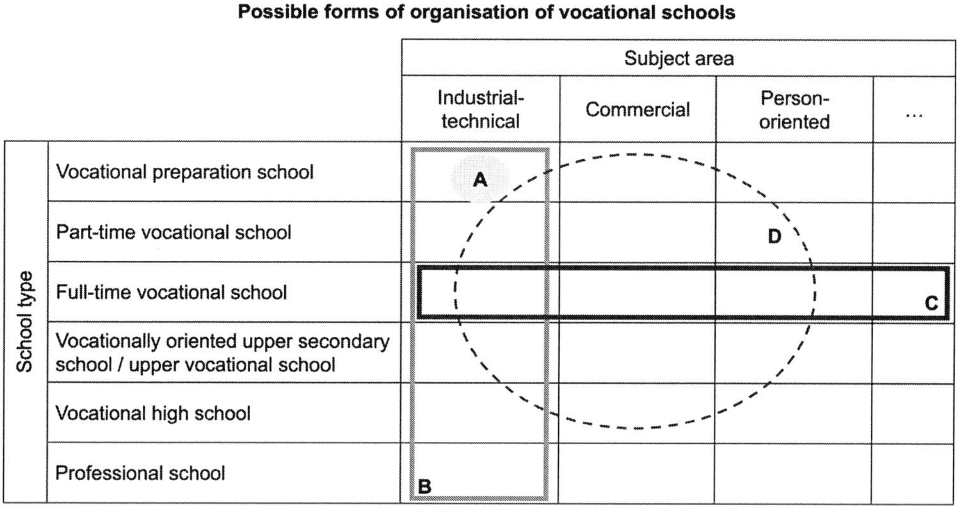


**Figure 8:** Possible forms of organisation of VET schools

*Note*: Based on Sloane et al., 1998, p. 229.

While the school types in the vertical structure primarily represent curricular differences with regard to the objectives, target group and duration of educational programmes (see previous section), occupational areas in the horizontal structure represent a subject-specific differentiation. For the organisation of the subject-related reference points of vocational education processes, differentiation in occupational groups and occupational areas has become established (Lipsmeier, 2014), although no uniform concept exists to date. With regard to the training of teachers for VET schools, the occupational areas are translated into so-called occupational specialisations and specialisation groups, to which reference is also made in part for the organisation of the BbS (Sloane et al., 1998, p. 229). Vocational specialisations are clusters of several occupations, occupational fields and occupational groups. They comprise a bundle of vocational requirements or profiles (Grottker, 2010, p. 25). However, the clustering is not consistent (Herkner, 2010, p. 52). A distinction is often made between commercial, industrial-technical, and people-oriented specialisations/occupational fields (Sloane et al., 2010, p. 246–263), although there may be school-specific differences.

Sloane et al. (1998, p. 229) derive three possible forms of organisation for VET schools from the differentiation of school types and occupational areas (see Figure 8), to which a further form has been added. These forms of organisation represent ideal types of organisation of VET schools and are considered specific for certain regional conditions (Sloane et al., 1998, p. 229).

The following describes the forms of organisation and shows how the VET schools in Lower Saxony are organised (see Table 7). The descriptions for the VET schools in Lower Saxony are based on the school directories of the Lower Saxony Ministry of Education and Cultural Affairs (MK NI, 2022a, 2022b) as of 15.11.2022. In 2022, there were a total of 211 VET schools in Lower Saxony, 61.1 % of which were publicly funded.

**Table 7:** Distribution of organisational forms of VET schools in Lower Saxony

| Sponsorship / School type | Public | Private | Total |
|---|---|---|---|
| **Mono-school** | 5 | 43 | **48** |
| **Vocational area school** | 51 | 27 | **78** |
| **Branch school** | 0 | 1 | **1** |
| **Bundle school** | 73 | 11 | **84** |
| **Total** | **129** | **82** | **211** |

*Note*: Data from MK NI, 2022a, 2022b.

## 4.1 Type A: Mono-school (Monoschule)

It can happen that VET schools 'only' combine the educational programmes related to a specific school type and vocational area. Such VET schools are referred to by Sloane et al. (1998, p. 229) as 'branch part-time VET schools'. However, since such schools do not focus solely on part-time VET schooling as a school type, the name is misleading. Therefore, these schools are referred to here as 'mono-schools'. Such forms of organisation are found above all in urban areas (Sloane et al., 1998, p. 229).

In Lower Saxony, 22.7 % of VET schools are organised as mono-schools. These are mainly private (89.6 %; see Table 8). One example is TEUTLOFF Technical Academy in the city of Braunschweig. TEUTLOFF claims to be Germany's oldest private technical school. Founded in 1903 as the School for Machine Technology in Braunschweig (TEUTLOFF, n. d.; author's transl.), it still offers technical courses at the professional school in Braunschweig. People with professional experience can complete the professional school there in the fields of electrical engineering and metal technology (MK NI, 2022b, p. 1). However, state schools can also be organised as mono-schools, for example the German Milling School (*Deutsche Müllerschule*), located also in Braunschweig. It is the "world's only technical school with a state qualification in grain and feed technology as well as mill construction" (DMSB, n. d.; author's transl.) People with professional experience can complete the course in mill construction, grain and feed technology here (MK NI, 2022a, p. 29).

**Table 8:** Distribution of mono-schools in Lower Saxony

| Subject area / School type | Industrial-technical | Commercial | Person-oriented | Total |
|---|---|---|---|---|
| **Vocational preparation school** | -- | 2 | -- | **2** |
| **Full-time VET school** | 5 | 2 | 20 | **27** |
| **Professional school** | 8 | 1 | 10 | **19** |
| **Total** | **13** | **5** | **30** | **48** |

*Note*: Data from MK NI, 2022a, 2022b.

In Lower Saxony, mono-schools can take the form of/integrate with the school types of vocational preparation school (4.1 %), full-time VET school (56.3 %) or professional school (39.6 %). Publicly run mono-schools exclusively are run as professional schools. The mono-schools in Lower Saxony are often full-time VET schools in person-oriented specialisations (41.7 %; e. g. CJD Schlaffhorst-Andersen full-time VET school in Bad Nenndorf, where breathing, speaking and voice teachers are trained; MK NI, 2022b).

## 4.2 Type B: Vocational area school (Berufsbereichsschule)

The vocational area school "offers the school types for an entire area of a school branch" (Sloane et al., 1998, p. 229; author's transl.) For example, the VET school in Bad Harzburg runs different types of schools (vocational preparation school, part-time VET school, full-time VET school and vocationally oriented upper secondary school) in the subject area of personal services. Students can attend a vocational qualification course in the full-time VET school 'nutrition, home economics and care' or in the part-time VET school 'specialist for gastronomy' or attend the vocational preparation school or the vocationally oriented upper secondary school in the subject area 'Health and Social Services' (MK NI, 2022a, p. 7).

**Table 9:** Distribution of vocational area schools in Lower Saxony

| Subject area / Sponsorship | Industrial-technical | Commercial | Person-oriented | Total |
|---|---|---|---|---|
| **Public** | 23 | 18 | 10 | **51** |
| **Private** | 2 | 0 | 25 | **27** |
| **Total** | **25** | **18** | **35** | **78** |

*Note*: Data from MK NI, 2022a, 2022b.

The vocational area school is the second most common organisational form of VET schools in Lower Saxony (37.0 %; see Table 7). They are predominantly found at public schools (65.4 %; see Table 9) and here primarily in the industrial-technical subject area (45.1 %). Most vocational area schools in the field of personal services are privately run (71.4 %; see Table 9).

### 4.3 Type C: Branch school (Zweigschule)

The branch school is an addition to the typology of Sloane et al. (1998). In contrast to the vocational area school, it does not refer to a specific vocational area but only delivers educational courses of a specific school type in different vocational areas. This is undoubtedly a rare form (see Table 7), which in Lower Saxony can only be found at the full-time VET school 'Professions with a Future' (*Berufe mit Zukunft*) in Oldenburg. At this private full-time VET school, courses are offered in the industrial-technical (biological-technical assistance) and personal fields (pharmaceutical-technical assistance; cosmetics) (MK NI, 2023b, p. 15).

### 4.4 Type D: Bundle school (Bündelschule)

Particularly in rural regions, VET schools are often run as so-called bundle schools, which combine educational courses from several school types and subject areas (Sloane et al., 1998, p. 229 f.). In Lower Saxony, 39.9 % of VET schools are such bundle schools, which are mainly publicly run (56.6 % of publicly run schools).

Examples of bundle schools in Lower Saxony are the BbS Georg-von-Langen Holzminden. Holzminden is a small town in the south of Lower Saxony. The Georg-von-Langen School "is a recognised competence centre for vocational education in the region and sees itself as a driving force for innovation in the field of education and training" (BbS Holzminden, n. d.) At the VET school Holzminden, students can attend the vocational preparation school, the part-time VET school, the full-time VET school, the vocationally oriented secondary school, the vocational high school or the professional school in industrial-technical, commercial or person-related fields. For example, the VET schools offer the part-time VET school for warehouse logistics specialists (commercial subject area), the vocational high school for technology (commercial-technical subject area) and the professional school for social pedagogy (person-oriented subject area) (MK NI, 2022a, p. 121 ff.).

## 5 Summary and conclusion

As an institutional framework, a VET school actually combines various school types that facilitate the acquisition of general education and occupation-related credentials. In contrast to the educational programmes offered by general schools, instruction in the educational programmes of VET schools fosters general and vocational education. It is divided into inter-occupational and vocationally related learning areas. The inter-occupational learning area comprises various general education subjects that are taught independently of the chosen vocational specialisation. The vocationally related learning area relates to a specific field of study which students have chosen, e. g. in the field of business, educational programmes convey basic and advanced commercial skills.

The main pillar of the VET school is the *part-time VET school*, where apprentices complete the school-based education of their dual apprenticeship. At the end of their apprenticeship, successful trainees receive a VET school certificate and can take the final vocational examination at the chamber to earn a vocational qualification. Although there are no formal prerequisites for entry into dual apprenticeship training, studies repeatedly demonstrate the link between socio-structural characteristics, such as a school-leaving certificate, and training opportunities (see Seeber et al., 2019, p. 31 ff.; Dohmen et al., 2023). The "rather stable underrepresentation of female youth in dual apprenticeships over time" (Heinrichs et al., 2023, p. 8, author's transl.) is also repeatedly shown and is also evident in the data for Lower Saxony.

Another option for vocational training is offered by the full-time VET school, where female youths, on the other hand, are overrepresented. The full-time VET school is itself a diverse type of school. In the vocationally qualifying courses of the full-time VET school, students can acquire various vocational qualifications outside the dual apprenticeship system, including training qualifications in federally regulated healthcare professions and professions regulated by a state. Unlike dual apprenticeship training, this type of vocational training is accounted the responsibility of the school but – as dual apprenticeship – includes extensive practical work-based training.

Those who do not (immediately) make the transition to vocational training after general school usually end up in the so-called transition system. The transition system comprises services and measures "that are below the level of qualified vocational training or do not lead to a recognised training qualification, but are aimed at improving the individual skills of young people to enable them to take up training or employment and in some cases enable them to catch up on their general school-leaving qualifications" (Konsortium Bildungsberichterstattung, 2006, p. 79; author's transl.). At the VET schools in Lower Saxony, two offers are provided in the transition system: The vocational preparation school is a state-specific type of school that primarily accepts young people without a lower secondary school-leaving certificate, prepares them for VET and enables them to obtain a lower secondary school-leaving certificate level one. It is not surprising that this type of school in Lower Saxony is mainly attended by students without a lower secondary school-leaving certificate. Contrary to expectations that vocational preparation school should help reduce the number of students without a lower secondary school-leaving certificate (Held & Straßer, 2012, p. 267), only a small proportion of graduates (27.3 % in 2020) succeed in obtaining a lower secondary school-leaving certificate level one.

In addition to the vocational preparation school, students with at least a lower secondary school-leaving certificate level one can also attend the one-year full-time VET school. This school imparts selected competencies acquired in the first year of training for occupations that belong to a vocational specialisation. The competencies acquired can be credited to the first training year of a dual apprenticeship. If the one-year full-time VET school is followed by the second class of the two-year full-time VET school, learners can obtain a higher school-leaving certificate.

The acquisition of higher school qualifications is also the focus of the vocationally oriented upper secondary school and the upper VET school. At the vocationally oriented upper secondary school, people with a lower secondary school-leaving certificate level two can acquire the entrance qualification for universities of applied sciences and thus the prerequisites for the upper VET school, which is aimed at acquiring the subject-specific or general entrance qualification for higher education. Students who wish to acquire the general higher education entrance qualification in the VET system can also do so at the vocational high school – the upper-level secondary school at VET schools. The vocational high school differs from the upper secondary school in the general education system only in having a profile subject that must also be chosen from a canon of vocational subjects.

In addition to these offerings, VET schools offer the opportunity to deepen and expand the acquired job-related competencies in further education and training. The courses of vocational further and continuing education are combined in the professional school and, in addition to the acquisition of vocational qualifications, enable the acquisition of the general higher education entrance qualification.

However, this diversity of educational offerings is not found equally at all vocational institutions. Depending on regional requirements and general conditions, schools can cover different school types and subject areas. The most focused form of VET schools are the so-called mono-schools, which combine educational offerings of one school type in one subject area. The broadest range is offered by so-called bundle schools, which offer courses in several school types and subject areas. In Lower Saxony, most VET schools are run as such bundle schools or as vocational area schools, which offer several school types within one subject area.

Overall, VET schools as institutions provide a more or less broad range of education for people with different educational and professional biographies. Therefore, the VET schools in Lower Saxony are considered a "central component of the school and educational landscape […]. No system is so permeable and offers so many degrees and opportunities" (MK NI, 2020, p. 3, author's transl.). The credentials that can be earned at VET school are assigned levels one (vocational preparation) through six (bachelor professional) in the German Qualifications Framework. This means that VET schools are the educational institutions that offer the broadest range of qualifications. The wide range of offerings requires a differentiated organisation of VET schools. Accordingly, reducing the VET schools to dual apprenticeship training falls far short of the mark, as VET schools are 'all-rounders' in the German school system.

## References

Althoff, H. (1999). Der Übergang in die betriebliche Berufsausbildung 1977 bis 1997. *Berufsbildung in Wissenschaft und Praxis, 28*(1), 7–11.

Autor:innengruppe Bildungsberichterstattung (2022). *Bildung in Deutschland 2022. Ein indikatorengestützter Bericht mit einer Analyse zum Bildungspersonal.* wbv.

BA (Bundesagentur für Arbeit) (2022): *Du entscheidest! Ausbildung. Beruf. Zukunft. Ausgabe Niedersachsen*. BA.

Baethge, M. (2005). Das berufliche Bildungswesen in Deutschland am Beginn des 21. Jahrhunderts. In K. S. Cortina, J. Baumert, A. Leschinsky, K. U. Mayer, and L. Trommer (Eds.), *Das Bildungswesen in der Bundesrepublik Deutschland* (pp. 525–580). Rowohlt.

BbS Holzminden (o. J.). *Leitbild der Georg-von-Langen-Schule.* https://www.bbs-holzminden.de/seite/395276/allgemeines.html

Berufsbildungsgesetz (BBiG) as amended 16 August 2023.

BMBF (Bundesministerium für Bildung und Forschung) (2023). *Berufsbildungsbericht 2023.* https://www.bmbf.de/SharedDocs/Downloads/de/2023/berufsbildungsbericht-2023-kabinettfassung.pdf?__blob=publicationFile&v=2

Clement, U. (2010). Gestaltungsoptionen für das berufliche Schulwesen. In U. Clement, J. Nowak, C. Scherrer, & S. Ruß (Eds.), *Public Governance und schwache Interessen* (pp. 63–74). VS/GWV.

DESTATIS (Statistisches Bundesamt) (2022a). *Bildungsfinanzbericht 2022.* DESTATIS.

DESTATIS (Statistisches Bundesamt) (2022b). *Berufsbildende Schulen. Schuljahr 2020/21. Fachserie 11, Reihe 2.* Wiesbaden: DESTATIS.

DESTATIS (Statistisches Bundesamt) (2023a, October 4). *Statistik der allgemeinbildenden Schulen – Absolventen und Abgänger.* Retrieval from the GENESIS-Online-database.

DESTATIS (Statistisches Bundesamt) (2023b, October 4). *Sozialversicherungspflichtig Beschäftigte am Arbeitsort: Deutschland, Stichtag, Geschlecht, Berufsabschluss.* ARetrieval from the GENESIS-Online-database.

Dietrich, H., Koch, S., & Stops, M. (2004). Lehrstellenkrise. Ausbildung muss sich lohnen – auch für die Betriebe. *IAB Kurzbericht, 6*, 1–7.

DMSB (Deutsche Müllerschule Braunschweig) (o. J.). *Für Studierende.* DMSB – Deutsche Müllerschule Braunschweig. https://www.deutsche-muellerschule-bs.de/fuer-studierende/

Dohmen, D., Bayreuther, T., & Sandau, M. (2023). *Monitor Ausbildungschancen 2023. Gesamtbericht Deutschland. 3.* Aufl. Bertelsmann Stiftung.

Ergänzende Bestimmungen für das berufsbildende Schulwesen (EB-BbS) as amended 1 August 2022.

Frommberger, D., & Lange, S. (2018). *Zur Ausbildung von Lehrkräften an berufsbildenden Schulen – Befunde und Entwicklungsperspektiven.* Working Paper Forschungsförderung (Hans-Böckler-Stiftung), 60.

Grottker, D. (2010). Fach und Fach-Richtung? Versuch einer Rekonstruktionsgeschichte der Beruflichen Fachrichtungen. In J.-P. Pahl & V. Herkner (Eds.), *Handbuch Berufliche Fachrichtungen* (pp. 15–35). Bertelsmann.

Heinrichs, K., Wuttke, E., & Stock, M. (2023): *Netzwerke – Strukturen von Wissen, Akteuren und Prozessen in der beruflichen Bildung.* URL: https://www.bwpat.de/profil8_fuerstenau/heinrichs_etal_profil8.pdf

Held, M., & Straßer, P. (2012). Übergänge schaffen – die Berufseinstiegs. In G. Ratschinski & A. Steuber (Eds.), *Ausbildungsreife* (pp. 267–284). VS.

Herkner, V. (2010). Berufspädagogische Wurzeln und Entwicklungen der Beruflichen Fachrichtungen. In J.-P. Pahl & V. Herkner (Eds.), *Handbuch Berufliche Fachrichtungen* (pp. 35–56). Bertelsmann.

Hillmert, S. (2004). Berufseinstieg in Krisenzeiten: ausbildungs- und Arbeitsmarktchancen in den 1980er und 1990er Jahren. In S. Hillmert & K. U. Mayer (Eds.), *Geboren 1964 und 1971. Neuere Untersuchungen zu Ausbildungs- und Berufschancen in Westdeutschland* (pp. 23–38). VS.

Kell, A. (1982). Das Berechtigungswesen zwischen Bildungs- und Beschäftigungssystem. In H. Blankertz, J. Derbolav, A. Kell, & G. Kutscha (Eds.), *Sekundarstufe II: Jugendbildung zwischen Schule und Beruf* (pp. 289–320). Klett.

Kell, A. (2006). Berufliches Schulwesen in der Bundesrepublik Deutschland. In F.-J. Kaiser & G. Pätzold (Eds.), *Wörterbuch Berufs- und Wirtschaftspädagogik. 2. Aufl* (pp. 89–92). Klinkhardt.

KMK (Kultusministerkonferenz) (o. J.). *Downloadbereich Rahmenlehrpläne.* https://www.kmk.org/themen/berufliche-schulen/duale-berufsausbildung/downloadbereich-rahmenlehrplaene.html

KMK (Kultusministerkonferenz) (2010a). *Rahmenvereinbarung über die Berufsoberschule. Beschluss der Kultusministerkonferenz vom 25.11.1976 i. d. F. vom 19.03.2020.* https://www.kmk.org/fileadmin/veroeffentlichungen_beschluesse/1976/1976_11_25-RV-Berufsoberschule.pdf

KMK (Kultusministerkonferenz) (2010b). *Rahmenvereinbarung über die Fachoberschule. Beschluss der Kultusministerkonferenz vom 16.12.2004 i. d. F. vom 01.10.2020.* https://www.kmk.org/fileadmin/veroeffentlichungen_beschluesse/2004/2004_12_16-RV-Fachoberschule.pdf

KMK (Kultusministerkonferenz) (2020a). *Definitionenkatalog zur Schulstatistik 2020.* https://www.kmk.org/fileadmin/Dateien/pdf/Statistik/Dokumentationen/Defkat2020_Anlagen.pdf

KMK (Kultusministerkonferenz) (2020b). *Rahmenvereinbarung über die Ausbildung und Prüfung zum Staatlich geprüften technischen Assistenten und zur Staatlich geprüften technischen Assistentin und zum Staatlich geprüften kaufmännischen Assistenten und zur Staatlich geprüften kaufmännischen Assistentin an Berufsfachschulen. Beschluss der Kultusministerkonferenz vom 30.09.2011 i. d. F. vom 25.06.2020.* https://www.kmk.org/fileadmin/Dateien/veroeffentlichungen_beschluesse/2011/2011_09_30-RV-Technischer-Kaufmaennischer-Assistent.pdf

KMK (Kultusministerkonferenz) (2021a). *Rahmenvereinbarung über die Berufsschule. Beschluss der Kultusministerkonferenz vom 12.03.2015 i. d. F. vom 09.09.2021.* https://www.kmk.org/fileadmin/veroeffentlichungen_beschluesse/2015/2015_03_12-RV-Berufsschule.pdf

KMK (Kultusministerkonferenz) (2021b). *Rahmenvereinbarung über Fachschulen. Beschluss der Kultusministerkonferenz vom 07.11.2002 i. d. F. vom 16.12.2021. https://www.kmk.org/fileadmin/Dateien/veroeffentlichungen_beschluesse/2002/2002_11_07-RV-Fachschulen.pdf*

KMK (Kultusministerkonferenz) (2022). *Rahmenvereinbarung über die Berufsfachschulen. Beschluss der Kultusministerkonferenz vom 17.10.2013 i. d. F. vom 24.03.2022.* https://www.kmk.org/fileadmin/veroeffentlichungen_beschluesse/2013/2013_10_17-RV-Berufsfachschulen.pdf

KMK (Kultusministerkonferenz) (2023). *Dokumentation der Kultusministerkonferenz über landesrechtlich geregelte Berufsabschlüsse an Berufsfachschulen. Veröffentlichung des Ausschusses für Berufliche Bildung vom 30.03.2023.* https://www.kmk.org/fileadmin/Dateien/veroeffentlichungen_beschluesse/2023/2023_03_30-Doku-Berufsabschluesse-BFS.pdf

Konsortium Bildungsberichterstattung (2006). *Bildung in Deutschland. Ein indikatorengestützter Bericht mit einer Analyse zu Bildung und Migration.* wbv.

Lipsmeier, A. (2014). Vom Berufsfeld zur Berufsgruppe – bloße Umbenennung oder Innovation? Über Irrungen und Wirrungen eines berufspädagogisch und berufsbildungspolitisch wichtigen Konstrukts. *Zeitschrift für Berufs- und Wirtschaftspädagogik, 110*(2), 295–304.

LSN (Landesamt für Statistik Niedersachsen) (2023a, November 1). *Berufsbildende Schulen im November in Niedersachsen.* Retrieval from the LSN-Online-database.

LSN (Landesamt für Statistik Niedersachsen) (2023b, November 1). *Allgemein bildende Schulen in Niedersachsen zum Schuljahresbeginn.* Retrieval from the LSN-Online-database.

LSN (Landesamt für Statistik Niedersachsen) (2023c, November 1). *Lehrkräfte an allgemein bildende Schulen in Niedersachsen zum Schuljahresbeginn.* Retrieval from the LSN-Online-database.

LSN (Landesamt für Statistik Niedersachsen) (2023d, November 1). *Lehrkräfte an berufsbildenden Schulen im November in Niedersachsen.* Retrieval from the LSN-Online-database.

LSN (Landesamt für Statistik Niedersachsen) (2023e, November 1). *Sozialversicherungspflichtige Beschäftigte am Arbeitsort in Niedersachsen.* Retrieval from the LSN-Online-database.

LSN (Landesamt für Statistik Niedersachsen) (2023 f, November 1). *Absolventinnen/Absolventen und Abgängerinnen/Abgänger an allgemein bildenden Schulen in Niedersachsen (einschließlich Abendgymnasien und Kollegs).* Retrieval from the LSN-Online-database.

LSN (Landesamt für Statistik Niedersachsen) (2023 g, November 1). *Schulabgängerinnen und -abgänger an berufsbildenden Schulen in Niedersachsen.* Retrieval from the LSN-Online-database.

Matthes, S., Ulrich, J. G., Flemming, S., & Granath, R.-O. (2017). *Die Entwicklung des Ausbildungsmarktes im Jahr 2016. Stabiles Ausbildungsangebot, leicht sinkende Nachfrage, mehr unbesetzte Plätze. Analysen auf Basis der BIBB-Erhebung über neu abgeschlossene Ausbildungsverträge und der Ausbildungsmarktstatistik der Bundesagentur für Arbeit.* BIBB.

MK NI (Niedersächsisches Kultusministerium) (2015). *Die Arbeit in den Schuljahrgängen 5 bis 10 des Gymnasiums. Informationen für Eltern, Schülerinnen und Schüler.* Broschüre. MK NI.

MK NI (Niedersächsisches Kultusministerium) (2020). *Das niedersächsische Schulwesen.* Broschüre. MK NI.

MK NI (Niedersächsisches Kultusministerium) (2022, November 15). *Bildungsangebote der einzelnen öffentlichen berufsbildenden Schulen.* https://www.mk.niedersachsen.de/download/5710/Bildungsangebote_der_oeffentlichen_berufsbildenden_Schulen_in_Niedersachsen.pdf

MK NI (Niedersächsisches Kultusministerium) (2022, November 15). *Bildungsangebote der einzelnen öffentlichen berufsbildenden Schulen.* https://www.mk.niedersachsen.de/download/97427/Bildungsangebote_der_berufsbildenden_Schulen_in_freier_Traegerschaft_in_Niedersachsen.pdf

MPhG – Gesetz über die Berufe in der Physiotherapie (Masseur- und Physiotherapeutengesetz) as amended 11 July 2021.

NSchG – Niedersächsisches Schulgesetz as amended 3 May 2023.

PflBG – Gesetz über die Pflegeberufe (Pflegeberufegesetz) as amended 11 July 2021.

Pimminger, I. (2012). *Junge Frauen und Männer im Übergang von der Schule in den Beruf.* Agentur für Gleichstellung im ESF.

Seeber, S., Wieck, M., Baethge-Kinsky, V., Boschke, V., Michaelis, C., Busse, R., & Geiser, P. (2019). *Ländermonitor berufliche Bildung 2019. Ein Vergleich der Bundesländer mit vertiefender Analyse zu Passungsproblemen im dualen System.* wbv.

Sloane, P. F. E., Liebberger, K., Ohlms, M., Pasing, R., & Reich-Zies, B.-T. (2010). Analyse von Studienplänen der Beruflichen Fachrichtungen – eine Synopse. In J.-P. Pahl & V. Herkner (Eds.), *Handbuch Berufliche Fachrichtungen* (pp. 245–263). Bertelsmann.

Sloane, P. F. E., Twardy, M., & Buschfeld, D. (1998). *Einführung in die Wirtschaftspädagogik.* Schöningh.

Steib, C. (2020). *Das der beruflichen Bildung ungeliebte Kind. Eine systemtheoretische Analyse der Herausbildung und Verfestigung des "(beruflichen) Übergangssystems" in der Bundesrepublik Deutschland.* Eusl.

TEUTLOFF. (o. J.). *Wo(für) wir stehen.* https://www.teutloff.de/teutloff/ueber-uns/

Troltsch, K. (2011). Betriebliche Berufsausbildung als Auslaufmodell? In M. Icking (Ed.), *Die berufliche Bildung der Zukunft. Herausforderungen und Reformansätze* (pp. 24–36). Heinrich-Böll-Stiftung.

BbS-VO – Verordnung über berufsbildende Schulen as amended 10 June 2009.

Wittmann, E. (2009). *Theorieentwicklung zur beruflichen Schule. Eine Mehrebenenanalyse.* Peter Lang.

## Short portrait of the author

**Silke Lange** has been Assistant Professor of Vocational Education and Training specialising in vocational teacher training research at Osnabrück University since 2021. She conducts research on various issues relating to vocational teacher training, the structures of vocational education and training (VET) and the development of disciplines and theories in VET research.
Contact: silke.lange@uni-osnabrueck.de

# Vocational teacher training in Germany and Lower Saxony – conditions, models and research needs

Silke Lange, Kristina Trampe, Christoph Porcher, Dietmar Frommberger

Abstract: A shortage of teachers has always been a problem for vocational education and training (VET) schools in Germany, at least for some vocational subjects. This is equally true for Lower Saxony, although the situation here is not as precarious compared to other federated states. At present, problems at VET schools are coming to a head in all of Germany's federated states and in all vocational disciplines. The implementation of measures to increase the number of teachers at VET schools is not an easy undertaking. A variety of measures are being taken at universities and colleges in an attempt to attract more students to the VET teaching profession. Heterogenisation is the central strategy. In this chapter, the heterogenisation tendencies in Germany are systematically assessed, and their consequences at the student level are analysed.

**Keywords:** Heterogeneity; Study Models; Vocational Education and Training Systems and Structures; Vocational Teacher Training.

## 1 Introduction

In times of demographic change in Germany, securing skilled workers is undoubtedly one of the central challenges facing society and the labour market. Vocational education and training (VET) in its various facets plays a central role in this. The VET system in Germany is currently burdened by a high and very likely increasing shortage of trained teachers (Frommberger & Lange, 2018). Current figures and available forecasts indicate that this situation will intensify over the next ten years (KMK, 2022a). In Lower Saxony, too, the demand for teachers for VET schools is expected to increase during this period (Niedersächsische Staatskanzlei, 2020).

The acute demand situation in VET schools is moving VET teacher training increasingly into the public eye in Germany. Universities, the so-called first phase of VET teacher training, are confronted with the requirement of attracting students to a course of study that has tended to be characterised by declining demand in recent years. In order to cope with these quantitative demands as well as to address equally relevant qualitative challenges, since the 1990s discussion has been increasing about alternative models of qualification for VET teachers and, above all, about alternative study models. As a result, numerous projects for the development of alternative study formats have emerged nationwide, projects which address new target groups, enable later entry into studies or shorten training periods. However, the extent to which these diverse study offers and formats meet these goals and to what extent they have an impact on the quality of VET studies and the professionalisation of students has remained largely unexplored.

Within the framework of the project DEIN-LBSCampus[1] funded by the Federal Ministry of Education and Research (BMBF) and carried out at Osnabrück University, the research deficit described above was addressed. Under the title LBS Monitor, a cross-location study was conducted on the professional development of students in different study formats. This article presents selected results of the project and a longitudinal analysis. The focus is first on Germany as a whole and then on the situation in Lower Saxony.

Before presenting the results from the project, the next section deals with VET teacher training in Germany and locates the study programme in the professionalisation process of teachers at VET schools. The basis of the analyses in the LBS Monitor is a structural analysis conducted by Porcher and Trampe (2021), which assigns the current offers of VET teacher training to seven study models with regard to their access modalities and study programme structures. This is presented in the third section, and the study programmes offered in Lower Saxony are located within it. In the fourth section, findings on students for the VET teaching profession are presented, and the findings on Lower Saxony are outlined against the background of the situation in Germany as a whole. Finally, different positions on the further development of higher education VET teacher training in Germany in general and in Lower Saxony in particular are discussed.

## 2 Professionalisation of teachers at vocational schools in Germany

Teachers at VET schools in Germany teach across the entire spectrum of the VET system (Lange, in this volume). Teachers in Germany are prepared for the associated requirements through two-phase training, which is part of teacher training in Germany. The term 'teacher training' is used to summarise the initial and in-service training programmes for teachers. Regardless of whether teachers teach in primary schools, secondary schools of general education or in VET, teacher training in Germany is characterised by a three-phase structure (see Figure 1) which enables (prospective) teachers to acquire experience and competences systematically and cumulatively and supports them continuously during their professional occupation. "This basic structure of teacher training is, on the one hand, the result of a historical development [...] closely connected with the development of the structure of the school system and the careers of the civil service [...]. On the other hand, it is the result of conscious educational policy

1 Funding code: 01JA2018 (Project duration: 01.03.2020 to 31.12.2023).

decisions and could therefore also look quite different" (Frommberger & Lange, 2018, p. 12; authors' transl.)

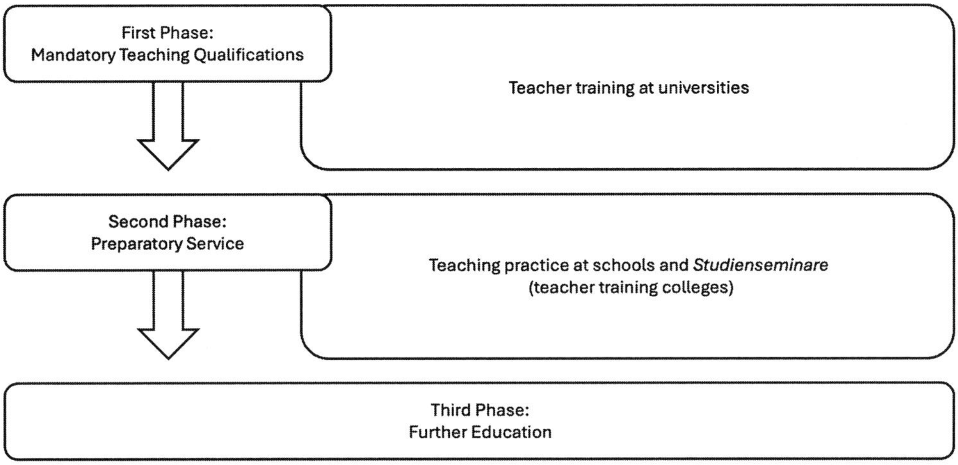


**Figure 1:** Structure of teacher training in Germany

Teacher training at a university or an equivalent institution of higher education represents the *first phase* of teacher training. It offers theoretical professional training of (prospective) teachers and provides the scientific basis for the development of professional competences (Terhart, 2000). In the teaching profession-specific tradition in Germany, the study programme takes place in two subject areas. Prospective teachers for VET schools usually combine a vocational subject[2] (see Table 1) and a general education subject (e. g. German, mathematics or politics). In addition, it is possible to combine two vocational specialisations, one vocational specialisation with a special educational need (e. g. learning, hearing or seeing) or two general education subjects.

2 Occupational specialisations are summaries or groupings of several occupations and occupational fields into a relatively closed construct of occupational requirements or profiles. "It is always the category of the occupation or occupational field that is at the centre of such a construct as the supporting basic idea of similarity" (Grottker, 2010, p. 25). In contrast to the subject, which stands for an intensive penetration of a specific (subject) matter, the vocational specialisation "directs the view into the broadness of an occupational field, the dimensions of the world of work and companies" (Gerds et al., 1999, p. 28).

**Table 1:** Vocational specialisations in the VET teaching profession in Germany

| **Vocational specialisations (according to KMK, 2018)**[3] | |
|---|---|
| **Commercial specialisations** | **Industrial-technical specialisations** |
| Economy and administration | Metal technology |
| **Person-oriented disciplines** | Electrical engineering |
| Health and body care | Civil engineering |
| Nutrition and home economics | Wood technology |
| Social pedagogy | Print and media technology |
| Care | Colour technology, interior design, surface technology |
| | Agriculture |
| | Automotive engineering |
| | Information technology |
| Further specialisations can be approved by the federated states. | |

Traditionally, a VET teacher training programme was completed with the first state examination. In the course of the Bologna Reform, VET teacher training was changed into bachelor and master programmes at most states and universities. Students first complete a professionally qualifying bachelor's programme, usually six or seven semesters in duration, in which they study the chosen subjects or subject area(s) as well as VET studies and subject didactics. However, the bachelor's degree (e.g. Bachelor of Education or Bachelor of Science) does not entitle the holder to enter the second training phase, namely the preparatory service (Referendariat), or the teaching profession. For this, a corresponding master's degree must be obtained; the master's programme usually lasts three to four semesters. In it, the two chosen subjects or subject area(s), VET studies and both subject didactics are also studied.

Academic training is usually followed by preparatory service. This *second phase* of teacher training is linked to the teachers' professional practice, supplemented by training phases in study seminars. In addition to the completed teacher training course, teacher trainees must provide evidence of at least twelve months of practical work experience related to the vocational subject area in order to enter the preparatory service (KMK, 2018). Depending on the federated state, the preparatory service lasts one to two years (KMK, 2018) and focuses on school-based and classroom-based training. The preparatory service is completed with the (second) state examination, which enables access to a public office. The (second) state examination concludes the formal training of teachers in Germany.

3 In order to reduce complexity, the individual occupational specialisations are combined into specialisation groups. This paper uses the classification of Sloane et al. (2010, pp. 246 ff.).

The longest phase is the *third phase* of teacher training – learning on the job. This phase takes into account the fact that with the completion of teacher training, important foundations for professional activity have been acquired, but that there is no "professional activity that can be directly implemented as well as lasting throughout professional life" (Terhart, 2000, p. 127, author's translation). The third phase includes formal, non-formal and informal learning processes of teachers at institutions and facilities for further and in-service training as well as within and outside the school.

Due to federal education policy in Germany, the basic structure of (VET) teacher training and teacher professionalisation is regulated and shaped by state-specific requirements in addition to uniform national standards and framework agreements of the Standing Conference of the Ministers of Education and Cultural Affairs in Germany (Kultusministerkonferenz, KMK).

In Lower Saxony, teacher training is also characterised by the three phases described above. Teacher training (six-semester bachelor's + four-semester master's) for VET schools takes place at universities in Göttingen, Hanover, Lüneburg, Oldenburg and Osnabrück. Students can combine one of the vocational subjects of civil engineering, electrical engineering, colour technology and interior design, health sciences, wood technology, cosmetology, automotive engineering, food science, metal technology, ecotrophology, nursing sciences, social pedagogy or economics with one of the general education subjects of biology, chemistry, German, English, Protestant religion, French, history, computer science, Islamic religion, Catholic religion, mathematics, Dutch, physics, politics, Spanish, physical education or values and standards (§ 6 Nds.MasterVO-Lehr). The master's programme is completed with a Master of Education. The preparatory service lasts 18 months. Upon completion of the preparatory service, the state examination is acquired, with which employment in the teaching profession in Lower Saxony is possible.

## 3 Typology of pre-service vocational education and training teacher training in Germany

This chapter explores the diverse pathways and structures that underpin the training of VET teachers in Germany. The discourse on VET teacher training research was and remains largely determined by the shortage of teachers at VET schools in the industrial-technical subjects, but also e. g. in the vocational subjects of social pedagogy or nursing science (KMK, 2022b, p. 28) and seems to be at an argumentative impasse: The reason for the shortage of teaching staff and low student numbers is often seen as resulting from the multitude of different study models and access routes, in that qualification and education paths for the teaching profession at VET schools are characterised by a high degree of confusion (Seidel & Wemme, 2011, p. 226). Conversely, it is precisely this lack of students at universities that is responsible for the structural heterogeneity of VET teacher training programmes, in that universities try to increase the attractiveness of their study programmes through alternative study models (Frommberger & Lange, 2018, p. 13).

In fact, there has been a broad differentiation of VET teacher training programmes in recent years: In addition to the university-based regular model (Bals et al., 2016, p. 8) of VET teacher training, consisting of a teaching-related, undergraduate bachelor's programme and a subsequent master's programme at a university, there have been cooperation models since the 2000s in which universities cooperate with universities of applied sciences (Faßhauer, 2012, p. 283). As a result of the amendment to the KMK Framework Agreement in 2016, it is also possible to design master's degree programmes for graduates of subject-specific bachelor's programmes that are not related to teacher training degree programmes without a teaching profession reference (KMK, 2016, p. 3). As a result, more and more locations have since offered teaching-related master's degree programmes that build on bachelor's degree programmes without reference to the teaching profession, that is, those whose curriculum is primarily made up of (subject) didactic and educational science content as well as subject science content from a second subject.

Against the background of these structural developments, this chapter develops and presents a typology of study models. The following objectives are associated with this typology:

- Increasing transparency by systematically mapping and classifying the study programmes
- Enabling cross-university comparability of different study programmes
- Creating common terminology for study models within the discipline of vocational education studies and
- Fixing a reference and starting point for further development and research activities in the discipline.

## 3.1 Development of the typology

As a basis for the development of the typology of study models, a survey of the study structures in Germany was carried out. For this purpose, all websites of study locations offering VET teacher training programmes (N = 52) were consulted. In addition, in the event of ambiguities, e. g. regarding the question of admission requirements, those responsible for the study programmes were consulted.

On the basis of the information provided on the websites in the form of study programme descriptions and regulatory documents (such as admission regulations, examination regulations and handbooks), the study programmes were classified in a simple analysis grid. Here, criteria were defined that relate to the federated state, the vocational specialisations and general education teaching subjects that can be studied, the necessary admission requirements as well as the academic degree to be obtained and the associated entitlement to enter preparatory service.

For the typology to be developed from these data, it was first necessary to clarify two questions that should be asked before any typologisation (Kelle & Kluge, 2010, p. 86):

- What elements or cases are the types about?
- What are the characteristics or features by which the types can be grouped and distinguished from one another?

Since the study programmes offered by higher education institutions differed greatly from one another within individual federated states and because individual locations also frequently offer different study programmes, in clarifying the first question, study programme models were first considered as 'cases' and grouped into types. However, upon closer examination of the individual cases this approach proved to be unfruitful, since a corresponding grouping according to study programme model would not have reflected the actual diversity of study options and the differences that constituted them. According to Kelle and Kluge (2010), for example, detachment from the case originally defined for data collection is necessary when a case can be assigned to several types (Kelle & Kluge, 2010, p. 86). In the present typology development, the situation arose accordingly that different access options existed for one and the same study programme and that this had to be assigned to several types as a result.

In the following, study models are understood as models that, from an output-oriented perspective, represent study options that qualify for the preparatory service and can differ in terms of their formal structure and organisation. In clarifying the second question, the characteristics were defined by determining which similarities (internal homogeneity) and differences (external heterogeneity) between the 'cases' can be recorded and which identified types can be characterised. This included determining characteristics (Kelle & Kluge, 2010, p. 91).

### 3.2 Presentation of the typology

After extensive research, we were able to identify 52 universities in Germany offering study programmes in pre-service VET teacher training. We studied the documents related to the programmes provided on the universities' websites. These documents provided information on curricula, examination regulations, and regulations on access and admission to the programmes. In order to prevent misconceptions, we contacted the assigned study programme coordinator to deal with any remaining questions regarding a programme. After this first step of our research, we were able to identify five characteristics which helped us to distinguish the numerous approaches in offering pre-service teacher training. These are degree structure, entry requirements, curriculum, consecutive/non-consecutive and cooperation.

*Degree structure* refers to the general logic of academic organisation in Germany. For teacher training, it is possible to study in bachelor's and master's degree programmes and the traditional state examination programme. After Bologna, the vast majority of study programmes are bachelor's or master's degree programmes. In most cases, a master's degree is required in order to work as a teacher. *Entry requirements* refers to access and admission to the master's degree programme. With this characteristic, we take the perspective of the master's degree programme and ask: What bachelor's degree must applicants hold in order to get access? We then distinguish two types of bachelor's degree programmes: teacher training programmes and non-teacher training programmes. A bachelor's degree in teacher training exists when classes in subject areas (i. e. mechanical engineering), didactics, and pedagogy are offered as well as mandatory school internships.

*Curriculum* refers to the structure of the master's degree programme and its targeted group of students. Very roughly speaking, we can distinguish two types of master's degree programmes: ones that are designed for bachelor's degrees in teacher training and ones that are designed for bachelor's degrees in any area other than teacher training, e. g. mechanical engineering, electrical engineering or chemical engineering. Speaking of the latter, we can imagine students who do not want to become teachers in VET initially but rather to work as engineers, in management or elsewhere. However, sometimes people want to change their career paths. Some master's degree programmes in teacher training are specifically designed for this target group. They do not bring all credits in the above-mentioned classes from their bachelor's, but they can still become teachers in VET without obtaining another bachelor's degree.

The second-last characteristic, *consecutive/non-consecutive,* is strongly linked to the aforementioned. However, while *curriculum* refers rather to the target group, this characteristic deals with the time needed to finish both bachelor's and master's degrees. The Framework Act for Higher Education, which is a federal law, defines that consecutive master's degree programmes must be no longer than one to two years. A bachelor's degree programme must be no longer than three to four years, which makes a total of five years for both degrees.

Finally, *cooperation* refers to the participation of other institutions in pre-service teacher training. These institutions can be other universities, VET schools or teacher's training colleges. Sometimes, universities agree to cooperate when they cannot offer all classes relevant to teacher training study programmes, e. g. classes in subjects such as engineering or the humanities, pedagogy or didactics.

Applying these characteristics to our research, we were able to identify seven study models. The pathway to each type is illustrated in Figure 1. We discuss each type in this section.

*Type 1: Bachelor's/Master's model: consecutive approach.* The first type could also be described as the standard model. Its major characteristic is the number of classes dealing with pedagogical or didactical questions, that is, both bachelor's and master's programmes offer a degree in teaching. Both programmes are complementary designed and to be studied in sequence. Universities require applicants to have earned a bachelor's degree in teaching.

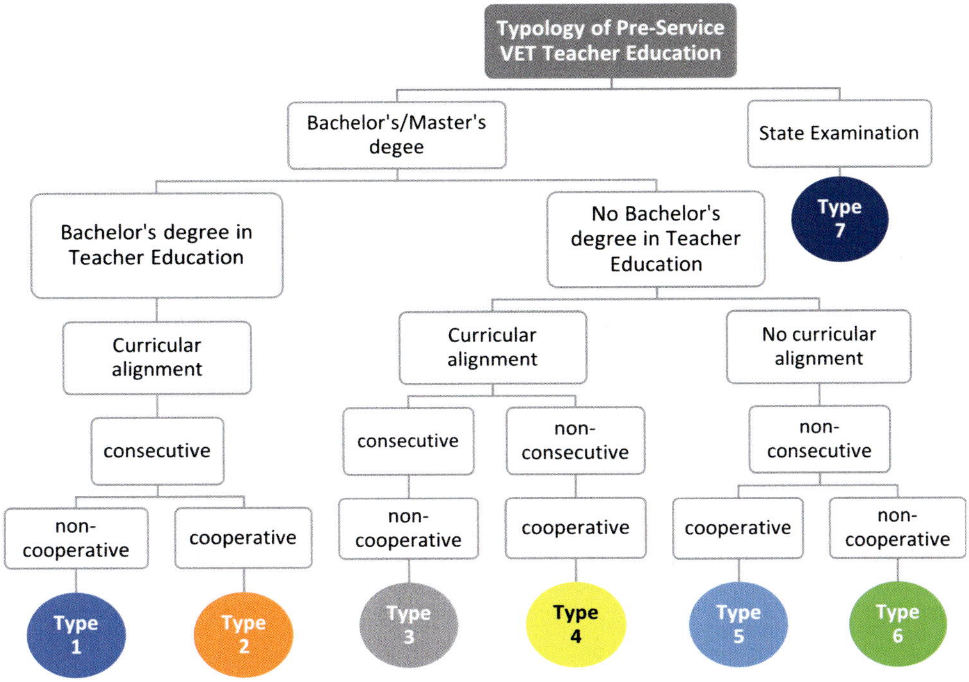


**Figure 2:** Typology of initial VET teacher training

*Type 2: Bachelor's/Master's model: consecutive + cooperative approach.* What was said for type one applies for this model as well. The only difference between type 1 and type 2 lies in its organisation. Usually, students apply for a study programme at a university; however, when a university cannot offer all aspects of the programme (e.g. classes in engineering, education etc.), they agree to cooperate with another university, often with a university of applied sciences[4]. We regard cooperation as when one of three pillars of teacher training is studied at an institution other than the university offering the programme.

*Type 3: Career change model: consecutive approach.* This study model is designed for applicants with a bachelor's degree that is not affiliated with teaching. The applicant may hold a bachelor's degree in engineering, nursing science, or electrical engineering. In the master's programme, students do not study a vocational subject, as they completed the mandatory requirement of credit points of this column (see the section on the professionalisation of teachers) with their bachelor's degree. Instead, they focus on non-vocational related subjects, e.g. English, maths, or physical education, and on lectures and seminars in vocational pedagogy and didactics. The general idea of this study model is to give students who did not plan to become VET teachers the opportunity to easily change their career.

4 In Germany, these schools are called *Fachhochschulen*. In the UK, the former oolytechnics were similar to the concept of *Fachhochschulen*.

*Type 4: Career change model: dual approach.* What was said about type 3 also applies to this study model, with the exception that students already work through a VET school during their studies. This practical experience is intentionally integrated in this study model. After getting their master's degree, the preparatory service may be shortened. There is also a variety offered where the preparatory service is systematically integrated, meaning that students simultaneously get their master's degree and finish the preparatory service. Due to this aspect, this type cannot be regarded as consecutive, since students may need more than two years to complete their studies.

*Type 5: Concurrent study model.* In this study model, a master's programme in teacher training is generally open for students who hold only a bachelor's degree in non-teaching-related subjects. This means that the curriculum is not specifically designed for this target group, as is the case with type 3. Instead, students have to accept that they might need more time to complete the master's programme, as they are given conditions with their admission to the master's programme, i. e. additional courses in vocational pedagogy. Additionally, this study model meets the criterion of *cooperation*. Application is limited to students of pre-defined universities, usually universities of applied sciences. The institutions usually sign an agreement to cooperate in order to limit the conditions given to students after their admission. Since this model might be confusing, we provide an example: Aachen University offers a master's programme in VET teacher training. In order to address the high demand in various vocational subjects, they signed an agreement with the universities of applied sciences in Aachen, Cologne and Niederrhein. Students in engineering programmes from these universities, and only these universities, are granted admission to the master's programme in VET teacher training without a detailed case-by-case review of their bachelor's degrees. However, they must deal with their given conditions and cannot complete the master's programme in two years' time.

*Type 6: Case-by-case review model.* What was said about type 5 also applies for this study model. The major difference is that there is no cooperation agreement in play. That said, it is obvious that universities who theoretically open their master's programme in VET teacher training to applicants without a bachelor's degree in VET teacher training evaluate applications on an individual basis.

*Type 7: State examination model.* The state examination is a degree programme that is unique to Germany and is offered by certain states and universities. The degree is awarded to students who have completed a programme in specific fields such as law, medicine or teaching. The state examination consists of two parts: theoretical and practical. The theoretical part of the examination usually involves written and/or oral exams which test the student's knowledge of the subject matter. The theoretical part of the exam is administered by the university and is designed to test the student's academic knowledge. The practical part of the examination involves articles, clinical rotations, or teaching practice, depending on the field of study. This part of the exam is designed to test the student's practical skills and their ability to apply their knowledge in real-world situations. The practical part of the exam is often administered by the relevant professional association or regulatory body. After completing the state examination, graduates are typically required to complete a period of practical training. The length of the training varies depending on the field of study, but it typically lasts between one and two years. During this time, graduates work as trainees under the supervision of experienced professionals and gain practical experience in their chosen field. Once graduates have completed the training, they are usually qualified to practise their profession and are eligible for certification or licensing. This allows them to legally work in their chosen field anywhere in Germany.

## 4 Effects of structural heterogeneity on students – insights into the results of the LBS Monitor

The typology of study models in the VET teaching profession (see section) illustrates a broad diversity of study paths. It can be assumed that this results in an equally broad diversity of the student body in the teaching profession at VET schools (Lange & Frommberger n. d.; Bals et al., 2016) and is also targeted with the diversity of study paths (Faßhauer, 2012). Above all, the possibility of entering teacher training with a master's degree (type 3 to type 6) is associated with the hope of enabling late entry into VET teacher training and thus increasing the number of graduates of VET teacher training programmes (e. g. Frommberger & Lange, 2018, p. 243). However, it appears unclear whether and by what characteristics the students in these alternative models differ from undergraduate students of types 1, 2 and 7.

### 4.1 Heterogeneity in higher education discourse

In general, higher education discourse on the opening of higher education institutions and the design of higher education teaching and learning opportunities refers to increasing student numbers (e. g. Hanft, 2015), differentiated higher education and study opportunities (Brockmeier, 2017) and an increasing diversity (heterogenisation) of students or student groups. Despite the problems associated with such a heterogenisation hypothesis (Becker & Heißenberg, 2018), current findings from nationwide student surveys demonstrate "that both the social composition and the study and living arrangements of students are diverse and heterogeneous" (Becker & Heißenberg, 2018, p. 12), at least when viewed across study programmes. At the level of individual degree programmes, however, the heterogeneity of students is much less pronounced; Bülow-Schramm (2015, p. 54) speaks of a "dialectic of heterogeneity and homogeneity". According to this, students differ greatly from one another in terms of socio-demographic characteristics such as age, gender, higher education entrance qualification and cultural capital. For certain study programmes and subject areas, however, there is a "lack of inclusion of certain study groups" (Bülow-Schramm, 2015, p. 54). Overall, Bülow-Schramm (2015, p. 55) speaks of a "segregation according to entrance qualification, academic background, migration and gender along university types and study programmes". The teacher training programme as an "interdisciplinary combination programme" (Bülow-Schramm & Merkt, 2013, p. 17) and especially the teacher training programme for VET schools unite in their study structures (as shown above) the different lines of difference between types of higher education institutions and study subjects. In this respect, a high degree of heterogeneity would also be expected among the study programmes of the teaching profession at VET schools. The extent to which the teacher training programmes for VET schools reproduce the homogeneity assumption at the degree programme level, or what heterogeneity the students in the teacher training programme for VET schools exhibit, is traced in the following using data from the LBS Monitor.

## 4.2 Sample of the LBS Monitor

**Table 2:** Characteristics of the student body in the VET teaching profession

| | | Women[5] | Average age in years (SD)[6] | Entrance qualification[7] | Vocational training[8] | Work experience[9] | Upper or high social origin[10] |
|---|---|---|---|---|---|---|---|
| Total sample | | 66.6 % | 26.8 (4.7) | 71.9 % | 61.1 % | 59.3 % | 33.0 % |
| Study model | basic | 71.9 % | 26.5 (4.6) | 74.1 % | 60.4 % | 55.3 % | 34.6 % |
| | cooperative | 58.0 % | 27.8 (4.9) | 75.7 % | 62.2 % | 66.9 % | 35.0 % |
| | alternative | 49.2 % | 28.3 (5.4) | 56.2 % | 65.3 % | 70.2 % | 39.2 % |
| First field of study | industrial-technical | 38.9 % | 28.1 (5.6) | 60.9 % | 67.3 % | 62.6 % | 36.5 % |
| | person-oriented | 86.6 % | 27.3 (4.6) | 69.5 % | 62.9 % | 63.2 % | 37.9 % |
| | commercial | 64.3 % | 26.3 (4.2) | 74.5 % | 63.8 % | 59.5 % | 36.1 % |
| Subsample Lower Saxony | | 77.8 % | 27.0 (3.9) | 64.1 % | 73.2 % | 66.5 % | 36.9 % |

With the LBS Monitor (Lange & Frommberger, 2022), a nationwide panel study of VET teacher training students, data are newly available that allow statements on the hetero-

5 The respondents assigned themselves to the gender 'female', 'male' or 'diverse'. However, the proportion of students who assigned themselves to a diverse gender is negligible at 0.7 %.

6 Age was collected only from the second wave onwards using an open response format; in the first wave, age was collected using age categories. The representations refer to the nominal age data of the students from the second wave onwards. Since the students were in different semesters of study at the time of the first survey, in the context of which the socio-demographic characteristics were collected, the age data were corrected in relation to the first master's year or the fourth year of teacher training. The following analyses are based on the corrected age data. The corrected age is not normally distributed according to the Shapiro-Wilk test ($p < 0.001$).

7 The higher education entrance qualification is surveyed in the LBS Monitor via the type of school at which the higher education entrance qualification was acquired (Lange & Frommberger, 2022, p. 76). The general higher education entrance qualification is considered the higher education entrance qualification acquired at the *Gymnasium*, comprehensive and community schools as well as a vocational *Gymnasium* or *Fachgymnasium*.

8 Completed VET is recorded (Lange & Frommberger, 2022, p. 80).

9 Work experience is defined as professional activities prior to studies outside of VET (Lange & Frommberger, 2022, p. 81).

10 Following the DZHW (2017, pp. 9–10), social origin is recorded via the educational and VET attainment of the parents. In the case of people with an upper or high social background, at least one parent has an academic degree.

geneity of the student group on the basis of a numerous study locations in the VET teaching profession. Statements are possible with regard to the heterogeneity factors of gender[5], age[6], higher education entrance qualification, vocational training[8], professional experience[9] and social origin[10].

After three survey waves, the LBS Monitor currently includes data on 1,033 students at 35 locations (see Table 2). Of these, 70.5 % studied in an 'undergraduate study model' (type 1 and type 7) and 16.4 % in an 'undergraduate cooperative study model' (type 2), i. e. at a university and a cooperating university, usually a university of applied sciences. Due to the small subsamples of students in study type 3 to type 6, these are combined into the 'alternative study models'. These alternative study models are characterised by the fact that entry into teaching-related training only takes place with the master's programme. In the sample of the LBS Monitor, 13.1 % of the respondents were assigned to such a study model.

With regard to the subjects of study, in the VET teaching profession (and especially in VET teacher training research), reference is made to the importance and differences of vocational specialisations. In the LBS Monitor sample, 93.0 % of students in the first subject are enrolled in a vocational specialisation[11], namely 36.4 % in a commercial specialisation, 32.4 % in a person-oriented specialisation and 24.2 % in a commercial-technical specialisation[12].

For Lower Saxony, the LBS Monitor has data on 188 students (18.2 % of the LBS Monitor sample; see Table 2) from the three locations Hanover, Lüneburg and Osnabrück[13]. At 74.0 %, the proportion of these students in the undergraduate model is somewhat higher than in the national sample, while 12.7 % of the respondents in Lower Saxony studied in the undergraduate cooperative model (thus somewhat less than in the national sample). However, students in undergraduate cooperative models are probably overrepresented in the Lower Saxony sample, as corresponding study programmes are only offered at Osnabrück, where participation was highest in Lower Saxony. At the same time, two of the five locations offering undergraduate programmes did not participate in the survey. At 13.3 %, the proportion of students in alternative models in the Lower Saxony sample hardly deviates from the national sample.

All students in the Lower Saxony sample study a vocational subject as their first subject, as no alternative subject combination is permitted in Lower Saxony. Since the largest locations for the commercial disciplines in Lower Saxony do not participate in the LBS Monitor, the proportion of students in these disciplines in the Lower Saxony sample is significantly smaller than in the federal sample (19.6 %). In contrast, the proportion of students in the person-oriented vocational disciplines in the Lower Saxony sample, at 66.3 %, is significantly higher than in the national sample. Students in industrial-technical vocational specialisations make up the smallest proportion in the Lower Saxony sample, just as in the national sample, at 14.1 %.

11 At individual locations, particularly in North Rhine-Westphalia, it is possible to combine two general education subjects in the VET teaching profession.

12 The grouping of the vocational specialisations into the three specialisation groups is done according to Sloane et al. (2010).

13 Oldenburg and Göttingen do not participate in the LBS Monitor surveys.

The subsamples of students in Lower Saxony in undergraduate cooperative and alternative study models as well as in industrial-technical and commercial subjects are so small that significance tests are not reasonable. Therefore, the group differences for the Lower Saxony subsample are not examined in more detail below.

## 4.3 Heterogeneity of students in the vocational education teaching profession

*Gender*: The teaching profession is considered a 'women's profession' (Lundgreen, 1999, p. 121); time and again, reference is made to the higher proportion of female students in the teaching profession (e. g. Neugebauer, 2013, p. 18). For the teaching profession at VET schools, the study situation is contradictory (Berger & Ziegler, 2021, p. 236; Goller & Ziegler, 2021, p. 165; Leon et al., 2021, p. 200). In the sample of the LBS Monitor, the proportion of female students predominates, both in the federal sample and in the partial sample from Lower Saxony (see Table 2). Two thirds (and in Lower Saxony even more) of the students are female; the VET teacher training programme is, accordingly, rather homogeneous in terms of gender – at least more homogeneous than the student body across all subjects, which has an almost balanced gender ratio (Lange & Frommberger, n. d.). Regarding the gender distribution of students in the VET teaching profession, there are considerable differences with regard to different structural features of the teacher training programme. For example, the proportion of female students in the federal sample is higher in person-oriented (86.6 %; $\chi^2(2) = 128.08$; $p < 0.001$) and commercial subjects (64.3 %; $\chi^2(2) = 33.57$; $p < 0.001$) and is significantly higher than in industrial-technical vocational subjects (38.9 %). There are also significant gender differences with regard to the study model: In the national sample, the proportion of female students in undergraduate study models is significantly higher than in undergraduate cooperative (71.9 % *vs* 58.0 %; $\chi^2(2) = 12.34$; $p = 0.002$) and alternative study models (71.9 % *vs* 49.2 %; $\chi^2(2) = 24.57$; $p < 0.001$). When controlling for vocational specialisation (first subject), the difference is no longer significant.

*Age*: Various empirical studies have come to the conclusion that students in the VET teaching profession are, on average, somewhat older than students in other degree programmes and subjects (Bülow-Schramm, 2015, p. 55; Leon et al., 2021; Göller et al., 2022; Lange & Frommberger, n. d.). This is entirely in line with expectations, since the VET teaching profession places extensive demands on the extracurricular professional experience of teacher candidates (KMK, 2018, p. 2), some of which must be provided during or before the start of the degree course. Furthermore, initial analyses of the data from the first wave of the LBS Monitor survey suggest that students in alternative study models are relatively older than undergraduate teacher trainees due to their path via a subject-specific (bachelor's) degree programme (Lange & Frommberger, n. d.). In the nationwide LBS Monitor sample, the uncorrected average age of respondents is 26.1 years (SD = 5.5 years) and, thus, almost three years older than the average age of students across all subjects (23.4 years; Destatis, 2021). The age distribution corrected to the first master's or fourth teaching degree year varies between 19 and 50 years, and the average age of the sample is 26.8 years (SD = 4.7 years). In Lower Saxony, the corrected age average of 27.0 years (SD = 3.9 years) is only slightly above the national average. Male students in the federal sample are, on average, slightly older than female students (27.5 *vs.* 26.4 *years*; $H = 30.39$; $p = 0.050$). With regard to subjects, there are significant differences between students in industrial-technical subjects and those in commercial subjects (28.1 *vs.* 26.3 *years*; $H = 38.54$; $p = 0.02$), which, however, are only significant for male students when controlling for gender (28.8 *vs.* 26.5 *years*; $H = 16.10$; $p = 0.052$). Age differences with regard to the study models (Table 2) are only significant for students in undergraduate and alternative models (26.5 *vs.* 28.3 *years*; $H = -50.25$; $p = 0.02$), whereby the differences remain nonsignificant when controlling for the first-subject variables.

*General matriculation standard*: The 'classic' target group of university studies, persons with a general university entrance qualification (Bülow-Schramm, 2015, p. 54), is significantly less represented in VET teacher training programmes than in other university study programmes (e.g. Ziegler, 2004, p. 380; Bülow-Schramm, 2015, p. 55; Lange & Frommberger, n. d.) In the federal sample, only 71.9 % of students have a general higher education entrance qualification; in Lower Saxony, the proportion is even lower at 64.1 % (see Table 2). For comparison: in the sample of the 21st Social Survey of Student Services in Germany as a whole, 95.0 % of students in all degree programmes had a general higher education entrance qualification (Lange & Frommberger, i. E.). Students in the VET teaching profession thus enter their studies more frequently with higher education entrance qualifications other than the general higher education entrance qualification. Significant differences can be seen in the federal sample of the LBS Monitor between students of industrial-technical and commercial subjects (60.9 % *vs.* 74.5 %; $\chi^2(1) = 11.09$; $p = 0.001$) as well as undergraduate and alternative (74.1% *vs.* 56.2 %; $\chi^2(1) = 16.00$; $p < 0.001$) and undergraduate cooperative and alternative study models (75.7 % *vs.* 56.2 %; $\chi^2(1) = 11.41$; $p < 0.001$). The study model-related significant differences only remain for commercial disciplines ($\chi^2/2) = 6.34$; $p = 0.042$).

*Professional training and experience*: Since VET teaching requires extensive professional experience outside of school (KMK, 2018, p. 2), students in the VET teaching profession are significantly more likely to have completed VET or have other professional experience (e.g. Ziegler, 2004, p. 380; Bülow-Schramm, 2015, p. 55; Lange & Frommberger, n. d.). In the federal sample of the LBS Monitor, 61.1 % of respondents have completed VET and 59.3 % of respondents have work experience that is temporally distinct from this (see Table 2). In Lower Saxony, 73.2 % of the respondents have completed VET; 66.5 % of the respondents state that they have work experience that is separate from VET (see Table 2). In all, 44.0 % of the respondents in the federal sample stated that they had completed VET and had (time-limited) work experience, while only 23.7 % had neither completed VET nor had any other work experience. In Lower Saxony, the proportion of students with VET and other work experience was as high as 56.9 %, while students without VET and other work experience made up only 17.4 % of the subsample. Subject-specific differences are not significant in the federal sample (*Berufsausbildung*: $\chi^2(2) = 1.10$; $p = 0.58$; *Berufserfahrung*: $\chi^2(2) = 0.99$; $p = 0.61$). Significant differences with regard to the study model are only found with regard to professional experience between undergraduate and undergraduate cooperative (55.3 % *vs.* 66.9 %; $\chi^2(2) = 6.56$; $p = 0.01$) and between undergraduate and alternative study models (55.3 % *vs.* 70.2 %; $\chi^2(1) = 9.27$; $p = 0.02$). The differences remain significant even when controlling for vocational specialisation.

*Social origin*: In terms of social background, teacher training is described as an 'upward mobility' field of study with a comparatively high proportion of students with middle or low levels of origin (Lange & Frommberger, n. d.; Neugebauer 2013, p. 7; Grunau & Petzold-Rudolph, 2021, p. 2). While across all fields of study just under half of students come from low or middle levels of origin (Lange & Frommberger, n. d.), the proportion of these students in the entire LBS Monitor sample is 63.6 % and in the Lower Saxony subsample 63.1 % (see Table 2). Differences between subjects and study models are not significant for the federal sample (*Studienfächer*: $\chi^2(4) = 2.78$; $p = 0.60$; Studienmodelle: $\chi^2(4) = 1.56$; $p = 0.82$).

In summary, the data did not support the homogeneity assumption at the programme level for VET teacher training. In detail, the analyses show

- that although VET teaching tends to be a female profession, the gender distribution cannot be assessed as heterogeneous. This is shown both for the entire federal territory and for the subsample of Lower Saxony. With regard to the professional disciplines, the lines of difference between engineering subjects, which tend to be male, and social science subjects, which tend to be studied by women, are reproduced. The different vocational specialisations in teacher training programmes thus contribute to a gender heterogeneity of the student body, although the occupation-specific gender differences remain clearly recognisable. However, under the assumption of gender-differentiated subject choice, the study models tend not to contribute to a gender heterogeneity of students;
- that student teachers for the VET teaching profession are characterised by a comparatively high heterogeneity, which is favoured by the combination of subjects. However, the study models do not seem to contribute to the heterogeneity of the students – contrary to previous assumptions (Lange & Frommberger, n. d.) – even with regard to age;
- that VET teacher training programmes have a comparatively high degree of heterogeneity with regard to university entrance qualifications, which is favoured by both the vocational specialisations and the study models;
- that students in the VET teaching profession have heterogeneous extracurricular, professional experiences. This heterogeneity is favoured by the different study models. This could be due to the integration of universities of applied sciences, where traditionally more students with professional experience are enrolled (Röwert et al., 2017, p. 18);
- that, regardless of the combination options and study models, it is possible to attract first-generation students to study to become VET teachers. Nevertheless, the group of students in the VET teaching profession cannot be assessed as homogeneous in terms of social origin either.

It can accordingly be stated that students of the VET teaching profession can certainly be described as a heterogeneous group with regard to the heterogeneity factors of gender, age, higher education entrance qualification, VET and occupation as well as social origin. Nevertheless, the lines of difference between types of higher education institutions and subjects of study are also reflected within the student groups of the teacher training programmes of VET schools. In this respect, subjects and study models in the VET teaching profession contribute to a high heterogeneity of the student group.

For Lower Saxony, group differences could not be systematically verified due to the small group size in the subsamples, but similar correlations can be assumed. Overall, it can be assumed that significantly fewer students study in undergraduate cooperative models in Lower Saxony compared to the rest of Germany, as the offer in Lower Saxony is limited to one location (Osnabrück) and a few subject areas (electrical engineering, automotive engineering, information technology, metal technology and ecotrophology), whose lack of demand is lamented nationwide (Lange & Sülflow, 2017). With the expansion of undergraduate cooperative study programmes, further student potential for the VET teaching profession could possibly be raised in Lower Saxony.

Furthermore, there are clear differences with regard to study entrance qualification. In Lower Saxony, more students without a classical higher education entrance qualification study in for VET teaching profession than in all other federated states combined ($\chi^2(1) = 6.19$; $p = 0.01$). In Germany, access to higher education is regulated by the higher education laws of the states, and there are considerable differences in some cases with regard to studying without a general higher education entrance qualification. In Lower Saxony, access to higher education is regulated comparatively liberally (Nickel & Leusing, 2009, p. 78): Applicants for university places with a master craftsman's qualification or other VET further training qualification (*Fachwirt, Techniker*) can study at the state's universities and universities of applied sciences without restrictions. People who have completed VET and have at least three years of professional experience can take up studies in subject-related proximity to their VET and professional experience at universities and universities of applied sciences (CHE, 2023). Nevertheless, Lower Saxony is only in 10th place in a comparison of the states in 2020, with a proportion of first-year students without general higher education entrance qualification of 2.34% across all subjects (Nickel & Thiele, 2022, p. 10). However, Lower Saxony performs better in VET teaching professions: In the LBS Monitor ranking of the proportion of students without general higher education entrance qualification, Lower Saxony comes fourth (35.9%) behind Bavaria (48.8%), Bremen (50.0%) and Hesse (63.6%).

Accordingly, students in Lower Saxony have completed VET ($\chi^2(1) = 12.62$; $p = 0.01$) and professional experience ($\chi^2(1) = 4.37$; $p = 0.04$) more often than students in the other federated states. This is partly due to the fact that in the personal subjects of nursing and social pedagogy, whose proportion in the Lower Saxony subsample is comparatively high anyway, proof of completed VET is generally required for entry into the school preparatory service; equivalent practical work experience can be recognised "in separate individual cases" (Nds.Master-VO-Lehr, Annex 5). In this respect, in Lower

Saxony more students with previously completed VET (50.0 % *vs.* 40.5 %; $\chi^2(1) = 0.50$; $p = 0.48$) and/or professional experience (62.5 % *vs.* 52.4 %; $\chi^2(1) = 0.55$; $p = 0.46$) enter a study programme. Since the vocational specialisation of nursing is combined with the vocational specialisations of health and personal care in the LBS Monitor sample due to problems of allocation (Frommberger & Lange, 2017, pp. 270–271), there are no significant differences between Lower Saxony and the other federated states.

# 5 Closing

VET teacher training in Germany is a dynamic field. In addition to many qualitative challenges in studies and in the preparatory service and as regards the system of in-service teacher training, a particularly acute challenge lies in the quantitative safeguarding of the demand for teachers at VET schools. This challenge also applies in principle (and at present) to teacher training for general education schools – and to the many other areas with a high demand for qualified specialists and graduates from colleges and universities. Against this backdrop, we have looked at the recruitment of students for a VET teacher training programme and determined the composition of the target group of students in this regard, which is related to supply structures.

Heterogenisation can probably be described as the central strategy of action with which attempts have been made to find answers to quantitative challenges in the VET teaching profession for years. With the heterogenisation of study structures described in the third section, attempts have been and continue to be made to attract new target groups to VET teacher training. These heterogenisation strategies are still being reproduced today. However, a look at the student body for the teaching profession at VET schools at least raises doubts as to whether the hopes associated with the structural heterogenisation efforts to develop new target groups for the profession can be fulfilled. Rather, the variety of offers for VET teacher training is already so great that the search for further new offer structures will probably no longer meet the quantitative challenges. The only conceivable success would be for programmes that allow students to study alongside their job. Current reform developments are directed towards so-called dual teacher training courses, with which the study and the transition into professional school practice are integrated or linked in terms of time. Furthermore, there seem to be changes with regard to the required combination of a vocational specialisation and a teaching subject in favour of single degree programmes.

However, it is not to be expected that decisions for or against pursuing the teaching profession at VET schools will be influenced by course structures alone. Increasingly, attention is also being paid to the outdated traineeships as well as the working and promotion conditions of teachers at VET schools. The high demand for teachers is now being met by an unmanageable variety of lateral and lateral entry opportunities that do not lead into the teaching profession via the traditional training structure. Graduates of subject-related study programmes either enter the teaching profession via the school preparatory service or are directly employed as teachers at VET schools. These individuals acquire pedagogical competences through further and in-service training.

As a tendency, all measures in the context of this growing heterogenisation go hand in hand with a reduction of previous formal quality demands and standards for teacher professionalisation. In the end, society and politics must decide how much to invest in the professionalisation of VET teachers in order to maintain and further develop a successful (and still attractive) model of VET in Germany. There is no doubt that problems in meeting demand are primarily related to the fact that teacher demand planning and the associated capacity developments for the study and training structures in the responsible ministries have completely failed.

However, with regard to questions of higher education didactics, it is not the quantitative aspect of teacher training that is central but above all qualitative safeguarding of the training already emphasised above and thus the contribution of the study programme to the professionalisation of prospective teachers. Here, too, the LBS Monitor provides opportunities for analysis, which must be used in the coming years to gain knowledge about professionalisation processes in study programmes – also in dependence on study structure and heterogeneity-related characteristics. Since training for teachers at VET schools does not end with graduation, at least in the public system, further analysis of the paths of graduates is necessary in order to be able to make further statements about career paths and professionalisation developments and thus to obtain a complete view of quantitative and qualitative aspects of the training of teachers for VET schools.

## References

Bals, T., Diettrich, A., Eckert, M., & Kaiser, F. (2016). Einleitung: Neue Formen der akademischen Ausbildung für das Lehramt an berufsbildenden Schulen. In T. Bals, A. Diettrich, M. Eckert, & F. Kaiser (Eds.), *Diversität im Zugang zum Lehramt an berufsbildenden Schulen. Vielfalt als Chance?* (pp. 3–26). Eusl.

Becker, K., & Heißenberg, S. (2018). Einleitung. In K. Becker & S. Heißenberg (Eds.), *Dimensionen studentischer Vielfalt. Empirische Befunde zu heterogenen Studien- und Lebensarrangements* (pp. 7–27). wbv.

Berger, J., & Ziegler, B. (2021). Bildungswege, Studien- und Berufswahlmotive, Überzeugungen und Interessen. *Zeitschrift für Berufs- und Wirtschaftspädagogik, 117*(2), 231.

Brockmeier, M. (2017). *Differenzierung im Hochschulsystem zwischen Bildungsauftrag und Selbstentwurf. Keynote der vorsitzenden Professorin Dr. Martina Brockmeier.* https://www.wissenschaftsrat.de/download/archiv/Keynote_VS_Brockmeier.pdf

Bülow-Schramm, M. (2015). Integration als Antwort der Hochschuldidaktik auf eine differenzierte Studierendenschaft. Aus Sicht der Hochschuldidaktik. In A. Hanft, O. Zawacki-Richter, & W. B. Gierke (Eds.), *Herausforderung Heterogenität beim Übergang in die Hochschule* (pp. 53–68). Waxmann.

Bülow-Schramm, M., & Merkt, M. (2013). Wie alles anfing: Genese und Reichweite des Projektes. In M. Bülow-Schramm (Ed.), *Erfolgreich studieren unter Bologna-Bedingungen. Ein empirisches Interventionsprojekt zu hochschuldidaktischer Gestaltung* (pp. 11–26). wbv.

CHE (Centrum für Hochschulentwicklung) (2023). *Studieren ohne Abitur Niedersachsen.* https://studieren-ohne-abitur.de/laender/niedersachsen/

Destatis (Statistisches Bundesamt) (2021). *Studierende an Hochschulen. Wintersemester 2020/21.* https://www.destatis.de/DE/Themen/Gesellschaft-Umwelt/Bildung-Forschung-Kultur/Hochschulen/Publikationen/Downloads-Hochschulen/studierende-hochschulen-endg-2110410217004.pdf?__blob=publicationFile

Faßhauer, U. (2012). Zwischen Standardmodell und "Sondermaßnahmen" – Rekrutierungsstrategien in der Lehrerausbildung aus Sicht von Schulleitern. In M. Becker, G. Spöttl, & T. Vollmer (Eds.), *Lehrerbildung in Gewerblich-Technischen Fachrichtungen* (pp. 281–300). Bertelsmann.

Frommberger, D., & Lange, S. (2017). Aktuelle Entwicklungen und neue Zielgruppen in der Berufsschullehrerbildung in Deutschland. In J. Wang, X. Feng, & J. Rützel (Eds.), *Berufsschullehrerbildung in der Volksrepublik China und in der Bundesrepublik Deutschland – Professionalisierung, Kompetenzen, Herausforderungen* (pp. 266–285). Tongji University Press.

Frommberger, D., & Lange, S. (2018). *Zur Ausbildung von Lehrkräften für berufsbildende Schulen: Befunde und Entwicklungsperspektiven.* WISO-Diskurs, 4/2018. https://library.fes.de/pdf-files/wiso/14169-20180306.pdf

Gerds, P., Heidegger, G., & Rauner, F. (1999). *Das Universitätsstudium der Berufspädagogen – Eckpunkte für ein Zukunftsprojekt: Reformbedarf in der universitären Ausbildung von Pädagoginnen und Pädagogen beruflicher Fachrichtungen in Norddeutschland; Gutachten im Auftrag der Länder Bremen, Hamburg, Mecklenburg-Vorpommern, Niedersachsen und Schleswig-Holstein.* Donat.

Goller, M., & Ziegler, S. (2021). Berufswahlmotivation angehender Wirtschaftspädagog*innen: Validierung des FIT-Choice-Ansatzes und Exploration der Gründe für das Studium der Wirtschaftspädagogik. *Zeitschrift für Berufs- und Wirtschaftspädagogik, 117*(2), 154–193.

Göller, R., Stellmacher, A., Lüdtke, S., Besser, M., & Freund, P. A. (2022). Motive für die Wahl des Studiengangs Wirtschaftspädagogik. Vergleichende Analysen für die Studiengänge Wirtschaftspädagogik, Grund-, Haupt- und Realschullehramt sowie Betriebswirtschaftslehre. *Zeitschrift für Berufs- und Wirtschaftspädagogik, 118*(2), 238–260.

Grottker, D. (2010). Fach und Fach-Richtung? Versuch einer Rekonstruktionsgeschichte der Beruflichen Fachrichtungen. In J.-P. Pahl & V. Herkner (Eds.), *Handbuch Berufliche Fachrichtungen* (pp. 15–35). Bertelsmann.

Grunau, J., & Petzold-Rudolph, K. (2021). First Generation Students in den Studiengängen des Lehramts an berufsbildenden Schulen. *Berufs- und Wirtschaftspädagogik online, Spezial 18*, 1–22. https://www.bwpat.de/spezial18/grunau_petzold-rudolph_spezial18.pdf

Hanft, A. (2015). Heterogene Studierende – homogene Studienstrukturen. In A. Hanft, O. Zawacki-Richter, & W. B. Gierke (Eds.), *Herausforderung Heterogenität beim Übergang in die Hochschule* (pp. 13–28). Waxmann.

Kelle, U., & Kluge, S. (2010). *Vom Einzelfall zum Typus. Fallvergleich und Fallkontrastierung in der qualitativen Sozialforschung, 2. Aufl.* VS.

KMK (Kultusministerkonferenz) (2016). *Rahmenvereinbarung über die Ausbildung und Prüfung für ein Lehramt der Sekundarstufe II (berufliche Fächer) oder für die beruflichen Schulen (Lehramtstyp 5).* Beschluss der Kultusministerkonferenz vom 12.5.1995 i. d. F. vom 6.10.2016. Berlin.

KMK (Kultusministerkonferenz) (2018). *Rahmenvereinbarung über die Ausbildung und Prüfung für ein Lehramt der Sekundarstufe II (berufliche Fächer) oder für die beruflichen Schulen (Lehramtstyp 5).* Beschluss der Kultusministerkonferenz vom 12.05.1995 i. d. F. vom 13.09.2018. Berlin.

KMK (Kultusministerkonferenz) (2022a). *Lehreinstellungsbedarf und -angebot in der Bundesrepublik Deutschland 2020–2035 – Zusammengefasste Modellrechnung der Länder.* Beschluss der Kultusministerkonferenz vom 10.12.2020.

KMK (Kultusministerkonferenz) (2022b). *Lehrkräfteeinstellungsbedarf und -angebot in der Bundesrepublik Deutschland 2021–2035.* Berlin.

Lange, S., & Frommberger, D. (n. d.). Die etwas anderen Studierenden? Thesen zur (besonderen) Heterogenität der Studierenden für das Lehramt an berufsbildenden Schulen auf dem Prüfstand. In S. Rahn, J. Seifried, & B. Ziegler (Eds.), *Beruf: Lehrer*in an berufsbildenden Schulen – eine Bestandsaufnahme der empirischen Forschung.*

Lange, S., & Frommberger, D. (2022). *Skalenhandbuch LBS-Monitor. Version 1.0.* https://doi.org/10.26249/FK2/LHFBD5.

Lange, S., & Sülflow, A. (2017). Aktuelle Entwicklungen der Studierendenzahlen in beruflichen Lehramtsstudiengängen – verlieren wir zu viele Studierende im Übergang vom Bachelor- in das Masterstudium? *Die berufsbildende Schule, 69*(2), 65–71.

Leon, A., Nagy, G., & Abele, S. (2021). Latente Profile der beruflichen Interessen Studierender des gewerblich-technischen Lehramts und ingenieurwissenschaftlicher Disziplinen. *Zeitschrift für Berufs- und Wirtschaftspädagogik, 117*(2), 194–211.

Lundegreen, P. (1999). Die Feminisierung des Lehrerberufs: Segregierung der Geschlechter oder weibliche Präferenz? Kritische Auseinandersetzung mit einer These von Dagmar Hänsel. *Zeitschrift für Pädagogik, 45*(1), 121–135.

Neugebauer, M. (2013). Wer entscheidet sich für ein Lehramtsstudium – und warum? Eine empirische Überprüfung der These von der Negativselektion in den Lehrerberuf. *Zeitschrift für Erziehungswissenschaft, 16*(1), 157–184.

Nickel, S., & Leusing, B. (2009). *Studieren ohne Abitur: Entwicklungspotentiale in Bund und Ländern. Eine empirische Analyse.* CHE.

Nickel, S., & Thiele, A.-L. (2022). *Update 2022: Studieren ohne Abitur in Deutschland. Überblick über aktuelle Entwicklungen.* CHE.

Niedersächsische Staatskanzlei (2020). *Lehrkräftebedarfsprognose passiert Kabinett.* https://www.stk.niedersachsen.de/startseite/presseinformationen/lehrkraftebedarfsprognose-passiert-kabinett-185394.html

Porcher, C., & Trampe, K. (2021). Das berufliche Lehramtsstudium in Deutschland. Eine Typologie von Studienmodellen. *berufsbildung, 75*(190), 13–16.
Röwert, R., Lah, W., Dahms, K., Berthold, C., & von Stuckrad, T. (2017). *Diversität und Studienerfolg. Studienrelevante Heterogenitätsmerkmale an Universitäten und Fachhochschulen und ihr Einfluss auf den Studienerfolg – eine quantitative Untersuchung.* Gütersloh: CHE (Arbeitspapier, 198).
Seidel, A., & Wemme, T. (2011). Nachwuchssorgen im Lehramtsstudium für berufsbildende Schulen? *Die berufsbildende Schule, 3*(7/8), 220–226.
Sloane, P. F. E., Liebberger, K., Ohlms, M., Pasing, R., & Reich-Zies, B.-T. (2010). Analyse von Studienplänen der Beruflichen Fachrichtungen – eine Synopse. In J.-P. Pahl & V. Herkner (Eds.), *Handbuch berufliche Fachrichtungen* (pp. 245–263). W. Bertelsmann.
Terhart, E. (Ed.) (2000). *Perspektiven der Lehrerbildung in Deutschland. Abschlussbericht der von der Kultusministerkonferenz eingesetzten Kommission.* Beltz.
Ziegler, B. (2004). *Professionalisierung im Studium – Anspruch und Wirklichkeit.* Shaker.

## Short portraits of the authors

**Silke Lange** has been Assistant Professor of Vocational Education and Training specialising in vocational teacher training research at Osnabrück University since 2021. She conducts research on various issues relating to vocational teacher training, the structures of vocational education and training (VET) and the development of disciplines and theories in VET research.
Contact: silke.lange@uni-osnabrueck.de

**Kristina Trampe** has been a Research Associate at Osnabrück University since 2011. Her research interests include vocational teachers and trainers as well as the history of vocational education and training in Germany.
Contact: kristina.trampe@uos.de

**Christoph Porcher** has been a Research Associate at Osnabrück University since 2020. His research interests include the structures and functions of vocational education and training (VET) in Germany as well as the statutory development of VET in Germany.
Contact: christoph.porcher@uni-osnabrueck.de

**Dietmar Frommberger** has been Professor (full) of Vocational Education at Osnabrück University since 2017. He previously held a professorship at the University of Magdeburg. His research interests include comparative aspects of vocational education and training (VET) research, especially with an international focus, as well as structures and functions of VET in Germany.
Contact: dietmar.frommberger@uni-osnabrueck.de

# The case of Lombardy

# Vocational education and training systems in Italy and Lombardy: Between light and shadow

Francesco Magni, Virginia Capriotti[1]

**Abstract:** This chapter explores the Italian vocational education and training (VET) system at the secondary level, with a particular focus on the Lombardy region, to highlight both its strengths ('light') and challenges ('shadow'). The VET system has long been the subject of attempts to strengthen its links with the world of work, increase the number of participating students, cope with early school leaving and educational poverty, and improve the quality of learning. Lombardy, one of the most industrially advanced regions in Italy, serves as a microcosm of the broader national trends. Through the course of our analysis, we consider the specific regional policies, institutional frameworks, and pedagogical approaches at play in the VET system. The paper ends with some recommendations for enhancing its efficiency and inclusivity, thereby ensuring that VET continues to meet the evolving needs of the workforce and the economy.

**Keywords**: Vocational Education and Training System; Strengths; Challenges; Education Policies.

## 1 Introduction

In these turbulent times, characterised by global uncertainty and economic instability, vocational education and training (VET) systems have gained importance throughout the world for providing younger generations with a quality education and the necessary training required for success in today's world (Pilz, 2017; Mulder, 2017; Guile & Unwin, 2019). VET in Italy has consistently been the topic of significant national discourse, which reflects the country's dynamic socio-economic landscape. Historically, Italy's commitment to fortifying its VET system has been evident through various legislative endeavours and innovative efforts, and especially so when considering its positive employment outcomes among graduate students (INAPP, 2019).

In February 2023, the National Institute for Public Policy Analysis (INAPP) published its latest report[2], which contains the following valuable insights into current VET trends:

1 Although this contribution is the result of a collaborative study by the two authors, Sections 2, 3 and 4 can be attributed specifically to Virginia Capriotti, and Section 5 to Francesco Magni. The Introduction can be attributed to both authors.

2 *XX Rapporto di monitoraggio del Sistema di Istruzione e Formazione Professionale e dei Percorsi in Duale nella IeFP. A.f. 2020–21*, Febbraio 2023. Inapp – Ministero del lavoro e delle politiche sociali. Available at: https://oa.inapp.org/xmlui/bitstream/handle/20.500.12916/3936/INAPP_XX-Rapporto-monitoraggio-sistema-IeFP-Duale_2023.pdf?sequence=4&isAllowed=y.

- Notable variations exist in training programme availability. For example, Sicily offers fewer courses, and enrolment is down in many regions. In general, the provision of courses is not stable, as regional tenders to fund them are typically issued on an annual basis;
- While most regions meet the required general service standards, some lag behind, which causes confusion due to the mixture of old and new specifications;
- There is inconsistency in regional data management. Specifically, informal databases in some areas could jeopardise accurate resource reporting;
- A mismatch between job availability and demand is evident. Sectors such as engineering and logistics face worker shortages, whereas wellness and catering have surpluses. This imbalance underlines the need for better job market strategies;
- Enrolments in IeFP (*Istruzione e Formazione Professionale*, or regional VET paths) are decreasing, especially in accredited institutions, which may be indicative of an increasing early school dropout rate;
- Raising awareness about the IeFP system's employment benefits is essential to addressing youth unemployment;
- Among the available IeFP pathways, there is a growing demand for those that follow a dual approach, either through dual apprenticeships, internships with on-the-job training hours ranging from 30 % to 50 %, or participation in a simulated work environment, with 27.8 % of students opting for this. Ensuring pathway quality and monitoring internship effectiveness are key objectives;
- Soft skills, such as problem solving, are vital for youth employability, and their prioritisation entails a national focus on transversal competencies;
- There is a need to clarify the technical-professional training standards and whether they cater to specific regional needs.

In a country such as Italy, where there is a significant number of individuals leaving education and training early (15 %), where there is a relevant number of NEET (Not in Education, Employment or Training) individuals aged between 18 and 24 years (22.5 %), and high levels of youth unemployment persist (approximately 28 % at the national level), VET is of paramount importance. There has been persistent demand in recent years, particularly from the European Union, for member states to improve their VET systems. These educational pathways provide a means of learning that integrates theoretical and practical approaches through innovative didactical methods (Bertagna, 2011; Potestio, 2020; Cegolon, 2019, 2020; Bertuletti, 2021; Massagli, 2023) and may be crucial in confronting the distinctive challenges of our era (Powell & McGrath, 2019). There is also a growing urgency to thoroughly reassess the pedagogical methodologies adopted by education and training institutions at large (Bertagna, 2020).

In today's context, a prominent status has been attributed to VET, since it holds the potential to effectively harness students' unique talents and potential while simultaneously aligning them with the demands of the professional world. Despite the progress made in recent decades, the VET system in Italy still has its shortcomings. Numerous regional disparities in educational opportunities continue to hamper the ability to overcome existing educational inequalities and poverty (Salerno, 2019). Against this background, this paper aims to outline some of the main features of the Italian VET model, with a particular focus on the Lombardy region, to provide an overview of the current situation and, based on a first reading of recent reform attempts, to outline possible options for the future.

## 2 The vocational education and training system in Italy: A first look at the history from today's perspective

Italy is currently the second largest manufacturing nation in Europe. According to Unioncamere Excelsior, the demand for skilled personnel in various fields, ranging from mechatronics to computer science, will require the employment of at least 500,000 people by 2027[3]. However, the national VET system will not be able to train those people, as it has not yet been sufficiently developed for this purpose.

The Italian VET system exhibits a significant contradiction, as it is split between the national level and the regional level: specifically, there is the five-year state VET path regulated at the national level (*Istruzione Professionale,* IP) and the three- or four-year regional VET pathways regulated at the regional level (*Istruzione e Formazione Professionale,* IeFP). The first is 'school-based', with face-to-face lectures and a teaching approach still modelled on the high school and other upper secondary school tracks, while the second is 'work-based', implying more significant teaching and organisational flexibility, the implementation of workshops, and the systematic integration of work-based learning in the form of internships.

This twofold/two-track structure has distinctive historical origins that merit a brief description. In 1970, with the launch of regional autonomy (a constitutional provision dating back to 1948), the responsibility for professional training and VET was transferred from the national to the regional level. This shift led to the coexistence of a national system of state VET schools and a parallel, mostly autonomous system of VET institutions developed by the regions (Bertuletti, 2021; D'Amico, 2015; Salini, 2014). Lombardy, as a region, played a pioneering role in regulating the professional school system during the 1970s. Specifically, administrators in this region created the Territorial Centres for Technical and Educational Innovation (*Centri territoriali per l'innovazione tecnica ed educativa,* or CITE) and adapted its educational systems and legislation to changing times. This collaboration between public and private institutions allowed for the development of a widespread system of VET institutions in Lombardy to meet the region's social and economic development needs. The national *Framework Law on Vocational Training* (Law No. 845/1979) marked the end of the transition period, thereby solidifying the dualism between 'school-based' VET (IP) governed at the national level and regional VET (IeFP). This legislation still allowed for state financing of

3 *La domanda di professioni e di formazione delle imprese italiane nel 2023*, Unioncamere-ANPAL. Available at: https://excelsior.unioncamere.net/sites/default/files/pubblicazioni/2023/Domanda_professioni_formazione_imprese.pdf.

the regional VET system and the promotion of modular teaching and training activities, work-based learning and traineeships in this sector.

Constitutional reforms in the early 2000s granted regions extensive legislative power and administrative competence in specific areas, including the VET system, leading to the successful development of VET in Lombardy and some other regions. As no government has yet established how to enforce the so-called 'essential levels of performance' (LEPs) in this sector (since the VET system's standards and services should be guaranteed uniformly throughout the entire national territory, according to Legislative Decree 226/2005), regional VET is still uneven across the country. As Zagardo (2019, 2022) points out, in certain regions, especially in southern Italy, VET pathways either do not exist or are available only on paper or in a significantly reduced manner. Therefore, the current situation indicates significant regional variation, resulting in unequal opportunities for learners (Censis, 2018) and a general failure to meet the constitutional obligation of providing equal opportunities to attend VET.

Both systems (IP and regional IeFP) aim to prepare students for work through a means of instruction that exists at the intersection between theory and practice. However, these systems have different providers and, consequently, differ regarding their work-based training and vocational qualification outcomes. While IP is regulated by the Ministry of Education and delivers training through public VET schools, IeFP is governed by the regions in compliance with state-set LEPs and is provided either by private vocational training centres (CFPs) or only as a subsidiary option at state schools accredited by the regions.

Approximately 600,000 high school learners in Italy, or roughly 25 % of the complete aggregate, participate in VET pathways. Around 440,000 of these learners are registered in educational pathways promoted by state VET schools, while over 150,000 are enrolled in regional VET centres. The latter courses have seen an increase in enrolment over time, while the state VET schools have experienced a sharp and rapid decline. In recent years, the percentage of students enrolled in IP has decreased from 18.6 % to 12.1 % of the total share of secondary students, with a decrease of almost 100,000 students within a few years (i. e. from more than 530,000 students in the 2015/2016 school year to around 440,000 students in 2021/2022).

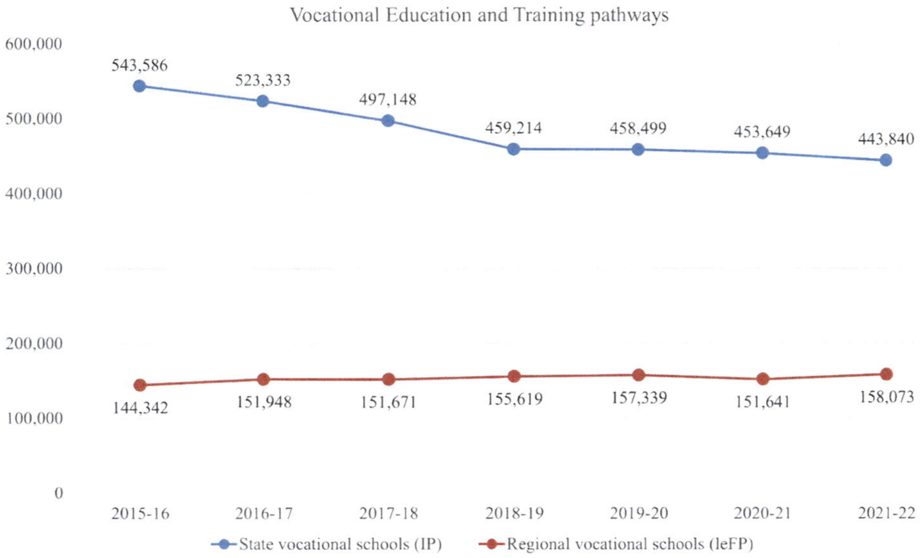


**Figure 1:** Students enrolled in IeFP and IP pathways 2015/2016–2020/2021.

*Note: Data obtained by Francesco Magni and Virginia Capriotti from INAPP (2023) and the Italian Ministry of Education (unified school data portal).*

## 3 Challenges arising from two co-existing vocational education and training systems

The implementation of this two-track system has resulted in numerous contradictions, shortcomings, and weaknesses. First, the inflexible and rigid nature of the IP system frequently fails to encourage genuine interaction with the world of work and creative laboratory-based teaching practices. Conversely, regional disparities and inequalities have intensified and expanded through the IeFP models. The result is a nationwide landscape characterised by both strengths and limitations.

Establishing a robust VET system in Italy is not a new endeavour. Law 53 of 2003 already emphasised the importance of VET, which had long been overdue. Furthermore, it is crucial to recollect the various specific calls from European Union bodies, including the Council, Commission, and Parliament, to support such initiatives. These calls began with the European Council's Communication in Bruges in 2010 and reached their culmination in the Riga Communication in 2015 (European Ministers for Vocational Education and Training, 2010). Together, they consistently underscored the need to strengthen and enhance the VET systems in member states to combat youth unemployment and achieve the goals outlined in the Europe 2020 Strategy. During the past decade, these calls have become more specific, especially since the establishment of the *European Alliance for Apprenticeship* in Leipzig in July 2013. This European shift towards a work-based approach to education has led to increased attention to 'dual system' models and reduced confidence in traditional schooling methods.

In this context, the Italian IP system, which remains uniform throughout the country and is financed directly by the state, also recruits teachers according to the same bureaucratic rules of competition as other sectors in general upper secondary education. As such, it seems to be struggling increasingly to respond to current challenges. However, over time, it has drifted towards a more academic approach, focusing on theoretical and school-based VET, which are far removed from the pathways chosen in other European countries, where VET is characterised by the promotion of work-related learning didactics, inductive methods, contextualised tasks, and learning environments concretely linked to the world of work. This has led to an increasing rate of dropouts from these programmes, as there is a significant gap between the type of vocational education offered and the specific needs of students and companies. The state VET schools have thus proved to be a weak link in the education system, despite the fact that they should instead be playing a crucial role in reducing the dropout rate.

The reform of the IP system through Legislative Decree 61/2017 initially seemed promising, especially in its clear orientation towards a 'European' VET model. However, the limitations of this decree are now becoming clear. On the one hand, the renewed VET institutes still retain the typical constraints of the organisation of the education system, including fixed teaching posts, limited subject areas, and a teacher's employment contract that is not adapted to an organisational model suitable for training pathways closely integrated with work. In addition, there is a lack of systematic support and the required teacher numbers to maintain permanent contact with companies. For these reasons, various regulations and bureaucratic-administrative processes need to be reconsidered. Specifically, learning activities should be organised in alignment with the dual system's principles, starting with the establishment of relationships with companies and a focus on teaching real-world tasks[4]. On the other hand, while the regional IeFP system seems to have had some success, it remains an incomplete and fragmented model.

There is thus a need to rethink the entire Italian VET system, both regionally and nationally, to overcome unnecessary duplication and ensure the harmonious improvement of the entire model.

## 4 The Lombardian model

Despite these broader limitations, in some cases, regulatory regional autonomy has enabled the successful implementation of an efficient VET system. An example is the Lombardy region (Magni, 2020), which stands out for two reasons. First, Lombardy's industrial history and its vibrant socio-economic-entrepreneurial environment (with

4 This is exactly as it was at the beginning of the 20th century for the so-called industrial technical schools, which used to have their own regulations, a board of directors, direct hiring of teachers, etc., as an expression of full autonomy in responding to the local production system's needs (see Bertagna, 2022).

over 10 million citizens contributing to more than 20 % of Italy's national gross domestic product, or GDP) are closely linked with VET institutions.

Second, Lombardy has experienced a greater diffusion and success of VET centres at the secondary and tertiary levels compared to other Italian regions, making it a compelling case study for this sector from a comparative perspective (Pilz & Li, 2020). In Lombardy, the youth population (aged 15 to 34) comprises almost two million people, with the majority (70.1 %) holding a high school diploma. This has resulted in lower rates of early school leavers (12.9 %) and NEET individuals (13.1 %) compared to the national average (Polis, 2019). Notably, Lombardy's focus on excellence through pluralistic, autonomous, and differentiated approaches has played a key role in its achievement of these favourable outcomes.

### 4.1 Vocational education and training pathways

Private or public VET centres accredited by the region or state VET schools offer the following:

- Three-year courses that lead to the achievement of the 'professional operator certificate' (*qualifica di operatore professionale*) at EQF Level 3;
- Four-year courses that lead to the achievement of the 'professional technician diploma' (*diploma professionale di tecnico*) at EQF Level 4, Enrolment requires at least a three-year qualification;
- One extra year to take a state exam that entitles the student to receive the general higher education entrance qualification. Enrolment requires at least a four-year diploma;
- One-year post-secondary courses leading to a 'high technical specialisation certificate' (*certificato superiore di tecnico*) at EQF Level 4. Enrolment requires at least a four-year diploma;
- Dual apprenticeship schemes (from 2016/2017 onwards);
- Customised pathways for disabled pupils, also offered in dual mode (from 600 hours to three years, with the option of a supplementary year).

The three-year and four-year pathways for qualifications/diplomas involve 990 hours of work per year. Currently, there are 36 qualifications and 54 diplomas awarded by the regions and recognised nationally. Each programme provides for a specific quota of learning activities identified by the single institutions with regard to the distinctive territorial peculiarities and educational needs of their students. In general, teaching units are divided by thematic areas, including languages and historical-socio-economic, mathematical-scientific, and technological subjects (35–45 % of the total hours); technical-professional subjects and work-based learning (40–50 %); and courses chosen individually by the respective institutions (15 %, corresponding to 445 hours). An internship is normally carried out in both the second and third years.

To those who already hold a four-year diploma, the Lombardian VET system also offers one-year post-secondary courses that lead to a higher technical specialisation certificate (still at EQF Level 4). These courses represent the so-called *Istruzione e forma-*

*zione tecnica superiore* (*IFTS*) and are designed nationally through a joint decree involving the Education and Labour Ministers, in coordination with the State-Regions Conference, which sets the minimum skill standards for each qualification. The delivery of these courses involves temporary associations of universities, higher technical schools, VET providers, job agencies, companies, and local authorities. These associations tailor the courses to meet the professional needs of the local area within each qualification sector. Financial support is thus limited, with funds being disbursed through annual regional calls. This limited funding contributes to the small and often unstable supply of these courses.

Furthermore, since 2015, with Regional Law 30/2015, Lombardy has implemented what is known as the 'dual system' for VET programmes. This system is characterised by a systematic, organised, and continuous connection between education and work. The law establishes a minimum and maximum proportion of work-based learning (internship or business simulation) within the annual hours of educational activities, starting from the age of 15. This proportion ranges from 15–50 % in three-year courses leading to the 'Professional Operator Certificate' and from 20–50 % in four-year courses leading to the 'Professional Technician Diploma'. Moreover, to receive funding through the dowry system (see below), accredited training centres must have a minimum of 5 % of their enrolled students as apprentices in the third and fourth years.

Educational institutions may also organise an annual extra course for access to the state exam, which allows students to enter higher education. However, this is only possible when the Regional School Office of Lombardy (*USR Lombardia*) ensures the placement of students in school institutions or under self-financing conditions. This is known as the VET 'fifth year' and was implemented starting from the academic year 2010/2011, with self-financing beginning in the academic year 2015/2016. This particular course of study has a duration of 990 hours. Annual courses can be activated only for students holding professional diplomas in the field of technology acquired in Lombardy. Basic or transversal skills (such as mathematics or communication in the native language or in English) range from a minimum of 70 % to a maximum of 80 %, while technical-professional competencies range from a minimum of 20 % to a maximum of 30 %. At the end of the programme, diplomas are awarded for entrance to a tertiary programme within the Italian educational system.

Here, we do not consider the non-academic tertiary technical education system, a sector that is on the cusp between higher VET and higher education, and formally under the jurisdiction of the Italian Ministry of Education (on this topic, see Bertuletti and Potestio in this volume).

## 4.2 Dual apprenticeship

In accordance with national law (Legislative Decree 81/2015) and ministerial regulations (Min. Dec. 18 October 2015), all VET courses in Lombardy can be offered as dual apprenticeships for individuals aged 15–24. Dual apprenticeships have a minimum duration of six months, and their maximum duration is determined by the length of the corresponding school-based programme in which they are enrolled. The exact duration is to be agreed upon by the company, the apprentice, and their school. If the apprenticeship in a company is terminated before its natural conclusion and cannot be replaced by another company, the learner may resume his/her studies at school.

Apprentices are required to attend school lessons and receive vocational training in their respective companies. Contractual hours are divided into work, formal learning at school, and in-company training. In-company training can take the form of on-the-job training or formal learning, either on the company's premises or elsewhere, but under the employer's responsibility. The number of effective working hours depends on the number of school hours necessary to achieve the corresponding qualifications. Regional regulations stipulate that in-company training cannot exceed 60 % of the learning hours at school in the second year of a VET programme or 50 % in the third and fourth year, as well as in the courses for attaining the so-called *certificato superiore di tecnico* (Regional Decree 4676/2015).

The learning outcomes associated with the final qualification must be equivalent to those in the corresponding school-based programme. While the final assessment is discussed with the company, it ultimately remains the responsibility of the educational institutions accredited by the region. In contrast, the in-company training content is jointly determined by the employer and the school.

### 4.3 Teacher training

As national essential levels of performance prescribe, VET teachers in all regions must have either a national teaching qualification in a specific subject (which in Italy requires a special training programme for teachers that must be attended during or after obtaining a master's degree in the teaching subject) or professional experience of at least five years in a specific sector (Legislative Decree 226/2005 Art. 18). In Lombardian VET, teachers must have either a national teaching qualification in a specific subject or a bachelor's degree with sufficient teaching experience in the national educational system (e. g. as substitute teachers). Such experience is elevated to a minimum of five years when the candidate teacher has received only an upper secondary education leaving certificate. Teachers of practical subjects can have professional experience (of at least 5 years) only within the same field in which they intend to teach (General Director's Decree 10187/13 November 2012).

According to school law, VET teachers of general subjects, VET theory, and practical subjects do not have to attend any professional development courses, but the collective agreements in the VET sector prescribe the attendance of at least 100 training hours for the professional development of the teachers. VET providers normally concur with their employees on which programmes to follow.

It is important to note that public funds for these purposes are not consistently available. The Ministry of Labour allocates funds to manage and govern national private VET providers with schools in various regions, often including the financing of teacher professional development (Law 40/1987). Occasionally, regions may provide funding for specific courses and bilateral funds, managed jointly by social partners (VET providers and teachers' unions), and may also support courses and in-company training periods. While it is generally permissible to hire professionals from the labour market, early-career teachers from an industry background, as well as professionals hired under part-time contracts, are quite rare, because teachers' wages are lower than those in other sectors.

### 4.4 Financing

One particularly innovative feature of the Lombardian VET system is its method of financing (Salerno & Zagardo, 2015). The introduction of the 'dowry' system in 2008 marked a significant shift in the way VET programmes are funded and managed. There are two key aspects of this financing method:

- Transition from a supply- to a demand-driven approach: Lombardy VET evolved from a rigid supply model that primarily focused on the needs and requests of the territories to a more flexible supply system. This shift means that it is now more responsive to the dynamics of student demand, which means that it reflects students' actual choices and the specific economic and social characteristics of different areas of Lombardy;
- Quota per pupil financing: funding for VET courses is based on a 'quota per pupil' criterion, which means that the economic resources allocated for the courses are directly tied to the number of students enrolled. This approach ensures that financial support matches actual student enrolment.

The value of the dowry depends on the type of VET course, with an annual cost per student ranging from EUR 4,000 to EUR 4,600. The recipients of the dowry are students living in Lombardy. These funds will be allocated in the chronological order of receipt of student application requests until the funds are fully allocated. It is important to note that the allocation of resources is subject to the availability of funds within the priority group. Overall, this financing system emphasises the importance of student choice and regional needs in the allocation of VET resources. It promotes a dynamic and adaptable approach to VET funding, with the goal of providing relevant and accessible VET to the residents of Lombardy while optimising the use of financial resources.

Finally, to understand the dual characterisation of the regional system, it is important to remember that since 2018 (under Law 205/2017), the Ministry of Labour has transferred additional financial resources to the regions to fund VET courses that include 'strengthened' work-based learning activities. These activities should account for no less than 40 % of the standard hours for the second year and 50 % for the third and fourth years, totalling a minimum of 400 hours annually. The same applies to courses conducted as apprenticeships up until the attainment of one qualification.

## 5 Recent developments and reform proposals: Toward a unified system?

The Italian 'double' VET system is still weak and imbalanced all across the country, with precarious economic sustainability being the norm. The exclusive regional competence in this matter, in the absence of adequate monitoring and verification of the essential LEPs, has led to further fragmentation of the system, as only some regions offer an adequate VET supply. Many regions, especially in central and southern Italy, offer VET at the secondary level exclusively in state VET schools. On the one hand, there is a tendency toward a school-based and theoretical approach, with an increasing number of disciplines in the curriculum; on the other hand, there are difficulties in implementing work-based learning and competency-based teaching. At present, there are two ways to provide IeFP programmes:

- Training pathways implemented by VET centres, which are financed by the regions through their budgets, the European Social Fund (ESF), and an annual transfer from the Ministry of Labour;
- Educational pathways implemented by schools based on an agreement between the State and the regions since December 2010 and later regulated by Legislative Decree 61/2017. These pathways are funded by the Ministry of Education, as they are considered regular educational programmes, with teachers paid by the Ministry.

For these reasons, the relationships and coordinated efforts between VET schools run by the state and the training centres accredited by the regions should be reconsidered, starting with a determination of how the courses to be delivered, as well as key professional resources and organisational methods between the two systems, can be effectively shared. In September 2023, the Italian government approved a draft law on the technological-professional training chain, which seems promising. As pointed out by Bertagna (2023), this project first aims to bring Italian schools up to European standards to develop qualifications and competences. In addition, the legislative project is designed to involve VET institutions, schools, and other territorial actors (i. e. families, companies, regions, provinces, and municipalities) in a broader effort to respect the principle of subsidiarity according to Article 118 of the Italian Constitution and achieve a real impact.

One of the backbones of the proposal is the new concept of an individual 'campus' (each comprising a virtual or on-site VET), each of which is to be united with the others by a common didactical approach. This concept should be promoted by the regions that currently provide VET courses (IeFP) and higher technical training courses (IFTS), the foundations that manage the ITS Academy (*Istituti Tecnici Superiori*; Magni & Capriotti, 2023), the state technical and VET schools, the other general education high schools (*Licei*), and possibly the universities and academies, as well as all the public and private entities operating within the territories (e. g. local authorities, companies, company networks, foundations, and non-profit organisations).

The main point of the proposed reform is to reduce the IP pathways, as well as the other upper secondary courses, into a four-year programme, as can be found in most European countries. It also provides for the personalisation and flexibilisation of learning pathways, the promotion of specific career guidance facilities, and internationalisation and strengthening of activities aimed at acquiring basic skills. At the end of the four-year regional VET pathways (IeFP), students who have obtained a regional VET diploma and, at the same time, an evaluation of the results of these pathways by INVALSI (*Istituto nazionale per la valutazione del sistema educativo di istruzione e di formazione*) have direct access to the ITS Academy, which is the non-academic tertiary education system. If they want to enrol in a university course, they will have direct access to the state examination to obtain a high school diploma, which would afford them the opportunity to do so.

Other points included in the reform are the strengthening of the basic subjects (especially Italian and mathematics), apprenticeship training and more work-based learning (up to 400 hours in the last three years), and the possibility of additional lectures by experts from the productive and professional world to broaden the existing educational offerings. Notwithstanding the competencies of the regions in the field of education and training, experimentation may include various measures, such as the following:

- Adaptation and expansion of the educational offerings, with particular attention to basic disciplines and new experimental paths, to respond to the specific needs of the regions;
- Promotion of transitions between different educational pathways;
- Reduction of upper secondary education to four years;
- Implementation of innovative teaching methods;
- Potential recruitment of teachers from the world of professional work.

Epistemological or pedagogical reasoning cannot be used to maintain the distinction between IP and IeFP, nor can it be applied to discern between professional roles in the world of work. The only reasons against the unification of IP and IeFP into a comprehensive Italian VET system today are to be found elsewhere, such as in historical factors, institutional and labour relations, and the actual governance of VET schools.

The VET system helps bridge the gap between theoretical knowledge and practical application. While the prevailing view used to be that work was a solution for those without sufficient intellect for 'higher' education, the VET system actually offers a transition to a new paradigm in the national education system. This approach focuses on providing multiple pathways of equal value (Bertagna, 2006; Berner, 2017), thereby allowing young people to exercise their freedom of choice. In addition, the notion of education and training as a service aims to identify and nurture the talents of each individual without exception.

Schools should not discriminate against young people based on abstract notions of intelligence or social status. Rather, they have a responsibility to recognise and cultivate the intellectual abilities of each student in their care, thus enabling them to develop into knowledgeable and skilled individuals (Bertagna, 2020, 2023). The VET system must also be integrated into a strategy of greater coordination between the regions and the central government. This coordination is essential to overcome the current regional fragmentation and to fully address the LEPs and thus the rights of all citizens. Legislative experimentation could serve as a prelude to broader regulatory reform, which would then pave the way toward the establishment of a unified national system of VET schools. This would, of course, require that the balance between national and regional regulations in this crucial sector of national education be reconsidered.

## References

Berner, A. R. (2017). *No One Way to School. Pluralism and American Public Education*. Plagrave Macmillan.

Bertagna, G. (2006). *Pensiero manuale. La scommessa di un sistema educativo di istruzione e di formazione di pari dignità*. Soveria Mannelli: Rubettino.

Bertagna, G. (2011). *Lavoro e formazione dei giovani*. La Scuola.

Bertagna, G. (2020). *La scuola al tempo del Covid. Tra spazio di esperienza ed orizzonte d'attesa*. Studium.

Bertagna, G. (2022). Il 'brutto anatroccolo' dell'istruzione e formazione professionale. Genetica di una pretesa ma insostenibile 'inferiorità'. In V. Boffo, G. Del Gobbo, & F. Torlone (Eds.), *Educazione degli Adulti: politiche, percorsi, prospettive. Studi in onore di Paolo Federighi* (pp. 29–50). Firenze University Press.

Bertagna, G. (2023). Nasce la filiera formativa tecnologico-professionale. Un primo commento al disegno di legge. *Nuova Secondaria, 2*, 5–6.

Bertuletti, P. (2021a). La strana duplicazione della formazione secondaria professionalizzante. Cause storiche e ragioni culturali di un'anomalia italiana. *Professionalità Studi, 4*, 70–76.

Bertuletti, P. (2021b). *Quale «formazione» professionale? Una rilettura di Georg Kerschensteiner (1854–1932)*. Studium.

Cegolon, A. (2019). *Oltre la disoccupazione. Per una nuova pedagogia del lavoro*. Edizioni Studium.

Cegolon, A. (2020). *Lavoro e pedagogia del lavoro. Origine, sviluppo, prospettive*. Edizioni Studium.

Censis. (2018). *52° Rapporto sulla situazione sociale del Paese/2018*. Roma.

D'Amico, N. (2015). *Storia della formazione professionale in Italia. Dall'uomo da lavoro al lavoro per l'uomo*. Franco Angeli.

European Ministers for Vocational Education and Training. (2010). *Communiqué of the European Ministers for Vocational Education and Training, the European Social Partners and the European Commission meeting in Bruges on 7 December 2010 to review the strategic approach and priorities of the Copenhagen process for 2011–2020. Bruges Communiqué on enhanced European Cooperation in Vocational Education and Training (2011–2020)*.

European Commission. (2015). *Declaration of the Ministers in charge of vocational education and training – of EU Member States, Candidate Countries, European Economic Area Countries.* https://education.ec.europa.eu/document/riga-conclusions-2015

Guile, D., & Unwin, L. (Eds.), (2019). *The Wiley Handbook of Vocational Education and Training.* Wiley.

INAPP. (2019). *Risultati dell'indagine sugli esiti formativi-occupazionali dei percorsi IeFP e IFTS.*

INAPP. (2023). *XX Rapporto di monitoraggio del Sistema di Istruzione e Formazione Professionale e dei Percorsi in Duale nella IeFP – a.f. 2020–21.*

Magni, F. (2020). The VET system in Lombardy (Italy): a first pedagogical outlook between history and future. In L. Moreno Herrera, M. Teräs, & P. Gougoulakis (Eds.), *Policies & partnership with the world of work – national and cross-national perspectives. Emerging issues in research on vocational education & training* (Vol. 6, pp. 26–50). Premiss förlag.

Magni, F., & Capriotti, V. (2023). Higher non-academic technical education in Italy: ITS Academy. In L. Moreno Herrera, M. Teräs, P. Gougoulakis, & J. Kontio (Eds.), *Learning, teaching and policy making in VET. Emerging issues in research on vocational education & training* (Vol. 8, pp. 258–293). Atlas förlag.

Massagli, E. (2023). *La didattica esperienziale. Apprendistato e impresa didattica nei percorsi del secondo ciclo di istruzione e formazione.* Edizioni Studium.

Mulder, M. (Ed.). (2017). *Competence-based Vocational and Professional Education. Bridging the Worlds of Work and Education.* Springer.

Pilz, M. (Ed.). (2017). *Vocational Education and Training in Times of Economic Crisis: Lessons from Around the World.* Springer.

Pilz, M., & Li, J. (Eds.). (2020). *Comparative Vocational Education Research: Enduring Challenges and New Ways Forward.* Springer.

Polis Lombardia. (2019). *I giovani in Lombardia, Polis Lombardia.* https://www.polis.lombardia.it/wps/portal/site/polis

Potestio, A. (2020). *Alternanza formativa. Radici storiche e attualità di un principio pedagogico.* Studium.

Powell, L. J., & McGrath, S. (2019). *Skills for Human Development. Transforming Vocational Education and Training.* Routledge.

Salerno, G. M., & Zagardo, G. (2015). *I costi della IeFP. Un'analisi comparata tra Istituzioni formative regionali e Istituzioni scolastiche statali.* ISFOL.

Salerno, G. M. (2019). *L'istruzione e la formazione professionale tra regionalismo e unitarietà. Una prima analisi.* Soveria Mannelli: Rubbettino.

Salini, A. (2014). Formazione professionale e mondo imprenditoriale Alto Milanese negli anni Settanta del Novecento: il progetto "Alternanza scuola-lavoro" del CFP di Gallarate. *Annali di Storia moderna e contemporanea, 2*(2), 149–172.

Zagardo, G. (2019). *La IeFP nelle Regioni. Tra consolidamento e stasi.* CONSFAP-MLPS.

Zagardo, G. (2022). *La IeFP nelle Regioni e nelle Province Autonome. L'anno del sorpasso.* CNOSFAP.

## Short portraits of the authors

**Francesco Magni** is Associate Professor at the University of Bergamo, where he is Deputy Director of the Centre for Quality Teaching, Educational Innovation, and Learning (CQIIA). His main research interests are education policies, teacher training, work-based learning, higher education and vocational education and training.
Contact: francesco.magni@unibg.it

**Virginia Capriotti** is a PhD Student at the University of Bergamo, Italy. Her research focuses on meritocracy in the educational system, specifically in secondary schools. During 2023, she was a Visiting PhD Student at Teachers College, Columbia University, New York, United States of America.
Contact: virginia.capriotti@unibg.it

# Historical Perspectives on the vocational education and training systems at the national and local level

EVELINA SCAGLIA

**Abstract:** The following contribution aims at reconstructing the historical roots of the conflict between the local and national levels in the vocational education and training system in Italy, which can be attributed to the changes in the school system outlined in Law 3725 of 13 November 1859 (known as the 'Casati Law') and have persisted since unification. Despite a few relatively insignificant changes, the system remained the same until 1962, when the first single middle school for 11- to 14-year-old pupils was introduced. At the local level, as in Lombardy, there are meaningful examples of institutions, such as the Pious Evening School in Bergamo Upper City and the Royal Technical Institute, that suffered from the uncertainties and difficulties associated with the hierarchical and centralist system of the Casati Law.

**Keywords:** 19th Century; History of Vocational Education and Training; Italian School System; School Dualism.

## 1 Invincible dualism

The Italian school system, as shaped by the Casati Law (1859), was characterised by its subdivision into three orders of studies (elementary, secondary and higher), which were structured in a hierarchical relationship with each other, due to the elitist and selective nature of secondary and, even more so, higher education. At this time, the law did not mention the vocational education and training (VET) schools provided by various local entities (e. g. religious bodies, professional associations, and private companies), which for decades had been operating in the central-northern areas for a heterogeneous population aged ten and over. Despite their strategic function for the economy of the newly-born Kingdom of Italy – a country characterised by the co-existence of under-development and growth, with a strong disparity between north and south, alongside high illiteracy rates – the VET schools were excluded from the national school system. This is because they were not considered proper schools due to their 'utilitarian' function of training for craft or industrial trades (Bonafede & Causarano, 2019, pp. 219–254).

A school system that was mainly concerned with the advanced education of the *elite* could not have guaranteed the foundations of generalised economic progress, which required the propulsive power of popular education, as evident in some areas of

Northern Italy, such as Lombardy, in the first decades of the 19th century. During this period, nascent industrialisation had found a valid ally in the early literacy offered by festive parochial elementary schools and in the special training provided by technical-professional schools. Only later, as economic development consolidated and expanded, did secondary and higher education become decisive for the growth of Italy (Zamagni, 1990, pp. 250–251).

The poor response of the Casati Law to addressing the educational needs of the working class reflected a strategic orientation toward 'popularising' elitist culture among the masses. It was also closely linked to the centralising principle of public education (Talamo, 1960, pp. 14–16). This choice, in the face of the heterogeneity of the political, economic, and scholastic systems in the pre-unitary states, accentuated the existing disparities, rather than seeking to reduce or even them out. The resistance that arose at the local level against King Savoia's intervention, worsened by the 'differences of regime and political feeling between the various parts of Italy', contributed to repressing any possible impulse for renewal (Castronovo, 2006, p. 4). The liberals in power were convinced that only a school, conceived as an 'apparatus' invested with a 'public and civil function', could justify a direct intervention of the state in promoting a particular field, namely that of education, which until then had been subject to a monopoly of the clergy, religious congregations, and local entities in the various territories (Morandini, 2001, pp. 9–10; Bertagna, 2008, pp. 25–26).

The public school, like the army, was conceived as an institution devoted first and foremost to realising the 'Italianisation' of the country (i. e. the construction of the linguistic, cultural, and value-based unity that was still lacking after 1861). From here, it was only a short step away to transforming the school into a device for the 'reproduction' of social inequalities. This was demonstrated by the oscillation between the primacy of the principle of selection and that of socialisation in the exercise of the scholastic function, which was particularly evident in the sphere of education for the 10- to 14-year-old age group, which saw the prioritisation of the classics, accorded to humanistic studies, remain unchallenged (Barbagli, 1974, pp. 18–21). Nothing could be further from a spirit of elevating the 'humble labours of the workshop' to a new civil dignity and freeing the workers from the subordinate conditions of their despised manual work. The latter objective was reflected in the animated demands of the Risorgimento debate, thanks to men such as Carlo Cattaneo, one of the staunchest supporters of simultaneous scientific, technological, and economic development (Lacaita, 1973, pp. 17–18). These recommendations were repeatedly expressed in Parliament by one of the 'founding fathers' of the united Italy, Camillo Benso, Earl of Cavour, who supported the promotion of popular and professional education to build a national education system in agreement, and not disagreement, with the needs of civil society.

In this way, the Casati Law showed its 'Achilles heel' – namely, its failure to overcome the opposition between liberal and scientific culture, on the one hand, and manual activity and instrumental knowledge on the other. Behind it, there was a twofold tendency, which was even stronger in the post-elementary schools, to consider school as a device for the selection, and not the promotion, of each single pupil, while the adjective 'public' continued to be interpreted as a synonym for the 'state' (Bertagna, 2008, pp. 5–19). This explains why, although the previous Boncompagni Law (1848) provided for a channel of 'special' (VET) schools alongside the secondary schools, Article 272 of the Casati Law considered the newly established technical school to be an integral part of the elementary order, and thus culturally inferior, despite its task of 'giving young people who intend to devote themselves to certain careers in public service, industry, commerce and the conduct of agrarian affairs, the appropriate general and special culture' (Art. 272, Casati Law). Also, as part of this operation, the pre-existing constellation of practical and VET schools (e. g. in the commercial, industrial, agricultural, and nautical fields) was placed under the direct control of the Ministry of Agriculture, Industry, and Commerce according to Article 308 of the Casati Law, as they were considered residual schools not worthy of recognition in their formative role, but only for the provision of an utilitarian and empirical application of technical-practical knowledge. Nevertheless, as illustrated by Mario Alighiero Manacorda, many of these schools were the embodiment of the ideals expressed by the Mutual Aid Societies, as afforded by the Albertine Statute in 1848 (Manacorda, 1992, p. 202), to prepare skilled workers. This is not to mention the schools founded by religious orders, such as the Lasallians and the Salesians, which were considered institutions of the 'ignorant' in the hands of the clergy and thus excluded from any form of recognition by the public school system.

Through these choices, the Italian ruling class exhibited their lack of a 'vision of the country's real needs, tendencies and aptitudes', which led to the spread in public opinion of the prejudice that the 'VET schools' were merely 'simple charitable conservatories of assistance for children less privileged by fortune' and thereby left to the 'goodwill of private individuals, charitable works and local administrations', as they were not worthy of state intervention (Castelli, 1915, p. 41). The same discourse could also be extended to apprenticeships, which were common experiences for many children and young people from the lower classes, who were often forced to skip compulsory education for an early start in the workplace. Apprenticeships were promoted in traditional settings (e. g. artisan workshops and merchant stalls) and industrial environments (e. g. factories and spinning mills), as well as in pious works, orphanages, and houses of correction, through forms of learning the trade by imitation on the job. In the first post-unification years, about 13,329 pupils were involved in apprenticeships. In the following decades, the Salesians, the Giuseppini, the Pavonians, the Artigianelli, and the Brothers of the Christian Schools stood out for enriching these learning experiences by systematically offering adequate tools and knowledge to cope with the needs of the new capitalist industrial context. These approaches reflected the cultural sensitivities that were to flow into Pope Leo XIII's encyclical *Rerum Novarum* of 1891, which was issued in response to the spread of secular and materialist ideologies of socialist inspiration among the working masses (Lacaita, 1973, pp. 72–73).

Behind the conditions of 'indeterminacy' and 'silence' in which these formative opportunities for Italian preadolescents emerged, thanks to the Casati Law, it is possible to discern the 'elitist and hierarchical' inspiration of the entire Italian liberal (moderate and radical) world. Italy at this time was affected by a sort of 'social classism' that also had among its effects an 'aristocratisation' of much of the bourgeoisie, who were ready to swell the ranks of the privileged few who had access to high school in the name of an assumed principle of 'social distinction' (Bourdieu & Passeron, 1972; Bertagna, 2013, pp. 62–63). Hence, the tendency emerged to use the term *zavorra* (ballast) to define all those young people – coming from the petite bourgeoisie and artisan classes – who were enrolled by their parents in grammar or technical school under the 'incautious aspiration' to climb the social ladder and reach future job positions in public administration. It was feared that this would turn the grammar school into a passepartout school, and the technical school into a general culture school with modest professional aims.

The 'inadequacy' with which the Casati Law tackled the problem of Italian VET can, at this point, be interpreted as a symptom of the 'incompleteness' of the bourgeois revolution in Italy and the 'impossibility' on the part of the school system to govern the tumultuous emergence of the popular classes on its own. Paradoxically, however, it represented the 'best coefficient' capable of prolonging the existing conditions, thereby initiating a condition of permanent reformism due to the 'inability' of the law itself to respond to the modernisation of Italian society in the central and northern regions. The Italian school system did not have up-to-date cultural tools capable of creating a real connection between education and the extension of its practical usefulness. The various attempts at change, often announced but almost never realised, went hand in hand with the difficulty of conceiving of 'less rigid and more open forms of schooling', but also with the refusal to make the most of what had already been done by non-state initiatives in terms of early literacy and professional training for workers; these latter forms of education were indispensable for breaking the vicious circle between unemployment/underemployment and the social and cultural lag of the country (Gonella, 1981, pp. 74–100).

The statistics were clear: the 1871 census, conducted ten years after the proclamation of the unification of Italy, still reported a worrying illiteracy rate of 72.96 % of both sexes among the population, with some negative peaks, especially in the most 'remote' regions of the South, such as Calabria and Lucania. The rate recorded after the first census in December 1861 had been 78 %, while in 1863, the schooling rate of the Italian population aged between 6 and 12 was 43 %, with a wide disparity between the 83 % recorded in Lombardy and the 14 % in Sicily (Vigo, 1971, p. 74). The fact that the Lombardy territories of the former Lombard-Venetian Kingdom had a higher literacy rate than other areas of Italy should be interpreted in light of what has already been stated above regarding the enduring presence of a network of parochial schools encouraged by Habsburg legislation and technical-professional schools for the training of workers – a heritage that the Casati Law was unable to exploit and extend to other regions.

Against this background, Dina Bertoni Jovine, a well-known communist scholar, did not hesitate to recognise that,

> "There was fear, in 1859, of accepting the lesson that came from Cattaneo, from Sacchi, from De Sanctis, there was fear of modern science and technology, fear of breaking away from the schemes of the Jesuit school, mistrust of the educated peasant who had been removed from superstition and submission, even if all these qualms ended up consecrat-

ing, at a time when the most serious national problems should have been set exactly, with the mind turned to the future, such a delayed pace of progress as to give the impression of stasis." (Bertoni Jovine, 1959, p. 117)

## 2 Bergamo at the 'dawn' of Italian unity

In the context of regional imbalances and the wider gap between North and South at the dawn of Italian unification, the city of Bergamo – located in the Lombardy region – represented an interesting case study. This is because it was characterised by an incipient process of industrialisation, favoured by the early introduction of textile machinery and a climate that prioritised the modernisation of economic and social relations, the roots of which were to be found decades earlier. An increasing number of entrepreneurs were particularly inclined to hire literate workers, who were considered better able to master 'the most elementary factory services' (Belotti, 1959; Fumi, 1997, p. 319).

The specificity of the local context shows how in a country such as Italy, still 'poised between backwardness and development', the presence of economic, social, and intellectual groups committed to changing the foundations of public life was able to make a difference in terms of exercising a propulsive drive for innovation (Castronovo, 2006, p. 4). Among the region's strengths, there was the fact that in Bergamo Province – despite the presence of a predominantly mountainous territory – there had been a significant diversification of production, with intensive agriculture (especially silkworms) emerging in the plains at the south of Bergamo, the industrial production of textiles taking place in the Seriana and Brembana valleys, and metalworking having developed along the course of the Brembo River. While there were several entrepreneurs from German-speaking Switzerland who had contributed to setting up the first cotton mills (i. e. the Honegger family in Albino and the Legler family in Ponte S. Pietro-Brembate Sopra), it should be noted that the number of small and medium-sized entrepreneurs of indigenous origin grew steadily around the time of the unification of Italy, thereby demonstrating how the process of industrialisation was taking root in a capillary manner (Fumi, 1997, p. 347).

In addition to these factors, a widespread popular form of education played a significant role in fostering overall economic growth in the Bergamo area, thanks to the effective work carried out since the times of the Austro-Hungarian dominion by the festive elementary schools opened in the parishes. These schools were an investment of the scholastic reform that took place in the Theresius-Joseph Era, with the fundamental task of promoting the literacy of the people. This confirms what Vera Zamagni emphasised about the propulsive role of elementary education in the early stages of economic development (Zamagni, 1990, pp. 250–251). Now, however, Bergamo was moving towards a new phase of consolidating this development, due in large part to the opening of new production sectors (e. g. cement, artificial fertilisers, flour, etc.) and the sedimentation of an attentive awareness to the spread of technology, capitalist development, and, consequently, the promotion of an education that went beyond the elementary level (Vigo, 1971, p. 3).

One of the liveliest examples of a fruitful interaction between the transformation of productive structures and a broader cultural shift was the Società Industriale Bergamasca (Bergamo Industrial Society), which as early as 1859 had launched an evening school for drawing and the plastic arts open to workers, and from 1860 had added evening literacy courses for men, who mainly included farmers, vegetable growers, carpenters, bricklayers, and blacksmiths. At the local level, there were also other initiatives, such as the Drawing School at the Academy of Fine Arts, called 'Giacomo Carrara', in Bergamo and the Pious Evening School at the Seminarino in Bergamo's upper city, already active for decades, which were supplemented with linguistic, civil, and technical literacy courses for adults of both genders due to the commitment of the Catholic movement to improving rural areas (Valota, 1983; Fumi, 1997, p. 347). What should be emphasised is the emergence of an increasingly urgent need to initiate a process of systematising the technical and professional training of workers on the basis of the valorisation of 'manual knowledge'.

## 2.1 The Pious Evening School in Bergamo upper city

The Pious Evening School in Bergamo upper city was born in 1796 as part of the broader process of launching new experiences in the field of youth pastoral work, which was undertaken a few years earlier by the archpriest of Bergamo's cathedral, Luigi Mozzi, a former Jesuit priest. Father Mozzi was one of the many priests who, embodying the post-Tridentine model, placed assistance and education activities aimed at the poorest population at the centre of his apostolate, with peculiar attention being directed to youth education, along with a new sensitivity to social challenges (Bassi, 1823; Altini, 1884; Zanchi, 1988, p. 196). The school, which aimed at providing young male workers with a first exposure to linguistic and technical literacy, was suddenly closed in 1797, because of the proclamation of the Napoleonic Republic in the Bergamo area. It resumed its activities in 1814, on the initiative of two priests, Giuseppe Benaglio and Marco Celio dei Passi, when Bergamo had by then come under Habsburg rule. Both priests belonged to the Apostolic College of Bergamo and wanted to follow the original project of Father Luigi Mozzi. In their view, they knew best how to interpret the new role of the priest in both the Church and society in Lombardy in the aftermath of the Restoration, which confirmed the reunification of the former Venetian and Habsburg lands of Lombardy (Valsecchi, 1869; Dentella, 1930).

The lessons started in 1814 in a makeshift room, while the following year, the school was moved to another location near the church of St. Matthew. It was only after 1845 that a permanent location was found at the Seminarino in Tassis Street, a 16th-century cloister that had long been the seat of the diocesan seminary. From 1853, the young priests of the Apostolic College settled at the Seminarino at the behest of Giuseppe Benaglio, who continued, from there, the apostolic work of preaching and assisting the youth. Giuseppe Benaglio was responsible for the selection and training of suitable personnel to run and manage the Pious Evening School, according to a model like that of the Christian doctrine schools: there was a prefect, responsible for the management of the entire institution, who was assisted by coadjutors and other volunteers who provided their services free of charge (Ghidini, 1848, pp. 10–12).

At that time, the school comprised seven sections, located in as many classrooms, in which "the young workers were instructed in reading, writing, arithmetic and letters", according to the provisions of Chapter I Article II of the *Compendio delle regole* (Compendium of Rules), which were in line with the original inspiration dictated by Father Luigi Mozzi in 1796 (Altini, 1884, p. 78). In the first six sections, the pupils were initiated into the acquisition of elementary culture, learning the rudiments of reading, writing, spelling, and mental and written arithmetic, while the seventh section, called the 'ornament and architecture' section – introduced a few years later than the others – was dedicated exclusively to learning drawing. The teachers and supervisors of the Pious Institute were recommended to study Joseph Peitl's *Insegnamenti di metodica* (Teachings of Method), in the Italian translation by Francesco Cherubini, as well as Jean-Baptiste De La Salle's *Guida delle Scuole Cristiane* (Guide to the Christian Schools). It has also been reported that "every semester there were examinations and merit awards for the best students, consisting of money or clothing" (Ghidini, 1848, p. 17).

The Pious Evening School was attended, on average, by 250 pupils who lived within the walls of Bergamo upper city, which at the time was inhabited by about 7,000 people, but exceptions were made for those who lived near the ancient doors of S. Lorenzo and S. Alessandro. The boys, all male, were between seven and 20 years old; many of them had never attended elementary school or had attended it only occasionally. During the first enrolment at school, the presence of one of their parents was formally required, as was the custom at the time; for enrolment in subsequent years, this obligation was waived. Most of the pupils were of humble origins, and almost all were already engaged in manual work during the day. For this reason, the Pious Institute opened its doors, under the supervision of a clergyman appointed for this purpose, when 'the public bell, one hour before evening, announces the end of the workday' (Ghidini, 1848, p. 20). The lessons began at dusk, and their duration varied according to the seasons; in winter, it was about two hours, and in summer less, because the workday was longer due to the greater number of daylight hours available. The school year began on November 21, the feast of the Presentation of the Blessed Virgin Mary in the Temple, and ended on June 30 (Ghidini, 1848, p. 128).

Once the lessons were over, the boys returned to their homes organised in squads, depending on the district or quarter from which they came. One of the main formative goals of the Pious Evening School was to safeguard the religious and moral conduct of the pupils, who were firmly recommended to attend the Marian congregation (if it existed in their own parish), parish mass services, and Christian doctrine on all festive days, even after the school year had ended. Moreover, the school tried to initiate a process of moral regeneration of families through the creation of a close interrelationship between school and family, in which the 'instructor' was a kind of second father for his pupils (Ghidini, 1848, pp. 40–41).

The Pious Evening School at the Seminarino experienced a brief interruption of activities between 1859 and 1863, coinciding with the Second Italian War of Independence and the ensuing political upheavals that led to the unification of the Italian peninsula. When it reopened its doors, the school had to come to terms with a number of changes that had taken place in the meantime, including the affirmation of the compulsory lower course of elementary schools for all children from six to eight years of age (under the Casati Law of 1859, which extended to the entire Kingdom of Italy) and the spread of the three-year royal technical schools, which had been set up as lower courses for access to technical institutes.

In that new historical and cultural context, its task as a popular school aimed at providing elementary education disappeared; it was left only as an evening drawing school 'with post-elementary intentions'. Therefore, only the old 'ornament and architecture' section continued to function, which was itself threatened by competition from other technical and professional training institutions that had sprung up in the meantime in the Bergamo area (Agazzi, 1989, p. 32).

## 2.2 First uncertain 'steps' of Bergamo's Royal Technical Institute

In 1860, Bergamo reached 44,765 inhabitants, out of a population of 357,220 in its province, thereby deserving recognition as a 'centre of significant industrial and commercial activity'. This designation made it suitable for the establishment of a Royal Technical Institute, as outlined by the conditions set forth in Articles 283 and 284 of the Casati Law. The proposal to open this kind of institute, 'at the mixed expense' of the local authorities and the state (with the possible contribution of the Royal Treasury up to half the amount of the teachers' salaries), was put forward thanks to the interest of the Provincial Council of Schools, the Chamber of Commerce and Industry, and the Municipal Representation (Zambetti, n. d., p. 4).

The control of the Royal Technical Institutes had passed, in the meantime, from the Ministry of Public Education to the Ministry of Agriculture, Industry, and Commerce (MAIC), entrusted under Royal Decree 347 of November 28, 1861, with the task of looking after institutions designed to increase agriculture and industry. Consequently, such a move opened up a rift of competition between the two ministries. It was therefore the MAIC that sent to Bergamo, with a dispatch dated June 30, 1862, the order and the programme of studies of the new institute, which included the administrative-commercial, physical-mathematical, and chemical sections, and not the agronomic section that was the subject of ministerial studies for improvement. After the inauguration took place on December 9, 1862 at the premises in the municipal building of the New Magistrate's Court in Bergamo lower city, the regular start was held the following January 23. The 16 'spacious, comfortable, and airy' rooms were attended in the first year by 41 students, of whom only 17 were full students, while four were paying auditors, and 20 were free auditors. Nine teachers delivered a total of 529 lessons (Zambetti, n. d., p. 5).

The users' area was potentially large, especially considering that this was the first Royal Technical Institute in the entire Province of Bergamo, in the territory of which as many as nine lower secondary technical schools were located, respectively, in Bergamo, Lovere, Treviglio, Martinengo, Clusone, and Celana in Caprino Bergamasco (Fumi, 1997, p. 347). In this context, it is interesting to see how the Royal Technical Institute exemplified the expression of genuine stakeholder activism from the local economic, industrial, and commercial world, with these stakeholders being particularly attentive to the modernisation and development of education in the technical-professional field, while the state was perceived as distant from the real needs of the territory. In fact, as early as in the second school year, the need to revise the educational offerings began to be perceived, with the suggestion to make it more 'attractive', at least on paper. A proposal was made by headmaster Luigi Ottavio Ferrero – a member of the Italian Society of Natural Sciences – to the Provincial School Council of Bergamo on June 18, 1864 to open a high school course for the preparation of head-miners and head-masters to be employed in the local mining and forestry industry (Scaglia, 2019, p. 109).

From the very first lines of his report, Ferrero warned his interlocutors of the difficulties encountered thus far in managing technical education within the complex interplay between the centre and periphery of the Italian state. Ferrero agreed to propose a reduction of the sections of the Royal Institute of Bergamo down to two, which included the administrative-commercial and the industrial-agronomic ones, the latter of which were organised in such a way that young people could, in their third year, also be introduced to university studies, as was already the case for the physical-mathematical and chemical sections. The real novelty was the opening of a higher course in mining and metallurgical studies, lasting two years and accessible only to those who had graduated from the industrial agronomy section and were destined to train miners and workshop managers. This would have represented an asset to the Bergamo Institute, which aimed at training 'intelligent chiefs' in guiding the excavation of minerals and ancillary operations within the mines, and workshop chiefs called upon to manage the plant of mechanical and metallurgical companies (Ferrero, 1864, pp. 3–4). For Ferrero, the 'inertia' and 'inability to manage' mining and industrial enterprises on the part of local technicians and engineers, still in many cases overcome by foreign personnel, could no longer be tolerated. Only a cultural project, such as the one he hoped for, would have ensured the preparation of professional figures who could serve as intermediaries between the 'man of concept' and the 'labourer'; these professionals would be capable of knowing 'practically' how to work and, at the same time, be in possession of a greater knowledge, as they themselves were the "bearers of a medium position between science and applied force" (Ferrero, 1864, pp. 78). Equipped in this way, they would be able to undermine the predominance of 'empiricism' in most local industries, which very rarely saw internally trained workers at the helm, and also combat the "sinister prejudice against the social inferiority of the worker by bringing science closer to work" (Ministero di Agricoltura, Industria e Commercio, 1875, pp. XIX–XX).

Despite their broad articulation, Ferrero's proposals were only partially accepted by the MAIC, since in the meantime, at the national level, the Royal Technical Institutes had undergone significant changes in their organisation and programme, in connection with their transformation from 'provincial governmental technical institutes' to 'royal special VET schools'; there were now 26 possible specialisations, pursuant to the Royal Decree of August 13, 1864 (Lacaita, 2009, p. 14).

The Bergamo Institute was thus transformed into a Royal Special Institute of Mineralogy and Industrial Metallurgy. The Provincial Deputation immediately intervened to issue a proposal of intermediation to the MAIC with respect to the established order, which concerned the possibility of also annexing a section of Accounting and Commerce to the Technical Institute, given the needs expressed in this regard by the local territory. The MAIC did not accept this, believing that a course of studies 'so disparate', or at any rate, 'not very homogeneous', could not be combined with a mining-metallurgical institute. The deputation did not give up, since under the same Royal Decree of August 13, 1864, it was allowed to make a request to have the technical institute's teachers work, duly paid, for other public courses designed for free learners. Thanks to this 'loophole', it was possible to open a Provincial Section of Accounting and Commerce, separate from the Royal Special Institute of Mineralogy and Industrial Metallurgy, but animated by its own teachers. Despite the regular start of classes, the MAIC did not recognise scholastic equalisation, so the new course of studies faced a challenging start due to the lack of a definitive set-up of the Institute (authorless, 1909, p. 5).

All those decisions showed a clear subordination – also in terms of economic investments – of the deliberations undertaken by the peripheral body to the directives coming from the centre. The course of studies offered by the Royal Technical Institute demonstrated its struggle to integrate itself within a socio-economic context that saw a fervent interest in technical education, almost entirely satisfied, however, by a constellation of training initiatives that could not be assimilated to the technical school-technical institute chain outlined by the Casati Law.

Two years after the start of the new system, the number of enrolments mirrored its difficulties: at the Royal Special Institute of Industrial Mineralogy and Metallurgy, there were four students, while at the Provincial Section of Accounting and Commerce, there were 16. What explains these low enrolment numbers? One of the plausible hypotheses concerned the lack of attractiveness of a 'high' technical-professional profile, such as that of a mining expert, accessible after completing studies in the industrial agronomy section, when most of the native labour force employed in the mines was still made up of simple workers, poorly paid and employed under unhealthy working conditions (there were numerous deaths due to silicosis in the Bergamo area in those decades; Scaglia, 2019, p. 113).

At this point, the Provincial Deputation felt that the project to open a certified School of Accounting, Administration, and Commerce could no longer be postponed, given the commercial and industrial nature of the local territory. The initiative obtained the support of the Municipality of Bergamo, the Provincial Council of Schools, the Institute's Teachers' Council, and the newly established local Board of Supervision, so much so that it was formally presented to the MAIC in September 1866, given the urgency of safeguarding the future fate of the institute (Tonelli, 1964, p. 23). This time, a favourable opinion was received from Rome, with the MAIC sending a note on the following November 3, containing the study plan for the new section. According to the Royal Decree of November 4, 1866, which provided for a balance between preparation for a wide range of professions and the provision of common fundamentals for all specialisations, the school took on the new name of the Royal Industrial and Professional Institute, with sections for mineralogy and metallurgy, as well as administration, commerce, and accounting. The cooperation of the local authorities and teaching staff proved indispensable in achieving the desired change, although once again, it was not enough. The enrolment of only five students in the entire three-year study period in the mineralogy and metallurgy section was a clear sign of a dilemma (authorless, 1909, p. 8).

Given the rather complicated situation, the ministry delegated Francesco Brioschi, one of the greatest exponents of 19th-century technical culture in Italy, Senator of the Kingdom, and member of the *Consiglio Superiore sopra l'Istruzione Industriale e Professionale* (Superior Council on Industrial and Vocational Education), to 'concretise' the desired reform (Lacaita & Fugazza, 2013, pp. 157–173). After all the necessary bureaucratic steps from the centre to the periphery, the new order was finally approved before the end of the calendar year and officially came into force with the Royal Decree of January 10, 1869. The solution identified by Brioschi was to immediately suppress the section of mineralogy and metallurgy and replace it with that of construction and mechanics, in the hope that the introduction of the professional profile of mechanical and construction experts would be the ideal choice to 'launch' the Bergamo Institute. The administration, commerce, and accounting section was retained, with slight modifications (Scaglia, 2019, p. 115).

Even in the latter case, the novelty introduced at the local level was short-lived due to the changes made to Royal Technical Institutes at the national level in terms of their organisation and culture, a sign of the difficulty for technical education in finding its own identity a decade after the implementation of the Casati Law in Italy. With the Royal Decree of March 30, 1872, and as a result of the reform project initiated by Minister Minghetti in August 1871, a sort of 'return to the past' was sanctioned. The increase in the length of studies to four years, with two years of general education of a propaedeutic nature followed by two years of special studies, did not help bridge the gap between school culture and work culture. On the contrary, it accentuated it, due to the hierarchisation created within the same Royal Technical Institutes between the physical-mathematical section (the only one open to higher education) and the sections for commerce, agronomy, mechanics, and construction (with no ladders to higher education; Tonelli, 1964, pp. 25–26).

Following the Minghetti reform, the Royal Technical Institutes in Italy found a more stable structure. After being moved to the Bergamo upper city in an old building overlooking the central place, formerly the town hall, the Bergamo Royal Technical Institute was dedicated in 1878 to the late King Victor Emmanuel II. Its definitive 'launch' took place in the 1885/1886 school year with the opening of the industrial section, thanks to which it gradually managed to gain a prominent role in the training of technicians to be employed in industries not only locally, but also regionally and nationally (Scaglia, 2019, p. 116).

Once again, the proposal was put forward by the periphery, starting from the Institute's local supervisory board and headmaster, Ottorino Luxardo, in December 1884, which suggested opening such a section as part of a broader project of interlinking the world of school and the world of work. Particularly shrewd was the decision to create a fruitful collaboration with the Bergamo Industrial Society; this would entail that the new section of the institute be annexed to the technical and professional training courses for workers that had been offered for some time, with both being realised on the same premises and taking advantage of more extensive teaching material. The purchase by the Bergamo Industrial Society of Buildings (formerly the Zuppinger cotton mill), located in Pradello Street in Bergamo lower city, with free use granted to the industrial section of the technical institute, sanctioned the definitive convergence of all "the forces from which the industrial life of the city was expressed to a single end, uniting the initiatives in a new school body designed to address the diverse need of the community" (authorless, 1909, p. 16).

Behind this synergetic understanding lies the conviction that "industrial education succeeds whenever, between real industry and the school founded for it, there is an intimate bond, a continuous exchange of ideas, desires and favours" (Scaglia, 2019, p. 117). Such a condition is indispensable for building the foundations of a professionalism based on a close circularity of theory and practice, which is itself capable of overcoming the dichotomy between general and specific skills and competences. The strong attendance numbers in the following years and the awards obtained by the Royal Technical Institute in the *fin de siècle* transition testified to the effectiveness of this choice.

## 3 Summary and outlook

It is worth concluding this contribution with the words of Dario Turri, a cotton entrepreneur who served as the president of the Royal Technical Institute's Supervisory Board in 1906. During the reorganisation of Italian VET into schools of arts and crafts initiated by Minister Francesco Cocco Ortu, Turri expressed his support for a model of a 'workshop school or school of things'. His intent was to refer to the experiences of Krefeld, Lyon, Zurich, and Vienna, but above all to the German *Gewerbeschule*, which was very similar to the school opened by the *Società di incoraggiamento d'arti e mestieri* (Society of Encouragement for Arts and Crafts) in Milan, with the hope of one day being able to open schools "to all classes of citizens, that is, to all intelligences and to all courageous vocations" (Turri, 1906, pp. 13–14). This is because the Casati Law had not been able to respond to the needs of the working people and the demands of industry due to a state-type conception of public education that did not respect and promote local autonomies.

Both the experiences of the Pious Evening School in Bergamo upper city and the Royal Technical Institute in Bergamo have demonstrated Lombardy's pioneering role in Italian vocational education and professional training since the 19th century, a role it still holds today (as highlighted in Francesco Magni and Virginia Capriotti's contribution in this volume). Furthermore, the region has served as a laboratory for innovation and future perspectives on the VET system, as explained in Giada Ragone's paper in the same volume.

## References

Agazzi, C. (1989). *Ogni bene. Scritti minimi di don Carlo Agazzi da "Il Seminarino" 1933–1964, notiziario periodico dell'oratorio interparrocchiale di Bergamo Alta.* Litostampa Istituto Grafico.

Altini, F. (1884). *Vita del p. Luigi Mozzi d. C. d.G. già arciprete della Cattedrale di Bergamo descritta dal p. Francesco Altini della medesima compagnia.* Tipografia S. Alessandro.

Authorless. (1909). *Cenni storici sull'ordinamento del Regio Istituto Tecnico V. E. II dalla sua fondazione ad oggi, con la Statistica dei licenziati dalla Sezione Industriale e dalla Annessa Scuola Biennale di Meccanica, Filatura, Tessitura fino a tutto l'anno scolastico 1906–07.* Mariani.

Barbagli, M. (1974). *Disoccupazione intellettuale e sistema scolastico in Italia.* Il Mulino.

Bassi, G. (1823). *Vita del padre Luigi Mozzi della Compagnia di Gesù.* Miglio.

Belotti, B. (1959). *Storia di Bergamo e dei bergamaschi. Vol. VI.* Bolis.

Bertagna, G. (2008). *Autonomia. Storia, bilancio e rilancio di un'idea.* La Scuola.

Bertagna, G. (2013). L'istruzione tecnica e la formazione professionale. In M. Bocci (Ed.), *Non lamento ma azione. I cattolici e lo sviluppo italiano nei 150 anni di storia unitaria* (pp. 59–92). Vita e Pensiero.

Bertoni Jovine, D. (1959). La legge Casati nella critica contemporanea. *I problemi della pedagogia*, 1, 77–117.

Bonafede, P., & Causarano, P. (2019). Istruzione tecnica e formazione professionale. In F. De Giorgi, A. Gaudio, & F. Pruneri (Eds.), *Manuale di storia della scuola italiana. Dal Risorgimento al XXI secolo* (pp. 219–254). Scholé.

Bourdieu, P., & Passeron, J.-C. (1972). *La riproduzione: teoria del sistema scolastico ovvero della conservazione dell'ordine culturale.* Guaraldi.

Castelli, G. (1915). *L'istruzione professionale in Italia.* Vallardi.

Castronovo, V. (2006). *Storia economica d'Italia. Dall'Ottocento ai giorni nostri.* Einaudi.

Dentella, L. (1930). *Il conte canonico G. Benaglio e un secolo di storia ecclesiastica bergamasca.* Secomandi.

Ferrero, L. O. (1864). *Modificazioni ed amplificazioni al piano degli studi tecnici locali. Relazione presentata al Consiglio scolastico provinciale dal prof. Luigi Ottavio Ferrero, preside dell'Istituto Tecnico di Bergamo con osservazioni in merito dell'ingegnere delle miniere del Distretto di Milano Cavaliere Axerio.* Bolis.

Fumi, G. (1997). L'istruzione professionale e tecnica dall'Unità al primo conflitto mondiale. In V. Zamagni & S. Zaninelli (Eds.), *Storia economica e sociale di Bergamo. Fra Ottocento e Novecento. Lo sviluppo dei servizi* (Vol. 5, Issue 3, pp. 319–391). Bolis.

Ghidini, A. (1848). *Dell'origine, della costituzione e dello spirito della scuola serale di carità pei giovani artisti della città alta in Bergamo. Discorso intitolato all'egregio signor conte Clemente Giacomo Suardo, cavaliere degli ordini de' Santi Maurizio e Lazzaro e di Santo Stefano di Toscana, letto in adunanza generale degli operarii e dei protettori del Pio Istituto, aggiuntevi note, pezze giustificative e formole di cancelleria.* Wilmant e figli.

Gonella, G. (1981). Dalla legge Casati alla Costituzione democratica. In G. Gonella, *Cinque anni al Ministero della Pubblica Istruzione. La rinascita della Scuola dopo la seconda guerra mondiale* (Vol. 1, pp. 74–100). Giuffré.
Lacaita, C. G. (1973). *Istruzione e sviluppo industriale in Italia 1859–1914.* Giunti-Barbera.
Lacaita, C. G. (2009). Istruzione tecnico-professionale e modernizzazione fra Otto e Novecento. In C. G. Lacaita (Ed.), *La leva della conoscenza. Istruzione e formazione professionale in Lombardia fra Otto e Novecento* (pp. 9–19). Giampiero Casagrande Editore.
Lacaita, C. G., & Fugazza, M. (Eds.), (2013). *L'istruzione secondaria nell'Italia unita 1861–1911.* FrancoAngeli.
Manacorda, M. A. (1992). *Storia illustrata dell'educazione. Dall'Antico Egitto ai giorni nostri.* Giunti.
Ministero di Agricoltura, Industria e Commercio. (1875). *L'istruzione tecnica in Italia, studi di E. Morpurgo.* Barbera.
Morandini, M. C. (2001). Da Boncompagni a Casati: la costruzione del sistema scolastico nazionale (1848–1861). In L. Pazzaglia & R. Sani (Eds.), *Scuola e società nell'Italia Unita. Dalla Legge Casati al Centro Sinistra* (pp. 9–46). La Scuola.
Scaglia, E. (2019). Il caso del Regio Istituto Tecnico di Bergamo nel primo quindicennio unitario. *Annali di storia dell'educazione e delle istituzioni scolastiche,* 26, 103–117.
Talamo, G. (1960). *La scuola dalla legge Casati alla Inchiesta del 1864.* Giuffré.
Tonelli, A. (1964). *L'istruzione tecnica e professionale di stato nelle strutture e nei programmi da Casati ai giorni nostri.* Giuffré.
Turri, D. (1906). *La scuola industriale di Bergamo. Proposte e programmi, dicembre 1906.* Bolis.
Valota, B. (1983). "L'istruzione tenuta nei giusti limiti…". La Società industriale bergamasca e le scuole popolari. *Studi e ricerche di storia contemporanea,* 20, 40–62.
Valsecchi, A. (1869). *Teresa Eustochio nobile Verzeri e Mons. Giuseppe conte Benaglio fondatori dell'Istituto delle Figlie del Sacro Cuore.* Sonzogni.
Vigo, G. (1971). *Istruzione e sviluppo economico in Italia nel secolo XIX.* UTET.
Zamagni, V. (1990). *Dalla periferia al centro. La seconda rinascita economica dell'Italia (1861–1990).* Il Mulino.
Zambetti, A. (n. d.). *Regio Istituto Tecnico Commerciale "Vittorio Emanuele II".* Stamperia Conti S. A.
Zanchi, G. (1988). L'età post-tridentina e il consolidarsi della tradizione bergamasca. In A. Caprioli, A. Rimoldi, & L. Vaccaro (Eds.), *Diocesi di Bergamo* (pp. 181–196). La Scuola.

## Short portrait of the author

**Evelina Scaglia** is Associate Professor in the History of Education at the Department of Human and Social Sciences, University of Bergamo, Italy. Her main research interests lie in the history of teacher training and the history of early childhood education.
Contact: evelina.scaglia@unibg.it

# Lombardy as a laboratory for innovations in vocational education and training: A constitutional perspective

Giada Ragone

**Abstract:** After the reform of Italian regionalism in 2001, vocational education and training (VET) was formally assigned to single regions. The first part of this chapter traces the issues and consequences related to VET that flowed from this reform, focusing on the well-known Law No. 53 of 2003 and on constitutional case law. The Italian Constitutional Court played a pivotal role in reframing Italian regionalism, reinterpreting the allocation of the legislative competences contained in Art. 117 of the Constitution in favour of the State; to some extent, this also happened in the case of VET. The question is whether there was truly room for regional innovation in VET. The second part of the chapter seeks to answer this by examining Lombardy's regulatory interventions in VET. This case illustrates how regional innovation and experimentation are essential for the broader implementation of constitutional rights, such as the right to vocational education.

**Keywords**: Duty to Education; Italian Regionalism; Right to Education; Vocational Education and Training in Lombardy.

## 1 Professional and vocational training within the Italian Constitution

According to *Françoise Gravier v. City of Liège* of the Court of Justice EC, February 13, 1985, "Any form of education which prepares for a qualification for a particular profession, trade or employment or which provides the necessary training and skills for such a profession, trade or employment is vocational training, whatever the age and the level of training of the pupils or students, and even if the training programme includes an element of general education." Following this definition, the Italian educational programmes that can be considered part of vocational education and training (VET) are (1) upper secondary education programmes, including technical schools (*istituti tecnici*) and VET schools (*scuole di istruzione e formazione professionale*, IeFP), and (2) higher technical education programmes, such as higher technical education and training courses (*istruzione e formazione tecnica superiore*, IFTS)[1], and higher technical institute

1 Leading to certification of EQF Level IV.

programmes (*istituti tecnici superiori*, ITS)[2]. However, in Italy, the term VET is used only for IeFP, IFTS, and ITS programmes (regulated by the regions), and not for technical schools (regulated by the state). The social-democratic Constitution of 1948 grounds the duty of the Italian Republic to guarantee its citizens access to VET. The Charter promotes, among other fundamental social rights, the right/duty to education in Article 34 (Part 1, Title II, Ethical and Social Relations). The next article – collocated in Title III, Economic Relations – states that the Republic "shall provide for the training and advancement of workers" (Art. 35.2).

Even if, in theory, the Italian Republic is 'one and indivisible', it "acknowledges and promotes local self-governments, and shall implement the greatest degree of administrative decentralisation in services which depend on the State" (Art. 5 Const.) Consequently, the regulation and management of the VET system has, over time, been devolved to the regions, which is in line with the assumed importance of VET for the economic growth of territories.

In particular, after the reform of Italian regionalism occurred in 2001[3] the state and its regions now have 'concurring legislation'[4] on education, with the exception of VET, which falls under the exclusive legislative powers of the regions (Art. 117 Const.). Accordingly, the state has legislative power over the general rules of education and determines its fundamental principles of education[5]; it also establishes the essential levels of performance (LEP) with respect to the education to be performed by the regions. Regions must comply with the general rules, fundamental principles, and LEP when concurring to legislate on general education and with the LEP when exercising exclusive legislative competence over VET[6]. To complete the constitutional framework under Art. 116.3 Const., additional special forms and conditions of autonomy related to the area of education[7] may be attributed to regions by state law upon the initiative of the region concerned (Maci, 2023).

The overall design of the reform was intended to decentralise the Italian legislative system, especially with reference to subjects with a strong connection to local territories (such as VET). Nonetheless, within the last two decades, the Italian Constitutional Court has played a pivotal role in reframing Italian regionalism by interpreting the allocation of the legislative competences contained in Article 117 of the Constitution in favour of the state. To some extent, this also happened in the case of VET.

2 Leading to certification of EQF Level V.

3 Before the reform, the regions could enact legislation for 'craft and vocational education and school assistance' within the limits of the fundamental principles established by the laws of the state.

4 "Concurring competence [...] means a legislative competence owned both by the state and the regions, on which the former indicates the main principles and the latters provide an extensive and articulated text" (Salone, 2017, p. 47).

5 On the uncertain distinction between *general rules of education* and *fundamental principles of education*, see *ex multis* in Zanon (2003).

6 *Contra*: according to respected doctrine, regions should comply with *general rules of education* and *fundamental principles* of the subject even when exercising exclusive legislative competence over VET. See Cardone, 2013, p. 437; Marra, 2013, p. 1197.

7 The request for greater autonomy can concern both *general rules* on education (Art. 117.2 lett. n) – of exclusive state competence – and education, which falls under the 'concurring competence' between the state and the regions (117.3 Const.)

## 2 Vocational education and training between the state and the regions

In the implementation of the 2001 constitutional reform, State Law No. 53/2003 (*Riforma Moratti*) introduced the VET system into the second cycle of education as a path under regional jurisdiction, thereby replacing previous programmes of VET under state governance (Bertelli, 2012, p. 160). The same year, an agreement between the state and regions[8] allowed the regions to start local VET experimentation, beginning with the 2003/2004 school year[9]. Afterwards, between 2005 and 2007, the state adopted a series of acts[10] that completed the regulatory framework necessary for the establishment of regional VET systems.

The way forward for regional experiments on VET appeared thus paved, but the Constitutional Court limited the regions' room for manoeuvring within these boundaries by theorising a sort of state pre-emption on this subject (Cortese, 2010, p. 525), which established a privileged role for the state in regulating this matter. In particular, Judgement No. 200/2009 (Cortese, 2010; Troisi, 2010) realised a 'clipping' of areas of state power into matters of regional competence (Poggi, 2009, p. 4), which would ensure uniform educational offerings throughout the national territory and the country's cultural identity (par. 24). On the one hand, the ruling gave the regions the power to legislate on school network sizing (e. g. number of schools in the territory, mergers between different educational institutes, closures of schools, etc.); this subject, indeed, "has a direct and immediate impact on situations closely related to the different territorial realities and related socio-economic needs of each territory" (par. 38.1). On the other hand, however, it established that among the *general rules of education*, reserved for state legislative power, are rules on the planning of integrated learning offerings between general education and VET. Therefore, it is the duty of the state to regulate the possibility of switching from general education pathways to VET programmes and vice versa.

Afterwards, other constitutional rulings followed the same vein. For example, Constitutional Judgement No. 219/2009 struck down the law of the Autonomous Province of Bolzano[11] that regulated the transition from upper secondary VET programmes to higher education pathways. The Court considered this subject a *fundamental principle* of education to be ruled exclusively by the central state. Another ruling worth mentioning is Judgement No. 287/2012[12]. Here, the Court clarified that only the state can regulate the training and advancement of workers when provided by employers (and not by an educational organisation)[13]. In contrast to the case of *Françoise Gravier*, the

8 Agreement No. 660/C.U. of June 19, 2003.
9 Among the first regions that approved a regional law to exercise this legislative power is Emilia-Romagna (see Regional Law No. 12/2003).
10 See Legislative Decree No. 226/2005; Laws nn. 296/2006 and 40/2007.
11 Trento and Bolzano have the same legislative powers as regions.
12 The ruling effectively summarises some previous approaches of constitutional case law on the topic. See, for example, Judgement nn. 50/2005, 279/2005, 286/2006, 425/2006, 24/2007, 250/2009, and 176/2010.
13 Cardone (2013) provides an in-depth analysis of the judgement.

ruling stated that this kind of offering is not proper VET: being a training offering descending from labour contracts, it falls under the subject of a 'civil order', which is reserved by Art. 117 to state power. It is barely worth mentioning that – in the Court's interpretation – regions are also prevented from identifying new professional figures on their own, since this function falls under the subject of 'professions', which is of concurring legislative competence (see Constitutional Judgement No. 230/2011).

In summary, regions have exclusive legislation over VET, but they must comply with the state LEP. Moreover, the particular subject of 'VET' – reserved for regional jurisdiction – has been eroded over time by constitutional case law. This scenario leads to the question of whether there is really room for regional innovation in VET.

# 3 The case of Lombardy

Exercising its legislative competence in VET, Lombardy established its own educational system for VET through Regional Law No. 19/2007, which has been amended multiple times over the years[14]. The section below describes the main characteristics of this system, and the following section will focus on ITS and IFTS (i. e. the higher technical education programmes provided in Lombardy).

## 3.1 Relevant characteristics

The system in Lombardy provides a rich and innovative VET offering, which includes (1) three-year courses for fulfilling the constitutional right and duty to education for students who have completed middle school[15], (2) non-academic higher education pathways (ITS and IFTS), which lead to advanced technical specialisation[16], and (3) annual courses to prepare for academic education (Art. 11)[17].

Different types of training institutions are eligible to provide the listed services, including regional training centres, educational institutions transferred under regional control after the reform of Title V of the Constitution, and accredited private operators admitted into the special register established by the Lombardy region (Art. 24). The provision of both public and private institutions is in line with the principle of horizontal subsidiarity, advocated by Article 118.4 of the Constitution, and embodies the idea of a "welfare mix" (Violini & Cerlini, 2011, p. 45), which is designed to be closer to the needs of citizens. An important agreement between the state and Lombardy, reached on March 16, 2009, also allows state schools to offer regional VET programmes (Violini & Cerlini, 2011, p. 48).

Among the most relevant characteristics of the Lombardian VET system, three stand out. First, it is a dual system, wherein theoretical education and practical work go hand in hand. Pursuant to Article 23*bis*, VET services must ensure "a systematic, or-

14 See Regional Laws nn. 6/2008, 37/2008, 11/2010, 3/2011, 7/2012, 7/2015, 30/2015, 14/2016, 35/2016, 15/2017, 23/2018, and 16/2021.
15 Leading to certification of EQF Level III.
16 EQF Level IV in the case of *IFTS*, and Level V for *ITS*.
17 Leading to certification of EQF Level IV.

ganised, and continuous connection between education and work, recognising the value and role of micro-enterprises." The regional provisions for VET offerings indicate the time modulation between theoretical education and in-company training. The importance of the link between VET and territorial economic actors underpins the entire regional legislative framework. Setting out the principles and purposes of regional policies on VET, Article 2 clarifies that it is the duty of the region to promote the connection of the VET system with the relevant territorial and productive spheres. Lombardy recognises the value of territorial partnerships and supports the establishment of networks between the educational system and the economic system, which are aimed at creating sectoral supply chains for employability and employment. The law also provides for the involvement of social partners (e. g. labour unions and employer associations) in the development and evaluation of training policies (Art. 4) in order to monitor labour market developments, detect skill needs, and orient the training supply.

A second important feature of the Lombardian VET system is its connection to the European dimension. Article 1 of Regional Law No. 19/2007 declares that the VET system is geared towards integration into the European (as well as national and regional) world of work and social context. Accordingly, the region promotes access to information on education and training opportunities within the European Union (Art. 2). In addition, the certifications issued by regional training institutions are in line with the standards set by European law and by the European Qualifications Framework (EQF)[18], which was developed by the European Union to support the cross-border mobility of learners and workers and to promote lifelong learning and professional development across Europe. Lastly, one of the most innovative aspects of Lombardy's VET provision is its resort to the *Sistema Dote* (endowment system)[19]. *Dote*[20] refers to the financial support given by the region directly to individuals – and not to institutions – who intend to enter a VET programme. It is given *ex ante*, before families have incurred the costs[21], and provided in the form of a voucher. This instrument aims to ensure freedom of educational choice for all citizens and to strengthen the constitutional right and duty to education. Indeed, Art. 34.4 Const. states that the Republic shall make this right effective by means of grants and scholarships, allowances to families, and other benefits.

As Violini and Cerlini (2011) note:

> "The *'Dote'* has been experimented and implemented [in Lombardy...] within the education sector since 2000, a sector in which, thanks to the new powers assigned to the Regions by the reform of Title V of the Constitution, Lombardy has pursued a reform project aimed at creating [...] a kind of parity between public and private schools. Through the school voucher, in fact, the Region, by reimbursing the family for part of the school fees, has provided support for the educational demand of families oriented to use the educational services of non-state schools" (p. 47).

18 See Council Recommendation of May 22, 2017 on the European Qualifications Framework for lifelong learning and the repealing of the recommendation of the European Parliament and of the Council of April 23, 2008 on the establishment of the European Qualifications Framework for lifelong learning (2017/C 189/03).

19 See Violini and Cerlini, 2011, pp. 44–57; Canavesi, 2011, pp. 61 ff.

20 The 'dowry system' includes *Dote formazione*, *Dote istruzione*, and *Dote lavoro*.

21 Any person resident or domiciled in Lombardy, aged between 16 and 64, may apply for the *Dote*.

After several years of experimentation with the *Buono Scuola* (school voucher), Regional Law No. 19/2007 codified the *Dote* for the VET system[22], albeit with the significant exclusion of non-academic higher education paths (e. g. ITS and IFTS). Those who attend these kinds of courses are currently excluded from regional financial support.

## 3.2 Higher technical education programmes in Lombardy: ITS and IFTS

The Lombardian VET system also includes non-academic higher education pathways: ITS as higher technical institute programmes and IFTS as higher technical education and training courses. ITS consists of technological specialisation courses in areas considered priorities for the country's economic development, such as sustainable mobility, energy efficiency, innovative technologies for cultural heritage and activities/tourism, information and communication technologies, new technologies of life, and new technologies for 'Made in Italy', which are divided in turn into the agro-food system, mechanical system, fashion system, business services, and construction. ITS courses have been offered from 2010[23] and lead to qualifications of EQF Level V (*Diploma tecnico superiore*). The Ministry of Education funds ITS on the basis of its results and quality. To address this aim, evaluation is entrusted to the National Institute for Documentation, Innovation, and Educational Research (INDIRE), which conducts periodic monitoring of all the courses activated.

The Italian Recovery and Resilience Plan has reserved a portion of its Next Generation EU funds specifically for strengthening and increasing the number of ITS in Italy[24]. ITS are also funded by regions that have exclusive competence in establishing them and planning the courses to be offered[25].

ITS pathways are provided by *fondazioni di partecipazione* (participating foundations). These foundations are made up of enterprises, universities[26], research centres, local authorities, and educational and training institutions. Lombardy provides a very wide range of these: 20 of the approximately 100 foundations operating in Italy in 2022 belonged to the Lombardian VET system[27], which together offered a total of 36 different courses[28]. According to the last monitoring by INDIRE (*Istituto Nazionale Documentazione Innovazione Ricerca Educativa*), 65.3 % of Lombardian ITS courses were awarded a prize due to their positive results.

As for the IFTS, these training paths are designed to meet the specific skill demands coming from the labour market and lead to EQF Level IV qualifications (*specializzazione tecnica superiore*). According to Article 69 of Law 144/1999, which established

---

22 According to Canavesi (2011), *Dote* is an evolution of *Buono Scuola* (p. 61).

23 These courses were established by State Law No. 49/2007 and the Decree by the President of Ministers (DPCM) of January 25, 2008.

24 See Mission 4 (1.5) of the Italian Recovery and Resilience Plan (PNRR).

25 See the report entitled *Monitoraggio nazionale 2022. Istruzione terziaria professionalizzante* published by INDIRE and the Italian Ministry of Education: https://www.indire.it/wp-content/uploads/2022/05/Monitoraggio-nazionale-2022.-Rapporto_originale.pdf

26 On the role of Lombardy universities in the offerings of both the ITS and IFTS paths, see Marra, 2013, pp. 1211–1212.

27 Marra, 2013, pp. 1211–1212.

28 The priority areas covered by these 36 courses are (1) energy efficiency, (2) sustainable mobility, (3) new technologies of life, (4) new technologies for 'Made in Italy', (5) innovative technologies for cultural goods and activities, including tourism, and 6) information and communication technologies.

the IFTS system, regions plan the development of courses on the basis of state guidelines. Universities, secondary schools, public research bodies, VET centres, accredited labour agencies, and enterprises, including those in the form of associations or consortia, are then called upon to provide the courses.

Also, by means of Next Generation EU funds and the rewards disbursed by the state as a result of the INDIRE evaluation, in 2022, the Regional Council of Lombardy allocated significant resources to both IFTS and ITS[29] to improve the existing offerings and permit the creation of new pathways.

## 4 Lombardy as a laboratory of innovation and future perspectives

Even within the limited room for manoeuvring that the constitutional framework provides, the case of Lombardy demonstrates that regional innovation and experimentation could be instrumental for the more effective implementation of constitutional rights, such as the right to (vocational) education. The close link between territory, economic fabric, and tertiary training requires that regions play a leading role in planning VET pathways, both at EQF Level III and Level IV. Paradoxically, it is exactly within this narrow range that the regions have shown particular courage in exercising their legislative powers[30].

The effort of regions such as Lombardy (but also Emilia-Romagna[31]) to continue to invest and experiment in this area can act as a driver for and inspiration for other regions. Indeed, the history of Italian regionalism – as well as of Lombardy, a region recognised for its representation as a vibrant laboratory of legislative innovation (Marra, 2013, p. 1204) – shows that the particular systems tested on a specific territory can be the engine of innovations that affect other regions as well as the entire country. This has, for example, happened in the fields of the right to health and the rights of people with disabilities, with the regional experimentation of 'health budgets', which refer to individualised welfare instruments first tested in individual regions and then implemented in national laws and policies (Arconzo et al., 2020).

This challenge is also underpinned in the current dialogue on the implementation of Art. 116.3 Const., which allows regions to ask for more autonomy in specific sectors of legislation. At present, the Italian government is studying those processes needed for realising differentiated regionalism, focusing on the definition of the basic levels of services (LEP) concerning civil and social rights – including the right to education – that must be guaranteed throughout the national territory, even in the case of more functions being devolved to regions. To this end, the Italian government has set up a committee to ensure the completion of this project.

29 See resolutions of the Regional Government No. 6547 and 6548 of June 20, 2022.
30 Such a paradox has been discussed by Campione and Poggi (2009, p. 105).
31 The so-called 'Emilia-Romagna Model' is explicitly mentioned by the Italian PNRR as an example to follow. The main features of this model are analyzed in Bertelli (2012).

There is still a long way to go to implement differentiated regionalism. However, it is important to note that among those regions that first moved forward to demand more autonomy is Lombardy[32]. With regard to education, Lombardy's demands include greater autonomy in the organisation of the regional educational system and its evaluation methods, the recruitment of school personnel[33], the regulation of the organisation of the 'participating foundations' providing ITS pathways, and the planning of the integrated learning offerings between general education and VET (Casilli, 2023, p. 119; Violini, 2021, pp. 146–149). Although Article 116.3 of the Constitution does not place substantial limits on regional requests for greater autonomy in education, according to some scholars (*inter alia*, Maci, 2023), there is a solid core of functions in this area that cannot be devolved to the regions.

It is not easy to make predictions, but certainly, if at least some of the regional requests are accepted, this would open up interesting new spaces for experimentation and innovation.

## References

Arconzo, A., Ragone, G., & Bissaro, S. (2020). Il diritto delle persone con disabilità al progetto individuale. *Le Regioni, 1,* 31–74.

Bertelli, C. (2012). Il sistema dell'istruzione e formazione professionale: il caso della Regione Emilia-Romagna. *Economia dei servizi, 1,* 159–173. https://doi.org/10.2382/38219

Campione, V., & Poggi, A. (2009). *Sovranità, decentramento, regole. I livelli essenziali delle prestazioni e l'autonomia delle istituzioni scolastiche.* Il Mulino.

Canavesi, G. (2011). La "Dote lavoro" in Lombardia: un nuovo modello di politiche del lavoro? *Rivista del Diritto della Sicurezza Sociale, 1,* 59–89. https://doi.org/10.3241/34058

Cardone, A. (2013). Il riparto di competenze legislative in materia di «formazione professionale»: alcune questioni aperte alla luce della sentenza n. 287 del 2012. *Giornale di diritto del lavoro e di relazioni industriali, 3,* 429–442.

Casilli, G. (2023). Verso la necessaria determinazione dei LEP: la Cabina di regia governativa, tra "pre-intese" e DDL "Calderoli. *Italian Papers on Federalism, 2,* 112–131.

Cortese, F. (2010). L'istruzione tra norme generali e principi fondamentali: ossia, la Corte costituzionale tra contraddizioni formali e conferme sostanziali. *Le Regioni, 3,* 511–531. https://doi.org/10.1443/33501

Maci, P. (2023). Autonomia differenziata e istruzione. Le intese Stato-regioni tra "principi generali" e "norme generali sull'istruzione". L'attuazione del terzo comma dell'art. 116 Cost nel solco del titolo V della Costituzione. *Dirittifondamentali.it, 1,* 61–101.

Marra, A. (2013). Il contributo delle Regioni allo sviluppo del sistema universitario. *Le Regioni, 5–6,* 1185–1215. https://doi.org/10.1443/76927

32 Together with Emilia-Romagna and Veneto.

33 On the possibility of regionalizing this matter, the Constitutional Court was initially open (see Judgment No. 13/2004) and then became much more cautious (see Judgment No. 76/2013). See Maci, 2023, pp. 80 ff.

Poggi, A. (2005). La legislazione regionale sull'istruzione dopo la revisione del Titolo V. *Le Regioni, 5*, 927–937. https://doi.org/10.1443/21283

Poggi, A. (2009). Dalla Corte un'importante (anche se non decisivo) monito di arretramento alle "politiche" governative sull'istruzione. *Federalismi.it, 15*, 1–6.

Salone, C. (2017). Questioning new regionalism from an Italian perspective, or the resistible rise of Italian regions. *Pole Sud, 1*, 43–61. https://doi.org/10.3917/046.0043

Troisi, M. (2010). La Corte tra «norme generali sull'istruzione» e «principi fondamentali». Ancora alla ricerca di un difficile equilibrio tra (indispensabili) esigenze di uniformità e (legittime) aspirazioni regionali. *Le Regioni, 3*, 531–539. https://doi.org/10.1443/33502

Violini, L., & Cerlini, S. (2011). Il sistema della "Dote" in Lombardia: prime riflessioni su un'esperienza in atto. *Rivista Del Diritto Della Sicurezza Sociale, 1*, 44–57. https://doi.org/10.3241/34057

Violini, L. (2021). *Una forma di Stato a regionalism differenziato? Percorsi e argomenti per l'attuazione dell'art. 116, III comma, Cost.* Giappichelli.

Zanon, N. (2003). Prime note sulle "norme generali" statali, sul rispetto dell'interesse nazionale e sulla legislazione di "rilievo (o di "ambito", o di "interesse") regionale" nel progetto di riforma dell'art. 117 Cost. *Federalismi.it*, 29.05.2003.

## Short portrait of the author

**Giada Ragone** is Associate Professor of Constitutional Law at the University of Milan, Department of Italian and Supranational Public Law.
Contact: giada.ragone@unimi.it

# How Lombardy's short cycle tertiary education promotes innovation

Paolo Bertuletti, Andrea Potestio[1]

**Abstract**: The contribution investigates and highlights the extent to which Lombardy's short cycle tertiary education fosters and supports innovation. This explorative research, which is grounded in semi-structured interviews conducted with nine higher technical education institutions across the region, sheds light on the nuanced role that this segment of regional vocational education and training plays. Contrary to the assumption that such education is necessarily and entirely market-driven, the findings suggest that, despite maintaining strong and substantial ties with the world of work, it is not fully aligned with market demands. Nonetheless, this branch of education could be considered a significant and crucial element within the broader skills ecosystem and play an essential role in promoting the development of new professional profiles, albeit within certain limits. Through this function, it contributes to shaping and enhancing the regional labour market, thus holding potential for long-term impact on innovation and economic growth.

**Keywords**: Innovation; Short Cycle Tertiary Education; Skills' Ecosystems; Vocational Education and Training; Lombardy.

## 1 Introduction

Higher technical education (*Istruzione tecnologica superiore,* ITS) is traditionally marginal within Italy's educational system: established only in 2008, in 2022 just 25,842 students had opted for this route (INDIRE – National Institute for Documentation, Innovation and Educational Research). Recently, the Italian Recovery and Resilience Plan of 2021 has made it one of its main targets: the ITS will receive EUR 1.5 billion in funding in the next two years with the explicit aim of doubling the number of enrolments until 2025. The government hopes to facilitate the development of the skills required to promote innovation and boost the economy, which has been suffering from low productivity rates for decades and more recently facing a lack of highly qualified technicians.

Lombardy is at the forefront of this process, since it is the Italian region with the largest number of ITS providers, covering all technological areas provided for by the

---

1 Although this contribution is the result of a joint work of the two authors, paragraphs n. 1,2,4,5,6 and 7 can be attributed to Paolo Bertuletti; paragraph n. 3 to Andrea Potestio.

ministerial regulations (Decree No. 8327, 7th September 2011). In 2022, there were 20 ITS academies, 173 courses and 4,423 students enrolled in this region, while in the whole country there were 120 academies, 800 courses and 21,253 students (Zuccaro, 2022). However, considering the size of the current public investment, it is legitimate to ask: (1) If and to which extent ITS academies have supported innovation so far and (2) whether they are market-driven institutions, i. e. whose curriculum choices are influenced by businesses skill's needs and powerful interest groups, or actors that active and independently contribute to the definition of novel professional profiles.

Many authors claim that higher education in the neo-liberal context is increasingly focusing on the instrumental task of creating a skilled workforce for the global market (Zajda, 2020). This shift would produce a commodification of higher education and its marketisation, since its governance is influenced by indicators and standards-driven policies (Moscati et al., 2015). This risk is real, as Italian (and Lombardy's) ITS academies are run as foundations in which companies participate, with representation on the academy board, and the employment rate of their graduates partially determines their annual public funding[2]. Nevertheless, when studying these institutions more closely, they seem to be able, at least in some cases, to act quite independently of partner companies as far as the choice of learning outcomes and the design of their curricula are concerned. Through an empirical inquiry, we clarify this point by considering the way ITS academies develop the skills that should enable future technicians to foster innovation. Our sample includes nine academies eight based in Lombardy and one in the neighbouring region Emilia-Romagna. The focus of our research is not on policy issues, but on curriculum design since we aim to shed light on the actual or potential role in promoting innovation played within skills ecosystems by Lombardy's ITS.

## 2 ITS academies in comparative perspective

Italian ITS may be categorised as 'short-cycle tertiary education' corresponding to level 5 of the ISCED 2011 taxonomy elaborated by the United Nations Educational, Scientific and Cultural Organization (UNESCO): Tertiary non-academic education programmes "designed to provide participants with professional knowledge, skills and competencies. [...] [T]hey are practically based, occupationally-specific and prepare students to enter the labour market", also providing, at least in some cases, "a pathway to other tertiary education programmes" (UNESCO, 2012, p. 48). Normally, short-cycle tertiary education trains specialised technicians, i. e. workers who solve practical problems in production, maintenance and management, applying upper or intermediate skills in science, technology, engineering, and mathematics (STEM).

ITS academies are managed by foundations, thus, private law bodies with a public purpose, endowed with statutory, teaching, research, organisational, administrative

2 In comparison with other Italian tertiary education institutions ITS academies have a much higher employment rate of their graduates: 80 % 12 months after graduation; among those who have found a job 91 % work in a sector related to their studies (Zuccaro, 2022).

and financial autonomy. According to the minimum organisational standards set by the national law, foundations are composed of one technical upper secondary school based in the province where the academy is located, a vocational education and training (VET) provider, one or more companies active in the same economic sector of the course provided by the ITS academy and a university or a research centre (cf. art. 4 Law No. 99 15 July 2022). The enrolment requirement is an upper secondary general education leaving certificate or a post-secondary VET diploma. ITS courses are structured over 4 or 6 semesters, with a minimum annual number of hours ranging from 900 up to 1,000 (cf. art. 5 Law no. 99 15 July 2022). Higher technical diplomas delivered by Italian ITS rank at level 5 of the European Qualifications Framework (EQF), six-semester courses at EQF level 6.

Every ITS academy belongs to one of the six 'technological areas' provided for by national law, these areas are split in 17 sub-fields that can be also divided into 29 technical profiles (cf. Table 1). Each course must refer to one profile, linked to a legally established set of core and technical skills, but the academies may customise their offer adding or shaping autonomously learning units and renaming the course[3].

**Table 1:** Technological areas, sub-fields and technical figures (Inter-ministerial Decree No. 8327, 7th Sept. 2011)

| Areas | Sub-fields | Technical profiles |
|---|---|---|
| Green energy | Power supply and generation | Higher technician for energy supply and plant construction |
| | High efficient and energy-saving processes and plants | Higher technician for the management and verification of high-performing energy systems |
| | | Higher technician for energy saving in sustainable building |
| Smart mobility | Mobility of people and goods | Higher technician for the mobility of people and goods |
| | Production and maintenance of means of transport and infrastructure | Higher technician for the production and maintenance of means of transport and infrastructure |
| | Infomobility and logistics infrastructure management | Higher technician for infomobility and logistics infrastructure management |
| Biotechnology | Industrial and environmental biotechnology | Higher technician for the research and development of biotechnological products and processes |
| | | Higher technician for the quality system of biotechnological products and processes |
| | Manufacturing of diagnostic and biomedical devices | Higher technician for the production of diagnostic, therapeutic and rehabilitation equipment and devices |

3 According to art. 3 Law No. 99 15th July 2022 technological areas and the corresponding core and technical skills will be reformed.

*(Continuing table 1)*

| Areas | Sub-fields | Technical profiles |
|---|---|---|
| Made in Italy | Food industry | Higher technician for agricultural, agro-food and agro-industrial production and transformation |
| | | Higher technician for the control, enhancement and marketing of agricultural, agro-food and agro-industrial productions |
| | | Higher technician for environmental management in the agro-food system |
| | Construction | Higher technician for innovation and quality of housing |
| | | Higher technician for process, product, communication and marketing for the furniture sector |
| | Mechanical industry | Higher technician for the innovation of mechanical processes and products |
| | | Higher technician for automation and mechatronic systems |
| | Fashion | Higher technician for the coordination of design, communication and marketing processes of the fashion product |
| | | Higher technician of process, product, communication and marketing for the textile, clothing and fashion sector |
| | | Higher technician of process and product for the ennobling of the textile, clothing and fashion products |
| | | Higher technician for the process, production, communication and marketing in the footwear-fashion sector |
| | Business services | Higher technician for marketing and internationalisation |
| | | Higher technician for product sustainability (design and packaging) |
| Cultural Heritage and Tourism | Tourism and cultural activities | Higher technician for communication and marketing of tourism and cultural activities |
| | | Higher technician for the management of hospitality facilities |
| | Cultural and artistic heritage | Higher technician for the management of restoration architectural sites |
| | | Higher technician for the production/reproduction of artistic artifacts |
| ICT | Methods and technologies for software systems development | Higher technician for software systems development |
| | Organisation and use of information and knowledge | Higher technician for the organisation and the use of information and knowledge |
| | Architectures and infrastructures for communication systems | Higher technicians for communication systems' architectures and infrastructures |

At least 60 % of teaching must be provided by staff recruited among professionals and the mandatory internship cannot take less than 35 % of the total amount of learning hours (art. 5 Law no. 99 15 July 2022). Courses can also be carried out as apprenticeships, in accordance with the provisions of art. 45 of Leg. Decree no. 81, 15 June 2015, and in compliance with the training standards set by the inter-ministerial Decree 12 October 2015 and regional regulations.

Italian commentators often compare ITS academies to the German Fachhochschule, but this is an undue comparison, since the latter offer academic courses leading to bachelor's and master's degrees and meet the criteria of the Bologna process, even if they do not award doctoral degrees. However, in our opinion not the German Fachhochschule but the German Fachschule/Fachakademie have much in common with Italian ITS academies, even if entrance requirements to ITS is not a completed vocational training but an upper-secondary general education leaving certificate. Moreover, it must be considered that academies originate not from initiatives held by the central or regional government, but through a bottom-up process involving local aggregations of stakeholders such as companies, VET schools, upper secondary schools, Universities, research centres, and local authorities).

# 3 Theoretical framework

The Italian Recovery and Resilience Plan states that ITS academies should promote innovation. However, nobody expects these institutes to make scientific discoveries, create technologies in their laboratories or develop new work process standards. Rather, they are supposed to train technicians who will be able to foster innovation in their own work contexts.

To understand how Lombardy's ITS academies may achieve this goal it might be useful to explore literature on innovation, with regard to the role of specialised technicians in the processes of acquiring and disseminating new knowledge.

## 3.1 Innovation as circular, iterative and distributed process

While extant literature describes the creation of new knowledge as an iterative and circular process which cannot be conceived without a specific application context (Gibbons, 1994; Etzkowitz & Leydesdorff, 2000; Chesbrough, 2006), studies on Marshallian industrial districts underline the fact that another type of innovation occurs through informal sharing of tacit knowledge normally embedded in companies and workers (Amin & Thrift, 1992; Lundvall & Johnson, 1994). Both well-known lines of research suggest that innovation may happen only within "systems" (Edquist & Johnson, 1997) or "ecosystems" (Finegold, 1999) of interdependent actors, including firms and educational institutions.

### 3.2 The skills ecosystem model applied to vocational education

The authors cited above focus on the relationship between the world of work and universities or research centres, whereas the impact on innovation of VET providers has not been granted as much attention in the literature. However, the skills ecosystem model, elaborated by Finegold studying high-tech companies (see Chapter 1 in this volume), has been adopted in some Australian and British studies to provide a new way of thinking about and reforming intermediate i. e. vocational skills (Dalziel, 2015; Hodgson & Spours, 2016; Buchanan et al., 2020). The fundamental idea behind the use of the skills ecosystem model in VET policies and research is the following: Education should not provide firms with the skills they ask for but make firms search for the right skills.

> "The nature of labour demand is far from self-evident. The challenge is not so much to predict specific skill sets which will be needed but rather what capacities and capabilities are best developed now to ensure the country has the capacity to adapt rapidly as circumstances change and, where possible, shape the way jobs are defined." (Buchanan *et al.*, 2017, p. 450).

### 3.3 The role of educational institutions

Some promising insights to better understand how higher VET may accomplish this task are given by Vona and Consoli's reflections on innovation and skill dynamics. As these authors have pointed out, at early stages of technological development knowledge transfer is reliant on the mobility of a few talented individuals. New knowledge is still tacit. Only the purposeful and explicit absorption of practical know-how in formal education enhances a process of 'knowledge systematisation' which helps firms to improve contents and assignments of work tasks and smoothes the adoption of technological and organisational innovations. Since novel and mostly tacit knowledge is not well known, educational institutions must take a proactive role in identifying innovations, incorporating them into their curricula and design innovative job profiles to "open up new opportunities by facilitating the translation of that technology to unforeseen contexts of use" (Vona & Consoli, 2014, p. 1408).

In this sense the 'fine-tuning' of existing educational programmes not only would facilitate the diffusion of skills already identified on the labour market, but also create the demand itself for new skills, which otherwise would remain the subjective property of individual talented workers. According to this perspective, a key role in the innovation process within skills ecosystems might be played by short-cycle education institutions, such as ITS academies, whose aim should be the training of skilled technicians who will lead the transition towards the application of new knowledge and solutions in their working context.

### 3.4 Technicians as contributors to innovation

The role of technicians in industrial innovation processes is well known. Using cross-industry and cross-country data from eight western nations, Mason *et al.* argue that "upper intermediate-skilled workers may contribute to spillovers that increase productivity" (Mason *et al.*, 2017, p. 27). In other words, they would enhance firms' "absorptive capacity", i. e. the ability to transform and exploit acquired external knowledge (Zahra & George, 2002, p. 191).

Inside their company technicians contribute to so-called 'incremental innovation', i. e. the gradual improvement of existing work processes and technologies through knowledge creation in the workplace[4].

> "The ideas behind such incremental gains are typically born out of intimate familiarity with technology of the kind technicians acquire through their experience of operating, maintaining and solving problems with the relevant machines and processes. In performing their duties, therefore, technicians learn how technology can be improved, enabling them to contribute to the creation of the knowledge required for incremental innovation" (Lewis, 2020, p. 622).

The point is to identify more precisely, which competence 'innovative' technicians must have to perform in this way. In other words, assuming that ITS academies 'systematise' and provide their students the basic knowledge to use cutting-edge technologies, as Vona and Consoli recommended, what are the personal characteristics that the future technicians must cultivate in order to make the most of them, once employed in a company?

The international appreciation of the German dual apprenticeship system of VET, characterised by a 'holistic' rather than a 'functional' approach (Bertuletti, 2021; Deißinger, Heine, & Ott, 2011, p. 398), suggests that an adaptive workforce with a broader professional mindset and a wide range of skills is the key for competitive and dynamic production (Tether *et al.*, 2005, p. 7). In this sense, the *forma mentis* of the typical German skilled worker, based on the systematic alternation between theory and practice (Potestio, 2020), seems to be suitable to support problem solving and incremental innovation (Toner, 2011, p. 48).

Following the Italian sociologist Butera, it can be said that future technicians must be 'broadband' professionals, in the sense that they will be asked to do a large number of activities "very different in terms of content, level, educational background" without losing their professional identity, because this identity will not be reduced to a list of tasks summarised in a rigid job description, but built around a 'script' to be interpreted in a singular and unique way within a specific organisational and working environment. That means that technical knowledge and skills can be made effective only by a clever, creative and sensitive 'interpreter' (Butera, 2017, pp. 294–296).

Then, it is not surprising that in the existing literature, alongside hard skills, soft skills are considered essential for fostering incremental innovation among technicians. The latter include communication skills, teamwork, leadership, initiative and accepting responsibility, constant vigilance regarding quality, flexibility, analytical skills and creative problem solving, capacity to learn and to teach (Toner, 2011, pp. 56–57). Moreover, the importance of non-cognitive skills for every career success has been now recog-

4 This has to be distinguished from "radical innovation", which corresponds to the introduction of completely new knowledge and is usually connected to purposeful R&D. The conceptual distinction between "radical" and "incremental innovation" is due to the historian of technology Nathan Rosenberg (1994).

nised (Heckmann *et al.*, 2006), as well as personal value orientation and social behaviour as a major part of professional competence (Weigel, Mulder & Collins, 2007).

# 4 Empirical inquiry

Our inquiry focuses on how and to what extent Lombardy's ITS academies support innovation within the ecosystem of upper technical skills. According to our theoretical premises three main matters related to the design of technicians' curricula have been investigated: (1) the provision of a broad professional mindset, (2) the presence of learning activities aimed at soft skills development and (3) the involvement of ITS institutions in the process of 'knowledge systematisation and spreading'.

Semi-structured interviews (Kvale & Brinkmann, 2014) were conducted with key collaborators (teachers, managers, directors or consultants) of nine academies, covering almost every technological area currently provided for by the Italian legislation on higher technical education[5]. Below is a table with the role held by the interviewees, the type of contract they have with the academy as well as their educational and professional background (Table 2).

**Table 2:** Role, work contract, educational and professional background of the people interviewed (n. of respondents)

| Role | Work contract | Education | Professional Background |
|---|---|---|---|
| Teacher (1) | Full-time (5) | In the same field of his/her Institution (4) | Experience in the same economic sector where students will be probably employed (4) |
| Manager of placement services (1) | Secondment (1) | In another field (5) *two of them in Educational sciences | Experience in another economic sector (1) |
| Institute's technical consultant (1) | Collaborator (3) | | Previous experience in Education (4) |
| Course director (4) | | | |
| Foundation's director or vice-director (2) | | | |

All interviews were audio-recorded, fully transcribed and thematic analysis (Bryman *et al.*, 2021, pp. 537–541) using MAXQDA. In the text, we will refer to the transcriptions as follows: '[interviewee's role], [ITS academy's sector], [date]'. Before the interviews, study plans were checked. Normally, academies offer several courses within the same technological area. It is important to note that for each institution, we considered one course only.

5 Biotechnology, Construction, Cultural Heritage and Tourism, Fashion, Food industry, Green energy, ICT, Mechanical industry, Smart mobility. One of the academies considered (Food industry) is based in the neighbouring region Emilia-Romagna. We did not manage to interview any academy active in the Business services area.

# 5 Results

## 5.1 Broad or narrow professional mindset?

Through the analysis of the study plans of the nine courses offered by the ITS academies considered, it is clear that the selection of subjects in their curricula is based on the main professional functions of the corresponding technical profile. However, all courses also include various learning units that focus on fundamental general subjects, which are necessary prerequisites for technical (and job-specific) ones, such as mathematics or physics, or on transversal subjects that are applicable to different job profiles and sectors, such as English or communication skills. The general and transversal subjects constitute a relevant portion of the total learning hours attended at school, ranging from 20 % (at the academies active in the food industry and tourism sector) to 50 % (at green energy ITS academy)[6]. In fact, as one interviewee notes, “approximately a good 30 % of the number of hours is aimed at creating a professional identity that is independent of the type of job or sector in which our students will be employed.” (Teacher, ICT, 18.11.2022).

All interviewees maintain that the job profile trained in their courses, while preparing students for direct job placement, at the same time provide a sufficiently wide education, which will allow them to also work in various sub-sectors in the same technological area (e. g. technicians for the design and development of food production who come from the ITS academy active in food industry may be employed either in the cereal or dairy or meat or wine or even in the fish industry) as well in different roles (laboratory analysis, production, quality control, health and hygiene, marketing and distribution). The same is true for the other institutions in the sample. For instance, graduates from the academy active in the mechanical industry (mechatronic manufacturing) may be employed as programming, quality and control or maintenance technicians: “they have a specific preparation, of course, but not too much, otherwise we stick them in fixed roles preventing them from professional development” (Course director, Mechanical industry, 16.01.2023). Industrial chemistry technicians from a biotechnology ITS academy may be hired as laboratory or quality and control technicians, but also as project managers or even in marketing; e-commerce marketing managers trained by the ITS academy active in fashion could work in digital marketing as well in the logistic or warehouse management.

The only exception is represented by the ITS academy active in smart mobility which trains highly specialised technicians: aircraft maintainers certified by the European Aviation Safety Agency (EASA). In this case, however, the complexity of the machinery that technicians must deal with, the rapid technological evolution and the need to operate in different countries (aircraft workshops are scattered all over the world), require young people with an open mind and who are ready to learn continuously: “for sure these technicians do not carry out routinary tasks” (Foundation’s director, Smart mobility, 11.02.2023).

6 See example table 3.

Nevertheless, it must be underlined that a considerable part of the overall training at ITS courses is covered by internships which are compulsory by law for at least 30 % of the total amount of hours[7]. Among the institutions considered in this research internship ratios range from 33 % (construction) up to 48 % (cultural heritage and tourism) (see Table 3). More oriented to specific job positions, internships represent the vocational moment of higher technical education: "we can say that ours is a funnel-shaped training path where the specialisation is given by the internship" (Course director, Mechanical industry, 16.01.2023).

**Table 3:** One example of study plan/Course: Mechatronic manufacturing – ITS Academy Mechanical industry

| | **N. of hours** | **%** |
|---|---|---|
| *Transversal learning units* | | |
| Communication, Marketing and Customer Management | 20 | |
| Corporate Organisation | 35 | |
| English | 40 | |
| Health & Safety and Quality System | 35 | |
| Job Market Orientation | 30 | |
| Machinery Legislation | 20 | |
| Maintenance Troubleshooting | 30 | |
| Metrology, Measurement and Testing | 20 | |
| Project Work | 50 | |
| Team Building, Project Management & Cost Accounting | 35 | |
| TOT | 315 | 15,75 % |
| *General learning units* | | |
| Fundamentals of Automation | 30 | |
| Mechatronic (Basic) | 90 | |
| Maths and Statistics (Basic) | 30 | |
| TOT | 150 | 7,5 % |
| *Technical learning units* | | |
| Computer Aided Manufacturing | 30 | |
| Computer Numerical Control | 40 | |
| Computing and Programming | 30 | |

7 According to the previous legislation (art. 4 D. P. C.M. 25th January 2008) which the courses considered followed. Now this quota has risen to 35 % (art. 5 Law no. 99 15th July 2022).

*(Continuing table 3)*

| | N. of hours | % |
|---|---|---|
| Design and 3D Simulation | 60 | |
| Industrial Design | 30 | |
| Industrial Drives | 40 | |
| Industrial Network and IoT | 40 | |
| Manufacturing Processes & 3D Printing | 80 | |
| Manufacturing Studies & Product Industrialisation | 30 | |
| Pneumatics & Oleodynamics | 60 | |
| Programmable Logic Controllers | 105 | |
| Robotics | 60 | |
| Smart Factory | 30 | |
| Switchboards Design | 60 | |
| Systems Supervision | 40 | |
| TOT | 735 | 36,75 % |
| Internship | 800 | 40 % |

## 5.2 Learning activities for soft skills' development

All people interviewed are aware of the importance for their students to develop not only technical skills (i. e. hard skills related to a specific profession), but also cognitive and social soft skills, which go beyond specific occupations and are needed across various job contexts (Pellerey 2016). The main idea is not to enhance the propensity for innovation among students, but to teach those behaviours and attitudes that will help them to positively integrate into the company context.

For this purpose, different didactical strategies are deployed to simulate corporate work organisation within the school context. All ITS academies use case studies or project works or both; some of them are authentic tasks assigned directly by a real company, solved or carried out with the tutoring of teachers chosen for their professional expertise (fashion; ICT).

Projects may be assigned at the end of the school year (mechanical industry) or, more commonly, at the end of single learning units. Sometimes (mechanical industry; fashion; green energy) project works are developed within contests (e. g. the one held by the Italian Ministry of Education on Industry 4.0 or hackathons for students). They may involve the creation of a product, from design to its presentation to a panel of experts, e. g. a furniture component (construction) or an energy-saving shower (green energy), as well as the drafting of a plan for the manufacturing process (mechanical industry) or the delivery of a hospitality service (cultural heritage and tourism).

Case studies normally adopt what one interviewee called a 'reverse engineering' approach: considering a production defect or a mistake in the process "students must carry out a backward analysis of what was the genesis of the problem" (Teacher, ICT, 18.11.2022). Future aircraft maintainers may be asked to solve the case of a notorious aircraft accident (smart mobility). Future Food industry technicians had to solve the case of a famous snack which had to be withdrawn from the market after the discovery of bacterial infections in some batches. They may also be asked to explain how they would employ an innovative sanitation method in the dairy industry after the recent introduction of novel hygiene regulations by an importing country (food industry). All these activities are supposed to enhance problem solving skills. It is important to stress that their realistic character depends on the fact that "they are proposed or supported by teachers coming from the world of work" (Course director, Construction, 26.01.2023). Sometimes "the task (e. g. how to eliminate a carcinogenic molecule from the final product or set the line according to the principles of lean production) is given by engineers who will provide the solution adopted in reality during a company visit a few months later. There, the best solution found by the students is awarded" (Manager of placement services, Biotechnology, 12.10.2022).

According to all interviewees these activities are carried out in groups in order to enhance teamwork skills. Specific teaching strategies are used to make the learning process more effective. Every team may, for instance, reproduce the company's functions: "we did a project based on a brief given by a big fashion house: students had to come up with a new catalogue of accessories. We gathered students from different courses: one had to deal with design, the other with financial matters, the third with marketing, and they had five days to make it. The student from the Fashion designer course wanted to be creative, one from the marketing course had his own ideas, the other was concerned about budget constraints, and they argued furiously. This is simply what happens in the companies" (Foundation's vice-director, Fashion, 26.08.2022). Team members are often intentionally chosen with different skill levels and educational backgrounds to facilitate peer tutoring (ICT; food industry; biotechnology). At the end of each project, students are normally expected to give a presentation, in order to also exercise communication skills. A role rotation within the group should guarantee that everyone is involved (biotechnology). To facilitate remote collaborative work, one academy (ICT) provides all necessary technological equipment (PCs, internet connection, software) for free.

Furthermore, all courses provide specific learning units on soft skills, such as team work (cultural heritage and tourism; mechanical industry: food industry; green energy), effective communication (cultural heritage and tourism; fashion; mechanical industry; food industry; smart mobility; green energy) and design thinking (fashion; mechanical industry; biotechnology; ICT; green energy). In its courses, two foundations provide 60 hours for 'soft skills workshops' (construction; smart mobility). Lessons are normally held by professional coaches, corporate trainers and psychologists.

Some ITS academies see soft skills development activities not only as opportunities to learn behaviours which are appropriate to the work context, but also to personal growth. In these cases, interviewees consider self-improvement to be closely intertwined with professional development. In fact, "the soft skills required by service professions are linked to ethical values that hit all dimensions of life" (Course director, Cultural Heritage and Tourism, 03.02.2023). In the so-called soft skills workshop "students become aware of their personal attitudes, which soft skills they have developed or not, and together with their trainers understand that the harmonious personal growth contributes to the building of a broader professional profile" (Course director, Construction, 26.01.2023). "Thoroughness and accuracy is an essential behavioural characteristic for professionals [aircraft maintainers] whose mistakes can cost people lives" (Foundation's director, Smart mobility, 11.02.2023). This is the reason why some academies are beginning to introduce a coach in their staff to support students' careers. "Our effort to educate on punctuality requires individual mentoring" (Course director, Cultural Heritage and Tourism, 03.02.2023). One institution starts this tutoring right from the very beginning of the course with an assessment followed by individual talks: "An analysis of students' learning style, their creativity and personal attitudes, as an opportunity that brings out strengths and weaknesses" (Foundation's vice-director, Fashion, 26.08.2022).

### 5.3 ITS involvement in knowledge systematisation and spreading

Regarding systematisation and spreading of new knowledge our inquiry revealed, among the cases considered, three different patterns of interaction between academies and companies. Regarding the choice of technical learning outputs, some ITS academies seem to be rather reactive, simply responding to the needs of businesses. Others take a more proactive role. Some even suggest to companies how to innovate their business.

Close to the first pattern there are four institutions, whose courses are designed according to business needs, within the frame of a constant information exchange between companies and the school. In this case the academies rely on the information about innovation provided by some big partner companies. Although they play a marginal role in the knowledge systematisation, in this model educational institutions may also support the spreading of innovations, helping businesses, especially small ones, to be aware of cutting-edge technologies or work-processes. "Our course manager [...] is constantly in contact with the training managers of some leading company [...] this reciprocal exchange is practically what leads all the processes forward, if we find something new and interesting we communicate it to our partners and vice versa, if there is something new in the company environment, we are informed about it, we adapt and then use it from an educational point of view" (Foundation's director, Smart mobility, 11.02.2023).

At the ITS academy active in the mechanical sector annual surveys and focus groups with partner companies are carried out to understand how to reshape courses. An expert (maybe an employee of a partner company or a freelancer) provides support in the curricula design. Typically, academies come to know of cutting-edge technologies through partner companies which are leaders in the automation industry. Corporate technicians show the applications of a new technology to the institute's teachers (e. g. a robotic cell). With the help of the same companies the academy may buy such technologies for its own laboratories and then update the corresponding learning unit (in this case: innovative machinery such as collaborative robots).

In the case of a biotechnology academy, too, companies which occupy a leading position in the chemical sector indicate evolving trends (lean production and management, industry 4.0 etc.) The academy takes these suggestions into consideration and eventually updates its courses. When training units on industry 4.0 were added, the institute asked a researcher from the National Research Center (CNR) to identify the essential knowledge and skills to integrate 4.0 technologies into chemical production. This work was carried out in synergy with corporate consultants and other teachers.

At least in three other cases, although course design is based on surveys and focus groups among partner enterprises, new skills trends have been identified and acknowledged first through consultation with experts (researchers or professionals) who are not employed by any companies. This is what we identify as the second pattern of interaction between academies and companies.

> "The course was born after a conference organised by *Politecnico di Milano* on sustainable mobility trends, such as: charging stations, sharing mobility and new fuels. These are actually three main points of our course, whose design took place in close contact with companies and experts consulted by our staff to understand what companies in this sector need." (Course director, Green energy, 21.12.2022).

It should be added that the aforementioned academy also provides learning units on biofuels and hydrogen, two technologies whose applicability is still controversial and not yet established on the market.

Finally, two ITSs appear to be active promoters of business innovation (third model), as conceptualised by Vona and Consoli (2014), i. e. redesigning their training programmes according to emerging knowledge and disseminating it among companies. One academy through the spread of fresh know-how, the other through what we can call a "systematisation" of new knowledge and skills linked to emerging job profiles. In the first case, one institution, which provides a course for marketing and internationalisation of wooden furniture, helps partner companies (usually SMEs) to renovate their business approach:

> "To digitise the whole aspect of communication but also marketing through e-commerce platforms [...] How did we do that? We recruited experienced freelance professionals keen on social media, multichannel marketing, and communication to teach in our course [...] our students [...] bring to the companies the knowledge they really need but are not able to acquire alone." (Course director, Construction, 26.01.2023).

Something similar occurs also for the course, provided by the same academy, on design and industrialisation of the furniture product. "Sometimes companies buy new machinery but don't know how to use its full potential. Our students who have studied to make these technologies work can help the company make the most of them"

(Course director, Construction, 26.01.2023). For the interviewee, the foundation's contribution to innovation is twofold: it trains young people who can lead innovation processes within SMEs and it urges partner companies to make investments on cutting-edge technologies.

The second, and more relevant case, is represented by an ITS academy which provides a two-year course to become a fashion designer. A few years ago, some of its teachers, fashion industry professionals hired to teach some learning units, reported the launch of a new powerful 3D clothing modelling software (Clo 3D). No Italian fashion house used this software at that time. Nevertheless, the academy decided to include a module on this subject in its fashion designer course.
Over the years this technology had evolved and it was clear that it could become the 'core' of a new professional profile. The academy then decided to open a new course for digital fashion design. A special scanner (VIZU) was also purchased to transfer the characteristics of fabrics (shine, grain etc.) to digital models, and a software to create avatars of customers wearing the digital clothes. The new training course was structured around the use of these new technologies.

The digital fashion designer did not yet exist in the market. However, after the first edition of the course, some companies that turned to the academy seeking for 'traditional' fashion designers, decided to hire these new technicians to change their organisation towards digital modelling.

In this case, it was not the companies that asked the educational institution to modify its training offer based on a predetermined professional profile, but the opposite: the ITS academy anticipated them, having realised the opportunities offered by some cutting-edge technologies. Thanks to the advice of some teachers, hybrid profiles coming from the world of work (not necessarily employed by a single company, but freelancing), it was possible to design the curriculum of future technicians who will be able to use those technologies to innovate production processes and transform the companies themselves. The design of study plans was partially based on the results of a survey conducted among companies and partially on suggestions coming from the teaching staff. For example, the photography teacher, an established photographer in the fashion industry who has been working for major brands, suggested how to conceive the digital photography learning unit, because "using Photoshop to retouch photos for a traditional catalogue is one thing, but using it to create realistic 3D renderings is another" (IFoundation's vice-director, Fashion, 26.08.2022).

In general, it can be said that in all academies – whichever pattern they belong to – teachers recruited among professionals play a key role in the interplay between the world of work and educational institutions, especially when innovation is concerned. At the ITS academy active in the ICT sector the packaging course was created on the explicit mandate of the Milan trade associations, but the role of teaching staff with different backgrounds is still fundamental for the steady update of the curriculum. "High profile professionals know the things that will enter in the work of work in a few years. Companies will come later" (Teacher, ICT, 18.11.2022). One teacher, who is also involved in the course design, said:

> "Yesterday I was in Bologna at the national flexography conference. New procedures for managing customer-supplier information exchange through packaging were presented. Currently, nobody applies these procedures, but ISO standards already exist, and they will spread in the coming years. I convey all this knowledge in advance to my students who are now attending the course to become a Packaging Specialist." (Teacher, ICT, 18.11.2022).

The same thing emerged during the interview with a teacher and consultant of the academy active in the Food industry. Also here, teachers hired from the world of work can quickly adapt the teaching contents of their lessons as soon as they realise that new procedures or technologies are emerging. The person interviewed spoke about the process of ozonisation for the sanitation of dairy industry environments, introduced in her learning unit shortly after new import restrictions were imposed by the American health authority on Italian imports, such as parmesan cheese.

Furthermore, the collaboration between students and companies during the course could enhance innovation's spreading. At one ITS academy

> "Teachers of a specific teaching unit may coordinate a project work assigned by a company to a whole class or a single student. Our foundation signs an agreement with the company that commissions a brief to one of our class groups. For example, the task is to design a three-dimensional model of slippers using new software. The company pays the teacher, who then becomes a sort of consultant, for coordinating the group and then for mentoring an intern (one of our students) that will try to carry out that project in the company – the experience represents also the chance to 'test' a possible future technician to be hired [...] This means that the company can try a new working method (in this case the digital design of its products) thanks to the work of an intern who knows the last release of one professional modelling software quite well, taking advantage at the same time of the support of an expert teacher." (Foundation's vice-director, Fashion, 26.08.2022).

# 6 Discussion

## 6.1 Broad or narrow professional mindset?

The collected information suggest that the nine academies considered, while preparing specialised technicians ready to enter in the job market, provide a (relatively) wide range of skills, which allow them to adapt in different professional positions thanks to – so we may argue – a sufficiently broad professional mindset. This is due to legislative, scholastic, practical and also – at least in some cases – pedagogical reasons.

Firstly, ministerial regulation, while leaving ITS institutions great autonomy in the curricula's design and learning outputs' choice, still indicates a set of quite broad professional profiles to reach at the end of the Italian higher technical education (Interministerial decree No. 8327 of 7$^{th}$ September 2011). This prevents the education offer from being too narrow:

> "the focus of the course is precisely green mobility. However, this does not mean that our 1100 hours of school-based teaching are exclusively on sustainable and electric mobility [...] our mandate is to prepare a technical figure recognised at a national level: the upper technician for the management and the verification of high-performing energy systems. For

> this reason, we give our students an elementary background useful to be employed not only into mobility-related fields [...] Thanks to this general preparation, after an internship in the right place, someone could be employed also by companies which deal with energy efficiency, both with technical or even managerial functions." (Course director, Green energy, 21.12.2022).

Secondly, as explicitly stated by three interviewees (smart mobility; biotechnology; mechanical industry) and confirmed also by the annual national monitoring released by INDIRE (National Institute for Documentation, Innovation and Educational Research), the educational background of students enrolled in ITS is very different, even in the same course, and not always consistent with the specialisation. Born as natural prosecution of the secondary technical education – in 2020 most of the students enrolled in the Italian short cycle tertiary education still had a technical upper secondary leaving certificate (58,7 %), but not always in the same technological field of the ITS course attended. In recent years, the number of enrolments coming from general upper secondary education has increased (up to 22.6 % in 2020). The number of those having an academic degree already has risen too (4 %). Students with a VET qualification were only 13.6 % in 2020. There is also a considerable number of students over 30 years of age (almost 10 %) (Zuccaro, 2022). This forces the academies to provide a series of preparatory teaching units at the beginning of each course.

Furthermore, providing a broad set of skills is also necessary because ITS students' employment destinations could be very differentiated: they are mostly SMEs in different sub-sectors.

> "If one student ends up in a large, highly structured company, then he or she can become a specialist (perhaps in Amazon sales) [...] But if he or she ends up in a smaller company, then he or she needs to be able to handle logistics, shipping, returns, inventory, a product catalogue on the site, omnichannel marketing etc." (Foundation's vice-director, Fashion, 26.08.2022).

Alongside these practical reasons, in the choice of a broad educational offer at least during some interviews, pedagogical motivations were also cited: "we need to develop in our students the ability to study and learn continuously" (Course director, Cultural Heritage and Tourism, 03.02.2023); "it is essential that they acquire a method and a mindset to evolve quickly following the rapid technological transformation" (Foundation's vice-director, Fashion, 26.08.2022); "we would also like to equip them with a personal method to progress on a path of professional growth" (Course director, Construction, 26.01.2023). This feature, though, does not seem to be explicitly related to the ability to innovate work processes.

## 6.2 Learning activities for soft skills' development

The attention of the nine interviewees paid to the development of soft skills is high. More than university teaching – in Italy often characterised by outdated teaching environments, overcrowded and frontal lessons (Rostan, 2014, pp. 102–104) – higher technical institutions manage to offer learning activities where the focus is actively exercising personal soft skills in small groups. During the interviews, the link between soft skills and the ability to find innovative solutions does not come out explicitly[8], despite a strong insistence on the importance of promoting problem solving strategies.

In general, soft skills are seen as functional character components for the effective adaptation to the relational dynamics typical of work contexts. As we have seen, this 'utilitarian' approach does not prevent the emergence of an explicit attention to the pedagogical dimension of personal growth. In this sense, the interweaving of professional and personal development might be the way to prepare technicians who will be able to support innovation processes.

### 6.3 ITS involvement in knowledge systematisation and spreading

Regarding the contribution of ITS academies to the innovations' systematisation and spreading the inquiry offer a twofold scenario. In the production sectors (aeronautics, mechanics, chemistry), where the use of new technologies directly impacts work processes, ITS curricula's design appears heavily influenced by skills needs expressed by some leading companies. In the service sector (marketing, hospitality, fashion design), where the use of new technologies has a more indirect impact on work processes, ITS institutions play a more proactive role in defining new job profiles.

In any case, teachers recruited from the world of work are crucial. These 'hybrid' professionals act as a 'bridge' between the production or service sector and academies for the acquisition of new knowledge, its integration and sometimes its original re-elaboration into curricula, as well as its dissemination among companies which are often not able to use or do not even know of it.

## 7 Conclusions

The enquiry presented here is still exploratory in nature. Based on the analysis of the internal documents of the organisations considered (study plans) and the voice of those who work for them, it can only provide interesting insights to understand the *modus operandi* of the Lombardy's ITS academies and the way they see their own function within the skills ecosystem.

However, the information gathered seems sufficient to give an objective idea of the relationship between academies and the world of work, which is more complex than the supply-demand model. Academies do not always play a merely passive role in the VET of future technicians but participate, with different levels of intensity, to the definition of professional profiles and the development of the respective field. This is possible thanks to a valuable job of re-elaboration of the emerging knowledge which corresponds to what some scholars call 'systematisation of innovations'. In addition to fulfilling demands of the labour market, academies play an important role in the spreading of new information and know-how among partner companies. In other words, they are equipping future technicians to drive the so-called 'incremental innova-

8 With the only exception of the academy active in the biotechnology sector, which offers a 12 hours teaching unit called team building, mindfulness and creativity.

tion'. One might assume that this also happens because of the collaboration between ITS academies and universities, but this aspect does not emerge in the interviews, as the interaction with researchers seems to be rather marginal.

Important limitations to the research obviously remain. Firstly, to evaluate the role played by ITS academies in the dissemination and systematisation of innovative know-how, we rely only on interviewees' testimonies about successful practices. We do not know how much these positive examples count in the overall activity of short cycle education in Lombardy. Secondly, although respondents are confident that their courses give an adequate preparation for different professional roles and fields, neither have data been collected on the professional careers of ITS graduates, nor evidence that their alleged broad professional mindset allows them to promote innovation at the workplace. Finally, teaching activities aimed at developing soft skills are surely relevant within ITS curricula, but we do not have evidence to assess the educational results of those activities.

More research is needed to find out whether academies are only providing skills which are supposed to foster innovation or whether they are also promoting the professional and personal development of future technicians. This is a crucial question, since the human factor is the key to organisational and economic development (Bertagna, 2006) and only the personal agency is the basis of innovation processes (Costa, 2013; 2018).

## References


Amin, A., & Thrift, N. (1992). Neo-Marshallian nodes in global networks. *International Journal of Urban and Regional Research, 16*(4), 159–175. https://doi.org/10.1111/j.1468-2427.1992.tb00197.x

Bertagna, G. (2006). *Pensiero manuale. La scommessa di un sistema educativo di istruzione e di formazione di pari dignità*. Rubbettino.

Bertuletti, P. (2021). *Quale «formazione» professionale? Una rilettura di Georg Kerschensteiner (1854–1932)*. Studium.

Bryman, C., Bryman, A., & Clark, T. (2021). *Bryman's social research methods*. Oxford University Press.

Buchanan, J., Anderson, P., & Power, G. (2017). Skill ecosystems. In J. Buchanan, D. Finegold, K. Mayhew, & C. Warhurst (Eds.), *The Oxford handbook of skills and training* (pp. 444–464). Oxford University Press.

Buchanan, J., et al. (2020). *Enabling renewal: Further education and building better citizenship, occupations and business communities in Wales*. CollegesWales. https://orca.cardiff.ac.uk/id/eprint/139414/1/Enabling%20Renewal%20-%20FE.pdf

Butera, F. (2017). Lavoro e organizzazione nella quarta rivoluzione industriale: La nuova progettazione socio-tecnica. *L'industria, 38*(3), 291–316.

Chesbrough, H. W. (2006). Open innovation: A new paradigm for understanding industrial innovation. In H. W. Chesbrough, W. Vanhaverbeke, & J. West (Eds.), *Open innovation: Researching a new paradigm* (pp. 1–12). Oxford University Press. https://doi.org/10.1111/j.1467-8691.2008.00502.x

Costa, M. (2018). Formatività e innovazione: Un nuovo legame per industry 4.0. In G. Alessandrini (Ed.), *Atlante di pedagogia del lavoro* (pp. 219–236). Franco Angeli.

Costa, M. (2013). Pedagogia e contesti di innovazione. *Prospettiva EP, 45*(3), 71–82.

Dalziel, P. (2015). Regional skill ecosystems to assist young people making education employment linkages in transition from school to work. *Local Economy, 30*(1), 54–66.

Deißinger, T., Heine, R., & Ott, M. (2011). The dominance of apprenticeships in the German VET system and its implications for Europeanisation: A comparative view in the context of the EQF and the European LLL strategy. *Journal of Vocational Education & Training, 63*(3), 397–416.

Edquist, C., & Johnson, B. (1997). Institutions and organizations in systems of innovation. In C. Edquist (Ed.), *System of innovation: Technologies, institutions and organizations* (pp. 41–63). Pinter.

Etzkowitz, H., & Leydesdorff, L. (2000). The dynamics of innovation: From national systems and "Mode 2" to a Triple Helix of university-industry-government relations. *Research Policy, 29*(2), 109–123. https://doi.org/10.1016/S0048-7333(99)00055-4

Finegold, D. (1999). High-skill ecosystems. *Oxford Review of Economic Policy, 15*(1), 60–81. https://doi.org/10.1093/oxrep/15.1.60

Gibbons, M. (Ed.), (1994). *The new production of knowledge: The dynamics of science and research in contemporary societies.* Sage.

Governo Italiano – Presidenza del Consiglio dei Ministri. (2021). *Piano italiano di ripresa e resilienza.* https://www.governo.it/sites/governo.it/files/PNRR.pdf

Heckman, J. J., Stixrud, J., & Urzua, S. (2006). The effects of cognitive and noncognitive abilities on labor market outcomes and social behavior. *Journal of Labor Economics, 24*(3), 411–482.

Hodgson, A., & Spours, K. (2016). The evolution of social ecosystem thinking: Its relevance for education, economic development and localities. Working paper Ecosystem Seminar – 22 June 2016, Centre for Post-14 Education and Work, UCL Institute of Education. https://discovery.ucl.ac.uk/id/eprint/1537510/

International Standard Classification of Education ISCED 2011. (2012). Montreal: UNESCO Institute for Statistics. http://uis.unesco.org/sites/default/files/documents/international-standard-classification-of-education-isced-2011-en.pdf

Lewis, P. (2020). Developing technician skills for innovative industries: Theory, evidence from the UK life sciences industry, and policy implications. *British Journal of Industrial Relations, 58*(3), 617–643.

Lundvall, B.-Å., & Johnson, B. (1994). The learning economy. *Journal of Industry Studies, 1*(2), 23–42. https://doi.org/10.1080/13662719400000002

Mason, G., Rincon-Aznar, A., & Venturini, F. (2017). Which skills contribute most to absorptive capacity, innovation, and productivity performance? Evidence from the US and Western Europe. *LLAKES Research Paper* 60. https://www.llakes.ac.uk/wp-content/uploads/2021/03/RP-60.-Mason-et-al-final_0.pdf

Moscati, R., et al. (2015). Marketization and managerialization of higher education policies in a comparative perspective. In T. Klenk & E. Pavolini (Eds.), *Restructuring welfare governance: Marketization, managerialism and welfare state professionalism* (pp. 46–72). Edward Elgar.

Pellerey, M. (2016). Orientamento come potenziamento della persona umana in vista della sua occupabilità: Il ruolo delle soft skills, o competenze professionali personali generali. *Rassegna Cnos, 32*(1), 41–50.

Potestio, A. (2020). *Alternanza formativa. Radici storiche e attualità di un principio pedagogico.* Studium.

Recommendation of the European Parliament and of the Council of 23 April 2008 on the establishment of the European Qualifications Framework for lifelong learning. https://ec.europa.eu/ploteus/content/descriptors-page

Rosenberg, N. (1994). *Exploring the black box: Technology and economics.* Cambridge University Press.

Rostan, M. (2014). Teaching and research at Italian universities: Continuities and changes. In J. Shin, A. Arimoto, W. Cummings, & U. Teichler (Eds.), *Teaching and research in contemporary higher education: Systems, activities and rewards* (pp. 89–112). Springer.

Kvale, S., & Brinkmann, S. (2014). *Interviews: Learning the craft of qualitative research interviewing.* Sage.

Tether, B., Mina, A., Consoli, D., & Gagliardi, D. (2005). A literature review on skills and innovation: How does successful innovation impact on the demand for skills and how do skills drive innovation? *ESRC Centre for Research on Innovation and Competition.* https://webarchive.nationalarchives.gov.uk/ukgwa/+/http:/www.berr.gov.uk/files/file11008.pdf

Toner, P. (2011). Workforce skills and innovation: An overview of major themes in the literature. OECD. http://www.oecd.org/innovation/inno/46970941.pdf

Vona, F., & Consoli, D. (2014). Innovation and skill dynamics: A life-cycle approach. *Industrial and Corporate Change, 24*(6), 1393–1415. https://doi.org/10.1093/icc/dtu028

Weigel, T., Mulder, M., & Collins, K. (2007). The concept of competence in the development of vocational education and training in selected EU member states: A critical analysis. *Journal of Vocational Education & Training, 59*(1), 53–66.

Zahra, S., & George, G. (2002). Absorptive capacity: A review, reconceptualization, and extension. *Academy of Management Review, 27*(2), 185–203. https://doi.org/10.2307/4134351

Zajda, J. (Ed.), (2020). *Globalisation, ideology and neo-liberal higher education reforms.* Springer.

Zuccaro A. (Ed.) (2022). *Istituti tecnologici superiori. Monitoraggio nazionale 2022.* Firenze: INDIRE; available at: https://www.indire.it/wp-content/uploads/2022/05/Monitoraggio-nazionale-2022.-Rapporto_originale.pdf

### Legal sources

D.P.C.M. 25th January 2008
Legislative Decree No. 81 15th June 2015
Inter-ministerial Decree 12th October 2015
Law No. 99 15th July 2022

## Short portraits of the authors

**Paolo Bertuletti** is Research Fellow at the Department of Human and Social Sciences, University of Bergamo. Currently his studies focus on philosophy of education with regards to apprenticeship and VET. He is Editor-in-Chief of the journals *CQIIA Rivista* and *Nuova Professionalità*.
Contact: paolo.bertuletti@unibg.it

**Andrea Potestio** is Professor (full) at the Department of Human and Social Sciences, University of Bergamo, where he heads the bachelor degree programme in Educational Science. His main areas of research are pedagogy of work and philosophy of education. He is also Director of the journal *CQIIA Rivista*.
Contact: andrea.potestio@unibg.it

# Comparative perspective

# Vocational education and training in Lombardy and Lower Saxony: An exemplary case for international comparative research into regions

Paolo Bertuletti, Johannes Karl Schmees

**Abstract:** In international vocational education and training (VET) research, countries are often the default unit of analysis, but this can overlook regional differences. The contributions in this volume suggest that comparative research cannot do without considering the regional dimension, using Lower Saxony and Lombardy as examples of how institutional settings, history, and local needs impact VET systems, which necessarily also changes the scope of analysis. In these two specific cases, this is particularly true with regard to the dual approach in VET, the organisation of school-based vocational pathways, the provision of higher VET and teachers's training.

**Keywords**: Comparative Research; Regions; Vocational Education and Training.

## 1 Reasons of a methodological choice

In international comparative vocational education and training (VET) research, the basic unit of a country is usually taken for granted. There are good reasons for this. First and foremost, legislation in general, and educational legislation in particular, are bound closely to national territory. In this line of thought, the International Handbook of Vocational Education and Training, in short IHBB, probably the most ambitious attempt to systematically build in-depth knowledge of VET systems, focuses primarily on studies of countries.

However, this logic begins to fall apart when it comes to federal systems. Federal states usually have at least some legislative power over education in general, as well as vocational education in particular. Taking Germany as an example, it is misleading to talk about the 'education system of Germany'. Rather, the 16 federated different states should be analysed individually and then, if possible, re-categorised into states with similar patterns. While there is more uniformity when it comes to the dual apprenticeship system, as workplace training is regulated at the federal state, school-based training, which is part of dual apprenticeship training as well as school-based VET in Germany, is by and large regulated at the federated state level. When it comes to Switzerland, another federal state, the dual apprenticeship system is dominant only in the German-speaking cantons (Bonoli & Vorpe, 2022) and by no means prevails in the other three language regions. Substantial differences between federated states can also

THEORY AND DECISION LIBRARY

*General Editors:* W. Leinfellner (*Vienna*) and G. Eberlein (*Munich*)

Series A: Philosophy and Methodology of the Social Sciences

Series B: Mathematical and Statistical Methods

Series C: Game Theory, Mathematical Programming and Operations Research

Series D: System Theory, Knowledge Engineering and Problem Solving

SERIES B: MATHEMATICAL AND STATISTICAL METHODS

VOLUME 14



*Scope:* The series focuses on the application of methods and ideas of logic, mathematics and statistics to the social sciences. In particular, formal treatment of social phenomena, the analysis of decision making, information theory and problems of inference will be central themes of this part of the library. Besides theoretical results, empirical investigations and the testing of theoretical models of real world problems will be subjects of interest. In addition to emphasizing interdisciplinary communication, the series will seek to support the rapid dissemination of recent results.

*The titles published in this series are listed at the end of this volume.*

be observed in Canada (Annen, forthcoming), Australia (Deißinger et al., 2017), and the United States of America (Zirkle & Martin, 2012).

But also, when it comes to unitary countries, the VET system does not necessarily expand across such territories in a uniform fashion. In Italy, there are two parallel systems, one governed by the central state and the other by the regions, which has resulted in great territorial differentiation. Such differences are even more stark when considering the autonomous region of South Tyrol, which, prior to the First World War, was part of the Austro-Hungarian Empire. Here, a dual apprenticeship system similar to the contemporary one in Austria is in place. The same situation holds for Hong Kong, where the VET system is closer in nature to that of the United Kingdom rather than the one found in mainland China (Pan et al., 2020).

Finally, we can even observe differences in systems that are governed by the very same legislation. Recent cross-border studies have unearthed some evidence suggesting a convergence of border regions due to their peripheral geography (push factor) as well as their proximity to regions in other states (pull factor) (Graf & Lohse, 2021), which results in a kind of cross-border skill ecosystem. Nevertheless, even without such proximity to other states, regions can develop their own unique VET profiles (Gjelstad, 2023), as in the case of the area around Bergen, a global centre for oil exploitation. Here, adaptation to regional industry has led to unique profiling and development.

In short, a comparison of dual VET models which does not assume a regional perspective cannot be insightful[1]. This is first because VET is driven by actors who operate regionally and locally and rely on the tangible and intangible infrastructures embedded in a specific area, as the theory of the 'skill ecosystem' illustrated by Fabienne-Agnes Baumann in this volume demonstrates. Additionally, the configuration of each skill system depends on distinctive institutional frameworks rooted in cultural, social, and economic contexts, which are often historically and locally anchored (Busemeyer & Trampusch, 2012). Furthermore, the role assigned to regional governance significantly influences the functioning of VET systems, as institutional and legislative decisions made at this level create substantial differences between systems. The comparison between two administrative regions similar in territorial extent and population, such as Lower Saxony, one of the 16 German *Länder*, and Lombardy, one of the 20 Italian *Regioni*, offers a good illustration of that.

Therefore, there is a strong case for attending to regional cases in particular when analysing VET systems, and, in line with Philips (2006), there is also a reason to be sceptical if the unit of comparison in international VET research is the state. Consequently, we support the use of regional cases in international comparative VET research, as such an approach allows for more accurate research designs to be established. Using John Stuart Mill's comparative approach as an example, either in terms of the most similar or dissimilar instances, it becomes obvious why regional cases pro-

1 Of course, the concept of a 'region' is itself rather vague and encompasses geographical, cultural, economic, political, and social dimensions. We understand the notion here as a territorial unit that is smaller in extent and administratively integrated within a nation-state.

vide a suitable unit for comparison for many research questions. The goal of both research designs is to establish causal connections by choosing cases that provide a certain degree of similarity or dissimilarity, respectively. If, however, a country is taken as the unit of comparison instead, it might be difficult to select those 'variables' that allow for a coherent evaluation. This accounts in particular for those systems where the legislation differs from region to region.

When it comes to the VET systems of Lombardy and Lower Saxony, we compare two regional systems that have a certain degree of independence with respect to their VET systems. Lombardy is regarded as a special case when it comes to Italy, while Lower Saxony is less special in this sense; however, due to the federal structure of Germany, it has legislative power when it comes to school-based VET. This justifies the use of Lombardy, as well as Lower Saxony, as cases to be considered on their own terms. Nevertheless, they remain situated in very different VET systems. Using Mill's most dissimilar case design, we argue that despite their differences, these systems share a lot of similar developments that must have a source beyond the national case. Here, we could argue that internationalisation (as a placeholder for reasons beyond the nation that would need to be further assessed case by case) in TVET policies play a substantial part.

## 2 Areas for interregional comparison

In this section, we use the rich data and descriptions from this book to elaborate on three topics that we find particularly interesting when it comes to analysing similar policy directions. The first is dual approaches in VET. While such a phenomenon is less surprising in Lower Saxony, what we might call 'symmetric' developments when it comes to dual approaches remain intriguing. The same accounts for school-based VET, as the unexpected diversification of school-based VET programmes in Lower Saxony is found to align with the traditional bipartite structure of VET in Lombardy. Furthermore, developments in higher VET can be observed in both study regions, mostly in the form of a combination of higher education and industry placements. Finally, when it comes to VET teacher training, the observed convergences are less likely to occur on a structural level, but more on the level of professionalisation, which is increasingly in demand.

### 2.1 Dual approaches

In the last two decades, the strong economic performance and low youth unemployment rates seen in nations that employ dual VET programmes have prompted several countries to introduce or implement vocational pathways based on the systematic alternation between on-the-job training and school education (OECD, 2017). Such is the case of Italy, a country that traditionally privileged school-based VET but recently tried to import the well-known and world-wide appreciated dual system found in Germany (Bertuletti, 2021). Despite the fact that a direct transfer of this model to a different cultural, institutional, and socio-economic context is not possible (Euler, 2013), similar attempts to assimilate a supposed 'national' paradigm attributed to a foreign country can be misleading and oversimplifying for another reason. As Dietmar Frommberger explains in his contribution to this volume, in Germany the provision of dual programmes goes far beyond the dual apprenticeship model and is very diversified indeed, as it must respond to various company-specific qualification requirements and local educational demands. In Lower Saxony, for instance, a peculiar variety of vocational pathways can be viewed as an important asset of the regional education system, as well as a strategy for coping with the emergent challenges that are now threatening VET in this region, such as the loss of attractiveness, high drop-out rates, matching problems, and gender bias in the choice of certain vocational careers (see Tim Migura in this volume).

The relevance of the 'regional scale' is even more evident in Italy, where VET governance and legislation rely on the exclusive competence of regional administrations, albeit within a national regulatory framework. The case of Lombardy shows how interventions at regional level can make a difference. As Virginia Capriotti and Francesco Magni show elsewhere in this collection, Lombardy is the Italian region in which company-based VET has flourished the most, as the system has been able to meet the demands of a strong, manufactory-oriented territory. This success is the result of a long history rooted in local initiatives carried out by VET schools and businesses since the 19th century, despite the partially successful attempt of the central state to take responsibility for technical and professional education after Italy's unification (see Evelina Scaglia in this volume). However, as Giada Ragone has pointed out, with the constitutional reform of 2001, which handed legislative authority over VET off to the regions, Lombardy has become a vibrant 'laboratory' of legislative and educational innovation, developing its own regional VET system characterised by unique features and the highest enrolment rate in Italy[2].

In both Lower Saxony and Lombardy, similar developments can be observed, though in opposite directions. In Lower Saxony, a multitude of VET programmes at specialised schools (e. g., those in health care or early education) were established to meet society's skill needs. Meanwhile, in Lombardy, it was precisely the demand for training programmes tailored to the local labour market that drove the development of dual apprenticeships and other forms of dual VET, in contrast to the traditionally more theoretical offerings of state VET schools.

The comparisons between the dual VET approaches in Lower Saxony and Lombardy reveal not only the importance of the regional dimension in the regulation, governance, and concrete implementation of VET, but also the permanent dialectic between central and local management regarding this segment of the education system. The centralised German dual apprenticeship system makes VET in Lower Saxony highly efficient but perhaps more rigid. However, in this region, the federated state government intervenes with its own legislation and provisions to create VET courses outside

2 While this rate would be calculated as such in absolute terms, it would actually be second after the autonomous province of Bolzano (South-Tirol) in relative terms (INAPP, 2023).

the dual apprenticeship system, thereby addressing additional local and individual needs. In Lombardy, the autonomy of a completely regional system, wherein providers can also organise their own training programmes with a certain degree of freedom, is probably more flexible and quicker to adapt to the needs of the local labour market. However, it also suffers from the weakness of a system that cannot rely on the vital support in forecasting, planning and coordinating VET provisions guaranteed by the national government and the tripartite governance typical of the so-called German 'dual apprenticeship system'. This fragility, combined with the chronic underfunding of dual VET, thus continues to result in limited development.

## 2.2 School-based approaches

The differentiation of VET systems into school-based, company-based, and dual approaches can be considered a classical distinction introduced by Wolf-D. Greinert (2010) based on his historical analysis of European VET systems and their development. In his analysis, the VET system of France served as the prototypical example of a school-based and statist system; the system in England held this role for market-driven systems, and Germany served as the archetype for dual and neo-corporatist approaches. However, to date, the dominance of school-based systems around the world remains striking. Newer analysis of the English system and the dominance of Further Education Colleges delivering VET qualifications even questions whether the prototypical case of Greinert is developing in other directions. Furthermore, when it comes to Germany, the second prototypical case, there is a growing presence of school-based VET. Currently, around half of the students in German VET are in either school-based qualifications or the so-called transition system, both of which can be subsumed under school-based VET. Therefore, the third prototypical case in Greinert's classification remains pending. From the English and the German examples, it becomes obvious that school-based VET is increasing its dominance, despite global dual apprenticeship transfer agendas. It is therefore legitimate and necessary to take a closer look at how school-based approaches are applied in the two study cases.

By and large, both cases exhibit school-based VET programmes with industry placements. While in Lombardy, this form of school-based dual VET, even if not as apprenticeship, is prevalent; in Lower Saxony, it represents around half of all students in VET (in line with the national average). Given the dominance of the German dual apprenticeship in the global discourse on excellence in VET, it is surprising, at least for an international audience, to see the diversity in school-based approaches in a particular federated state like Lower Saxony. As Silke Lange explains in this volume, VET schools in Lower Saxony go far beyond being just the second learning venue in the dual apprenticeship system. They also offer full qualifications in certain trades, provide vocation-related qualifications for secondary and upper secondary education, and are an essential part of the transition system through which general vocational skills are trained, sometimes combined with qualifications for secondary education. In general, school-based VET is growing with respect to student numbers in Lower Saxony and in Germany.

In Lombardy, with a much less developed dual apprenticeship approach, schools play an even more dominant role in VET. It must also be considered that since World War II, two different vocational education channels have developed in Lombardy: the five-year programmes regulated at the national level by the central state (*Istruzione Professionale,* IP) and the three- or four-year programmes regulated at the regional level (*Istruzione e Formazione Professionale,* IeFP). The first ones are 'school-based' (with face-to-face lectures and an organisation of teaching still modelled on high schools and other upper secondary school tracks), while the second are 'work-based', with more significant teaching and organisational flexibility, workshops, and the systematic integration of work-based learning in the form of internships. The need, due to financial reasons, for a subsidiary offer by the central state for the first type of VET, which overlaps with regional ones, makes the system less transparent and hinders the full development of a dual VET system in alignment with European standards. This happens in Lombardy, but even more so in the rest of Italy (Zagardo, 2022).

While the differentiation between work-based and school-based systems makes sense from an Italian perspective to systematise these two models of VET, in the classification of Geinert, which assumes the governance structure as the most prominent indicator, both models would represent school-based VET; accordingly, such a categorisation does not account for the complexity of the regional system in its actual reality.

## 2.3 Higher VET

Higher VET is a contemporary topic of interest not just in academic discussions, but also when it comes to global policy discourses. Generally, there are three forms in which higher VET can be developed. One would be to systematise further vocational education and ascribe it to tertiary levels of a qualification framework, making it, at least nominally, an alternative to higher education. The second would be to make existing higher education more vocational, for example, by adding industry placements or combining them with a vocational qualification. The third would be to create new higher education institutions. While there are specific examples of all of these developments, it is worth noting that they are simultaneously observable in different parts of the world.

When looking at the specific cases of Lombardy and Lower Saxony, both regions have undergone different developments in higher VET, which are attributable to the first and third forms, respectively. In Lower Saxony, as in the rest of Germany, higher VET was systematised by the last reform of the Vocational Education Act in 2020. Here, three levels of higher VET were systematised as Vocational Specialist, Bachelor Professional, and Master Professional (Frommberger & Schmees, 2020), listed at Levels 4, 5 and 6 of the EQF, respectively. Parallel to these developments, the dual-study scheme (see Tim Migura in this volume) is an established programme that combines VET with applied higher education studies. While Lower Saxony does not have its own dual study or cooperative university, these courses are offered at the universities of applied sciences.

In Lombardy, as in the rest of Italy, efforts have been concentrated on relaunching a new short-cycle tertiary education model (*Istruzione tecnologica superiore,* ITS), established only in 2008, through the funding received from the Recovery and Resilience Plan approved in 2021. ITS academies, similar to German *Fachschule/Fachakademie*, do not originate from initiatives spearheaded by the central or regional government, but through a bottom-up process involving local aggregations of stakeholders, such as companies, VET schools, upper secondary schools, universities, research centres, and local authorities. Where greater autonomy is given to stakeholders, the local dimension becomes more prominent. In this sense, Lombardy's short-cycle tertiary education represents a paradigmatic example of how the convergence of local initiatives, territorial professional needs, and national legislation can create the right conditions for establishing innovation-oriented vocational courses – which is exactly what is expected from VET (see Paolo Bertuletti and Andrea Potestio's contribution in this volume).

### 2.4 VET teacher training

Teacher education, a key issue with regards to VET quality, is normally managed at the regional level. Currently, both Lower Saxony and Lombardy are struggling to attract the right candidates to the VET teaching profession. A common challenge here is the maintenance of high standards for teacher professionalisation while increasing accessibility to this career path for a larger number of people.

In Germany, the initial training of VET teachers is regulated by national legislation and agreements established by the Standing Conference of the Ministers of Education and Cultural Affairs (KMK 2018), which are then supplemented by state-specific requirements. In Lower Saxony, as in all German federated states and for all school levels, training occurs in two phases: a master's degree must first be obtained, followed by a preparatory service based on teaching practice (the so-called *Referendariat* or *Vorbereitungsdienst*).

It should be noted that the initial academic course must include the study of the educational sciences, with a focus on vocational education, as well as didactics pertaining to the vocational subject area. Additionally, teachers of technical subjects are required to have practical work experience (of at least twelve months) related to their vocational specialisation. Consequently, individuals pursuing a career in VET teaching are significantly more likely to have completed VET vocational training or possess other professional experience. As reported by Lange et al. in this volume, prospective VET teachers in this condition are proportionally more abundant in Lower Saxony than in other German federated states.

To cope with VET teacher shortages, a problem that all regions in Germany are now suffering from, Lower Saxony has established a wide range of different study models and access routes into this profession (see Lange et al. in this volume). These models and routes may be associated with different entry requirements, curricula, and forms of cooperation with other institutions in pre-service teacher training (e. g., other universities, VET schools, or teacher's training colleges). Such heterogenisation represents an attempt to attract new target groups to VET teacher training and careers. As a general tendency, all measures in the context of this growing differentiation go hand in hand with a reduction of previous formal standards for teacher training. This could potentially undermine the level of the teachers' pedagogical and scientific preparation.

In Lombardy, professional conditions for qualifying as a teacher in the VET system are much looser than those in Lower Saxony. Specifically, VET teachers must possess one of the following alternative requirements: either a national teaching qualification in a specific subject (obtained at the national level through a special training programme for teachers during or after the course of a master's degree in one's own teaching subject) or a bachelor's degree with 'sufficient' teaching experience in the national educational system (e. g., as substitute teachers). Such experience is set to a minimum of five years, when the candidate teacher has got only an upper secondary education leaving certificate. Those who want to teach practical subjects must have a minimum of five years of professional experience directly related to their field of instruction. It is also possible for VET providers to hire professionals active in a job sector congruent with their teaching subjects (e. g., an engineer for a mechanic course or an employee of a big retail company for a marketing course), but early career teachers coming from a previous experience in one company, as well as professionals hired under part-time contracts, are quite rare, given that teachers' wages are lower than those in other sectors.

One critical point worth emphasising is the continuous training of VET teachers. According to Lombardy's legislation, participation in professional development courses is not compulsory for VET teachers. However, national collective agreements stipulate a minimum of 100 training hours annually for teacher development. Nevertheless, it is important to note that public funding for these initiatives is not guaranteed, and teaching personnel often rely on self-financing by their employers.

In summary, in Lower Saxony, VET teachers' initial education ensures a high level of pedagogical preparation, as well as solid theoretical and technical knowledge. However, the region is now facing recruitment challenges due to a shortage of candidates. Lombardy has not encountered this issue, possibly because VET is less widespread there, resulting in a lower demand for VET teachers. At the same time, another concern in this region is the quality of teaching, which may be compromised due to lower professional requirements. Lower Saxony is attempting to address the teacher shortage by creating new ways to enter this occupation. In the future, lateral entry opportunities that bypass traditional training paths, such as hiring professionals active in fields congruent with teaching subjects, could be considered. To counterbalance the potential shortcomings in pedagogical preparation among such personnel, investing in continuous teacher training could be a solution. Such an approach may also be beneficial for the entire VET system in Lombardy.

# 3 Summary and conclusion

In international comparative research on VET, it is often assumed that countries are the appropriate unit of analysis. However, this perspective is problematic in federal systems, where education laws may differ significantly between federated states. Even in unitary countries, such as Italy and China, there are regional differences in VET. Consider, for example, the dual apprenticeship system in South Tyrol, with its historical connections to Austria, or the VET system of Hong Kong, with its long-term associations with the United Kingdom. Differences in VET systems can also arise within the same national legislation, such as the unique regional profiles shaped by local industries found in the area around Bergen, Norway. Such patterns and disparities highlight the importance of considering regional perspectives. Therefore, we argue that the use of regional cases in VET research can provide more accurate and insightful comparisons than a nation-based approach.

As far as Lombardy and Lower Saxony are concerned, we have examined their dual approaches to VET and found that while certain patterns were expected in Lower Saxony, the parallel developments in Lombardy were surprising. Similarly, the diversification of school-based VET programmes in Lower Saxony is unexpectedly in line with the traditional bipartite VET structure in Lombardy. Both regions have also exhibited developments in higher VET, which often entails a combination of higher education and industrial placements. Finally, we observed a convergence in VET teacher training – not so much in structure, but in the growing demand for professionalisation.

In conclusion, while dual apprenticeships are on the rise in Lombardy, school-based VET programmes are increasing in Lower Saxony. Although these two regions make different choices with regard to higher VET and teacher training, they face similar issues and challenges. In general, the VET systems of the two regions show some dialectical tension in the regulation and governance of VET. On the one hand, there is a need for standardisation at the national level to ensure stable and high-quality provision. On the other hand, further differentiation is required in response to local needs. Historical reasons and the institutional culture of each nation influence the resolution of this dialectic, but this does not diminish – on the contrary, it highlights – the importance of regional characteristics in determining the concrete form that VET takes in different areas.

# References

Annen, S. (forthcoming). *Kanada* (Internationales Handbuch der Berufsbildung). Barbara Budrich.

Bertuletti, P. (2021). *Quale "formazione" professionale? Una rilettura di Georg Kerschensteiner (1854–1932)*. Studium.

Bonoli, L., & Vorpe, J. (2022). Swiss VET between national framework and cantonal autonomy: A historical perspective. *Education Sciences, 12*(2), 114. https://doi.org/10.3390/educsci12020114

Busemeyer, M. R. & Trampusch, C. (2012) (eds.). *The Political Economy of Collective Skill Formation.* Oxfrod University Press.

Deißinger, T, Gulden, S. & Herdrich, M. (2017). *Australien* (Internationales Handbuch der Berufsbildung, Bd. 46). W. Bertelsmann.

Euler, D. (2013), *Germany's dual vocational training system: a model for other countries?* Bertelsmann Stiftung.

Gjelstad, L. E. (2023, September 27–29). Collaborating through crisis: Shifting geographies of academic-vocational education in Western Norway. VET & Culture Workshop 2023: VET in the academic drift, Oslo, Norway.

Graf, L., & Lohse, A. P. (2021). Conditions for cross-border policy transfer and cooperation: Analysing differences between higher education and vocational training. *Research in Comparative and International Education, 16*(4), 361–383. https://doi.org/10.1177/17454999211057747

Greinert, W.-D. (2010). Governance Models of Training for Employment: A European Perspective. *Research in Comparative and International Education, 5*(3), 251–260. https://doi.org/10.2304/rcie.2010.5.3.251

INAPP (Istituto Nazionale per l'Analisi delle Politiche Pubbliche) – Ministero del lavoro e delle politiche pubbliche (2023). XX Rapporto di monitoraggio del Sistema di Istruzione e Formazione Professionale e dei Percorsi in Duale nella IeFP a. f. 2020–21, febbraio 2023. Roma. https://www.lavoro.gov.it/temi-e-priorita-orientamento-e-formazione/focus/xx-rapporto-di-monitoraggio-iefp-e-sistema-duale

KMK (Kultusministerkonferenz) (2018). Rahmenvereinbarung über die Ausbildung und Prüfung für ein Lehramt der Sekundarstufe II (berufliche Fächer) oder für die beruflichen Schulen (Lehramtstyp 5). Beschluss der Kultusministerkonferenz vom 12.05.1995 i. d. F. vom 13.09.2018. Berlin.

Pan, W., Chen, L., & Zhan, W. (2020). Implications of Construction Vocational Education and Training for Regional Competitiveness: Case Study of Singapore and Hong Kong. *Journal of Management in Engineering, 36*(2). https://doi.org/10.1061/(asce)me.1943-5479.0000750

Phillips, D. (2006). Comparative Education: Method. *Research in Comparative and International Education, 1*(4), 304–319. https://doi.org/10.2304/rcie.2006.1.4.304

Valiente, O., Scandurra, R. (2017). Challenges to the Implementation of Dual Apprenticenships in OECD Countries: A Literature Review. In: Pilz, M. (Eds.), *Vocational Education and Training in Times of Economic Crisis. Technical and Vocational Education and Training: Issues, Concerns and Prospects.* Vol. 24. Springer. https://doi.org/10.1007/978-3-319-47856-2_3

Zagardo, G. (2022). La IeFP nelle Regioni. L'anno del sorpasso. Quaderni n. 11. Cnos/Fap - Ministero del lavoro e delle politiche sociali. https://www.cnos-fap.it/sites/default/files/crea_allegati/cnos_quaderni_11_zagardo_ultimabozza_2.pdf

Zirkle, C., & Martin, L. (2012). Challenges and Opportunities for Technical and Vocational Education and Training (TVET) in the United States. In Pilz, M., *The Future of Vocational Education and Training in a Changing World* (pp. 9–23). VS Verlag für Sozialwissenschaften. https://doi.org/10.1007/978-3-531-18757-0_2

## Short portraits of the authors

**Johannes Karl Schmees** was, during the formation of this volume, Postdoctoral Fellow at the Norwegian University of Science and Technology. Currently, he is Associate Professor (Research) in Technical and Vocational Education and Training (TVET) and Post-14 Education. His focus lies in international and international comparative technical and vocational education and training.
Contact: j.schmees@derby.ac.uk

**Dr. Paolo Bertuletti** is Research Fellow at the Department of Human and Social Sciences, University of Bergamo. Currently his studies focus on philosophy of education with regards to apprenticeship and vocational education and training. He is Editor-in-Chief of the journals *CQIIA Rivista* and *Nuova Professionalità*.
Contact: paolo.bertuletti@unibg.it

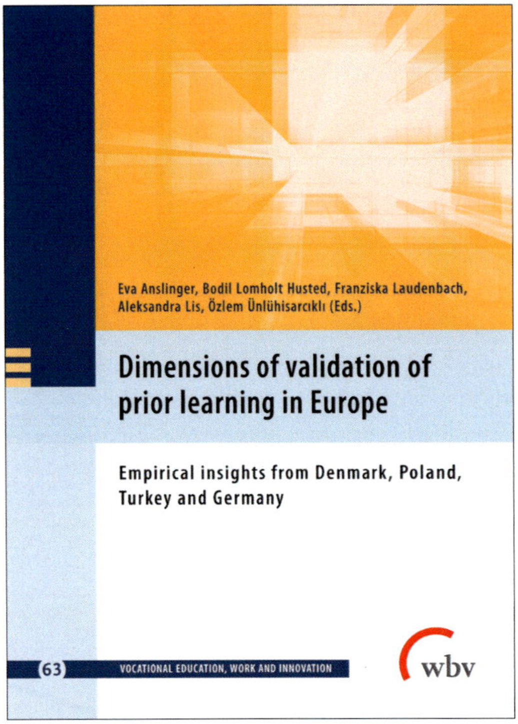
Eva Anslinger, Bodil Lomholt Husted, Franziska Laudenbach,
Aleksandra Lis, Özlem Ünlühisarcıklı (Eds.)
Dimensions of validation of prior learning in Europe
Empirical insights from Denmark, Poland, Turkey and Germany
63
VOCATIONAL EDUCATION, WORK AND INNOVATION
wbv